Guitar Legends

"He was the ultimate role model"

Nile Rodgers

THE DEFINITIVE GUIDE TO THE WORLD'S GREATEST GUITAR PLAYERS

Guitar Legends

By CHRIS GILL
of GUITAR PLAYER® magazine

HarperPerennial

A Division of HarperCollinsPublishers

For Anna Le, whose warm friendship gave me inspiration and motivation.

GUITAR PLAYER IS A REGISTERED TRADEMARK OF MILLER FREEMAN, INC.
USED WITH PERMISSION. ALL RIGHTS RESERVED.

HarperCollins books may be purchased for educational,
business, or sales promotional use. For information please write: Special
Markets Department, HarperCollins Publishers, Inc.,
10 East 53rd Street, New York, NY 10022.

FIRST EDITION

Editor	**Michael Downey**
Art director	**Peter Champion**
Book design	**Dave Farrow**
Editorial	**John Boteler**
Consultants	**Iain Scott, David Woodman**
Picture research	**Kay Rowley**
Index	**Eric Downey**

Music written by Iain Scott

Library of Congress Cataloging-in-Publication Data
Gill, Chris.
   Guitar legends: the definitive guide to the world's greatest guitar
players / by Chris Gill.
         p.   cm.
   Includes discographies.
   ISBN 0-06-273352-4
   1. Guitarists — Biography.
ML399.G56 1995
787.87′166′0922 — dc20
[B]   95-3165
                                                                CIP
                                                                MN

95 96 97 98 99   10 9 8 7 6 5 4 3 2 1

Printed and bound in Spain

Contents

Introduction 7

Introduction

There are hundreds, perhaps thousands, of great guitarists. One of the world's most versatile and popular musical instruments, the guitar has been used to perform almost every genre of music, including classical, jazz, rock, blues, country, bluegrass, gospel, folk, and numerous ethnic styles. But although each genre boasts many notable players, only a few guitarists have earned legendary acclaim.

Guitar Legends provides comprehensive, detailed information about the playing techniques, equipment, recordings, lives, and influences of 36 of the world's greatest guitarists. If you've ever wondered what Albert King's "secret" tuning was, or needed to know when Jimmy Page played on his first recording session, you'll find those details here. We've also included several musical examples for each guitarist that show you how to play a few of their characteristic licks. This book is a veritable encyclopedia of almost everything you need to know about a guitarist from a musical focus.

Considering that there are thousands of great players, choosing three dozen of the world's greatest guitarists is no small feat. Everyone has differing opinions on who they think is the best, and there is no set criteria for determining what makes one player better than another. Guitar playing is not an Olympic event, where excellence can be measured merely by technical expertise, accuracy, and speed. Emotion, imagination, and other intangible attributes are equally, if not more, important than measurable skills.

So how did we come up with the players that were chosen for this book? For the sake of continuity, we decided to limit the musical styles to the two most popular genres of guitar music – rock 'n' roll, and blues. Of course, even within these two styles, hundreds of possibilities exist. By breaking down the genres into several categories – such as early style-defining players, timeless favorites, and modern rule-breaking virtuosos – we were able to narrow down the list considerably, but it still left open a wide range of possibilities.

After much consideration, we selected 36 players who we feel represent the widest possible cross-section of rock and blues guitarists. There are blues artists who were active in the 1920s and '30s, rockabilly and urban-blues players who brought the electric guitar to the forefront in the '50s, rock guitarists who reached massive audiences in the '60s and '70s, musicians who expanded the guitar's role in the '80s, and players who are breaking new ground in the '90s.

Some of our choices were easy. No one can dispute that Jimi Hendrix was one of the most highly respected and influential rock guitarists. His impact on guitar playing was monumental, affecting everything – from playing techniques, to guitar and equipment designs. The British rock triumvirate of Jeff Beck, Eric Clapton, and Jimmy Page, and the three Kings of the blues – Albert, B. B., and Freddie – are consistently cited as players who shaped the way we think about the guitar. Their influence remains as strong today as it was decades ago. Eddie Van Halen and Steve Vai are two recent visionaries who have shown that the guitar still has potential to create new and exciting sounds.

Many of our other choices haven't quite achieved household-name status, but their impact on the guitar community was nonetheless universal. Lonnie Johnson, T-Bone Walker, and Muddy Waters all helped form the foundation of modern blues guitar. Johnson, who enjoyed a career that spanned seven decades, was one of Robert Johnson's biggest influences, and his playing inspired

several generations of players. Walker gave the blues a jazzy sophistication, and was also one of the first blues artists to use an electric guitar. Waters merged Delta and urban blues styles, creating what came to be known as Chicago blues.

Chuck Berry, Scotty Moore, Cliff Gallup, and Duane Eddy were all seminal figures in the development of rock 'n' roll. Many of Berry's licks have become a common part of the rock guitarist's vocabulary. Gallup and Moore were the primary influences on

many of today's most respected players, including Jeff Beck and Jimmy Page. Duane Eddy pioneered the rock 'n' roll guitar instrumental, and his early hits presaged the '60s surf-guitar craze.

Buddy Guy, Stevie Ray Vaughan, and Robert Cray are a few of the world's most highly regarded blues guitarists. Guy, who started recording in the late '50s, developed a modern blues style that many guitarists continue to pattern their own styles after. Vaughan and Cray were both pivotal figures

Born in Mississippi in 1917, boogie guitar legend John Lee Hooker has recorded more than 100 albums spanning five decades. His rich voice and foot-stompin' guitar style captures the essence of the blues.

in the re-emergence of the blues in the '80s. Their best-selling records introduced the blues to a new generation of fans, one that is still going strong today.

Of the hundreds of noteworthy rock guitarists, we decided to concentrate on a few of the most original stylists. With his mixture of Latin rhythms and jazz-influenced lines,

Carlos Santana is one of rock music's most innovative soloists. Ritchie Blackmore added classical music influences to the rock guitarist's repertoire, and his Bach-inspired lines were important influences on many of the guitar heroes who emerged in the late '70s and '80s. David Gilmour has consistently provided exemplary performances with Pink Floyd, and few guitarists have developed such a distinctive tone and touch. Steve Howe, one of progressive rock's most versatile instrumentalists, showed that jazz, classical, and country licks could all work in a rock-music context.

Of the more recent guitarists, Slash has gained notoriety for his hard-rock style that is deeply rooted in the blues-based playing styles of '70s rock guitarists. Joe Satriani, one of rock's most successful instrumental musicians, is notable not only for his extremely well-developed technical skills and application of music theory, but also for his superb melodic chops.

We also chose a couple of guitarists for their rhythm-playing skills. Keith Richards' rhythm-playing style is so distinctive that he can be identified within a few chords. Although he is also a noteworthy lead player, Pete Townshend's driving, aggressive rhythm style was the centre-piece of many of the Who's finest songs. Finger-stylists Mark Knopfler and Richard Thompson are notable for their ability to seamlessly merge lead lines into flowing rhythm patterns. U2's The Edge, Johnny Marr, and Andy Summers are all highly original rhythm players whose textural styles rely as much on tone and space as they do on note choice and chord progressions.

Slide guitar is another important aspect of rock-guitar playing, and few can dispute that Ry Cooder and Duane Allman are two of the world's best slide guitarists. Allman's performances with the Allman Brothers Band are timeless classics, and few slide players have been able to match his melodic sense, intonation, and inventive phrasing. Cooder is a true master of the slide guitar who has been able to merge many types of music with his playing, including blues, Indian, African, and several other ethnic styles.

Rock guitar is distinguished by several iconoclasts who have greatly expanded the boundaries of the genre. To call Frank Zappa a rock guitarist is an understatement, as his expertise encompassed many talents, including composition and social commentary. His playing style possessed a rhythmic complexity and imagination that few players can match. Robert Fripp has consistently explored new musical territory since the early days of King Crimson, and he continues to break new ground with his electronic effects experimentation and unorthodox scales and time signatures.

We are sure that you will agree that all of these players deserve accolades for their excellent playing and contributions to the guitar. Unfortunately, we did not have room to

Albert Collins, also known as the "Iceman," was a big influence on many latter day rock guitar players. His showmanship and biting raw emotion coupled with a "frosty" Telecaster guitar sound drew capacity crowds.

Steve Morse created a unique brand of rock music drawing on country, jazz-rock, heavy metal and bluegrass. His band, the Dixie Dregs, played intricate arrangements with super-accurate technique, great tone, and tasteful phrasing.

Malmsteen and Randy Rhoads; punk guitar stalwarts the Sex Pistols' Steve Jones and Black Flag's Greg Ginn; modern metal mavens, such as Metallica's Kirk Hammett, Megadeth's Marty Friedman, and Living Colour's Vernon Reid; '70s icons, such as Aerosmith's Joe Perry, UFO's Michael Schenker, Queen's Brian May, and Black Sabbath's Tony Iommi; blues/rock stylists ZZ Top's Billy Gibbons, Fleetwood Mac's Peter Green, Gary Moore, and Bonnie Raitt; contemporary funk figures Prince and Nile Rodgers; modern-day minimalists Nirvana's Kurt Cobain and Sonic Youth's Thurston Moore; perennial favorites Dave Edmunds, Jerry Garcia, and Neil Young; slide demon Lowell George; rockabilly revivalist Brian Setzer; inventive adventurist Adrian Belew; blues-country rocker David Grissom; and new-wave guitarist the Pretenders' James Honeyman-Scott.

There are also countless blues guitarists worthy of accolades, including: country-roots players, such as Big Bill Broonzy, R. L. Burnside, John Cephas, Reverend Gary Davis, Skip James, Blind Lemon Jefferson, Robert Johnson, Mance Lipscomb, Mississippi Fred McDowell, Johnny Shines, and Son Thomas; urban-blues guitarists, such as Guitar Slim, John Lee Hooker, J. B. Hutto, Elmore James, Magic Sam, Jimmy Reed, Jimmy Rogers, Otis Rush, and Hubert Sumlin; Texas-blues guitarists, such as Clarence Gatemouth Brown, Albert Collins, Lightnin' Hopkins, and Johnny "Guitar" Watson; and white-blues greats, such as Mike Bloomfield and Johnny Winter.

Because we limited ourselves to rock and blues musicians, two of the world's all-time greatest players were not included, because their playing crossed so many styles. Telecaster masters Danny Gatton and Roy Buchanan were both incredible players who were fluent at almost any

include many other greats who are certainly noteworthy as well, particularly those of other genres. Other rock players who deserve mentioning include: instrumental virtuosos Eric Johnson and Steve Morse; rockabilly pioneers James Burton, Paul Burlison (the Rock And Roll Trio), and Carl Perkins; instrumental proto-punk Link Wray; rhythm masters Steve Cropper and Curtis Mayfield; surf-guitar king Dick Dale; early funkateers, such as the Meters' Leo Nocentelli, James Brown's sideman Jimmy Nolen, Funkadelic's Eddie Hazel, and the Isley Brothers' Ernie Isley; '80s heavy-metal heroes Yngwie

style of music, including jazz and country, as well as rock 'n' roll and blues.

The world's great jazz guitarists also deserve a mention, including: early jazz pioneers Charlie Christian and Django Reinhardt; traditional jazz artists Herb Ellis, Tal Farlow, Jim Hall, Wes Montgomery, and Joe Pass; fusion architects Al Di Meola and John McLaughlin; perennial favorites George Benson, Larry Carlton, Allan Holdsworth, and Pat Metheny; two-handed tapping genius Stanley Jordan; '50s jazz/pop hero Les Paul; ground-breaking experimentalists Bill Frisell and Sonny Sharrock; and John Abercrombie, Lenny Breau, Pat Martino, Howard Roberts, and John Scofield.

Country music has boasted its own fair share of incredible musicians who have made noteworthy contributions to guitar playing. Some of the top country guitarists include '50s and '60s kingpins Chet Atkins, Jimmy Bryant, Roy Clark, Hank Garland, Joe Maphis, Grady Martin, Roy Nichols, and Merle Travis, as well as recent guitar terrors Vince Gill and Albert Lee, the Hellecasters (Jerry Donahue, John Jorgenson, and Will Ray), and Tele- and flat-picking master Clarence White.

Many of the great guitarists opt for acoustic instruments instead of electrics. Some of the world's best acoustic players include Martin Carthy, Michael Hedges, Bert Jansch, Leo Kottke, Adrian Legg, Joni Mitchell, John Renbourn, Martin Simpson, and Doc Watson, and bluegrass flatpickers Lester Flatt and Tony Rice. Classical guitarists Elliot Fisk, Carlos Montoya, Christopher Parkening, Andres Segovia, and John Williams also deserve accolades for their achievements on the guitar.

Then there are the many ethnic styles of guitar music. Many guitar fans consider flamenco the ultimate guitar music, and its masters, such as Paco De Lucía, Ramón Montoya, Sabicas, Mânolo Sanlúcar, and Tomatito, make exceptionally exciting music. African guitarists Doctor Nico and King Sunny Ade have highly distinctive styles that have influenced many adventurous rock musicians. Hawaiian musicians Sal Hoopii, who was a master lap and steel guitarist, and Gabby Pahinui, one of Hawaii's finest slack-key players, have also been monumental figures in the guitar community.

While we regret not having the space to include the guitarists mentioned above, when you see the breadth of the material on each guitarist who was chosen for this book, we hope that you will understand why we couldn't include everyone. Our goal with *Guitar Legends* was to provide a complete source of details spanning the artist's entire career in a manner that makes the information easy to find. Even if you don't entirely agree with out choices, we're sure that if you are a guitar enthusiast, you will be fascinated by the information included in this book.

Yngwie Malmsteen, influenced by Ritchie Blackmore, incorporated classical harmony into the heavy-rock tradition. His incredible technique enabled him to re-create virtuoso masterpieces by composers such as Paganini.

Duane Allman

In his brief, 24-year life, Duane Allman became rock music's pre-eminent slide guitarist. As the creative force behind the Allman Brothers Band, Duane pioneered the "Southern rock" sound with his distinctive, blues-influenced slide playing and the melodic dual-lead guitar interplay between himself and Dickie Betts. Duane's performance on the band's live album, At Fillmore East, *took electric bottleneck slide playing to new heights that few players since have been able to equal.*

The Player

Influences

Although Duane's initial interest in music was inspired by his father, who sang and played guitar, he was killed before Duane began to play an instrument. Duane became interested in playing guitar after his younger brother Gregg purchased an inexpensive acoustic. When Duane acquired his first guitar, Gregg showed him how to play a few chords. Later, Duane made friends with Jim Shepley, a guitarist who taught him a few licks and exposed him to the blues styles of Jimmy Reed and B. B. King. "What he really liked was my finger-picking blues," Shepley recalled. "Lightnin' Hopkins, John Lee Hooker, Muddy Waters – he was always in awe of that." Duane never took any formal lessons.

Gregg recalls that Duane liked to listen to Kenny Burrell, Robert Johnson, and Chuck Berry albums. He was also inspired by the music he heard on R&B radio stations. As Duane got more and more into the blues, he enjoyed the music of Albert King, T-Bone Walker, and Blind Willie Johnson. Duane and Gregg often watched the local black musicians play in clubs in Daytona Beach. One of their favorite bands was the Lindsey Morris Band, which often played at a club called the Surf Bar.

As the brothers started getting involved in their first bands, Duane became heavily influenced by Jeff Beck with the Yardbirds. When Duane and Gregg formed the Allman Joys, they started to play gigs beyond their home town. In New York City they met the Blues Magoos who were a significant influence on Duane. He bought his first distortion box from one of the members of the Blues Magoos.

Duane got into slide playing while with Hour Glass in California. According to Pete Carr, who played bass with Hour Glass and was Duane's roommate in Los Angeles, Duane decided to learn to play slide guitar after he heard Ry Cooder perform Blind Willie McTell's "Statesboro Blues" with Taj Mahal at a Los Angeles club. Duane enjoyed using his slide to imitate harmonica licks that he heard on records by Little Walter, Slim Harpo, and Sonny Boy Williamson.

At the time of the *Layla* sessions, Duane admitted that playing with Eric Clapton had challenged him to become a better player. He considered Clapton and Robbie Robertson the best white blues guitarists there had

Background

1946 *Duane Allman is born on November 20 in Nashville, Tennessee.*

1949 *His father is murdered by a hitchhiker.*

1957 *The Allman family leaves Tennessee and moves to Daytona Beach, Florida.*

1960 *Duane trades a pile of parts from a wrecked motorcycle for his first guitar.*

1964 *Duane and his brother Gregg join the House Rockers, a rhythm section for a black group called the Untils. Duane and Gregg then form their first band, The Shufflers. Gregg was originally the guitar player, but Duane convinces him to get a Vox organ and become a singer.*

1965 *Duane and Gregg form the Allman Joys.*

1966 *The Allman Joys record their first 45, featuring a cover version of Willie Dixon's "Spoonful".*

1967 *After the Allman Joys break up, Duane and Gregg form Almanac.*

1968 *The brothers move to Hollywood and form the band Hour Glass, which records two unsuccessful albums for Liberty Records. Duane then returns to the South and lands a job as a studio guitarist at Muscle Shoals Sound Studio. Gregg stays in Los Angeles.*

1969 *Duane forms a band featuring Dickie Betts on guitar, Berry Oakley on bass, and Butch Trucks and Jai Johnny Johanson on drums. He coaxes his brother Gregg back from California, and the Allman Brothers Band is born. The band travels to New York and records* The Allman Brothers Band *for Capricorn records.*

1970 *The band releases* Idlewild South. *Duane teams with Eric Clapton for the Layla sessions.*

1971 *The Allman Brothers Band records the live album* At Fillmore East. *While working on the studio album* Eat A Peach, *Duane dies in a motorcycle accident in Macon, Georgia on October 29.*

ever been. Later, Duane also came to appreciate the work of jazz horn players, such as Miles Davis and John Coltrane.

Approach and Style

Duane Allman is best-known for his slide playing. When playing slide, he usually tuned his guitar to open *E (E, B, E, G♯, B, E*, low to high), although he often used standard tuning as well, particularly if he was going to switch between playing slide and fretting notes during a song. The songs "Dreams" and "Mountain Jam" are a couple of examples in which he plays in standard tuning. The *Layla* outtake "Mean Old World" is Duane's only recorded performance where he uses open-*G* tuning (*D, G, D, G, B, D*, low to high).

When playing in open *E*, Allman used the box approach (playing a pattern of closely-placed notes) instead of traditional open-string blues styles. The box patterns made it easier for him to play in any key. In standard tuning, Duane often preferred to use a linear approach to play slide, playing most of the notes by sliding up and down a single string. This approach may have been inspired by the playing styles of Duane's jazz influences, Miles Davis and John Coltrane.

Allman's slide work consisted primarily of single-note lead lines. He'd often extend beyond the box pattern by ascending up a minor third on the first or fourth strings, or he would use the minor-third spacing between the second and third strings, three frets above the tonic, to produce a dominant 7th-chord fragment. Duane sometimes also played the 2nd, 9th, 6th, and 4th above the tonic chord as grace notes or for adding pentatonic-major color. He also made effective use of microtones. On his long, extended leads, he relied on repetition, elongation, rhythmic displacement, and retrograde to add variety to his playing.

The Allman Brothers were also known for

their two-guitar harmonies. Duane and guitarist Dickie Betts worked out melodic counterpoint and unison lines that served as a backbone for the guitarists' extended solos. These harmonies were unlike anything heard from any previous American rock 'n' roll band, and they remain the distinguishing factor of the Allman Brothers' music.

Techniques

Duane developed his style to such an advanced level that it was often difficult to discern between his slide and standard playing techniques. His intonation with the slide was exceptionally accurate, and his phrasing while fretting notes was so fluid that it didn't sound like conventional guitar playing. His intonation was the result of his well-developed listening abilities, as evidenced by his

One of the most influential electric slide guitarists, Duane Allman decided to play slide guitar after seeing Ry Cooder perform. About a year later, Duane recorded several classic slide performances on The Allman Brothers Band.

accuracy when his playing extended well above the range of the fingerboard.

When playing slide, Duane picked with his thumb, index, and middle fingers. This allowed him to damp strings effectively and to pluck triads with his right hand. He wore the slide on his left-hand ring finger, and also damped behind the slide with his left-hand middle and index fingers. To achieve his accurate intonation, Allman aligned the tip of his left-hand ring finger over the fret. He often used a flatpick when he played leads that called for fretted notes, but he always used only his fingers for slide.

The neck- and middle-position pickup settings provided the warm, fluid tones that Duane favored for slide. He rarely used the bridge-pickup setting unless he was playing lead by fretting notes on the guitar's neck.

The Hardware
Guitars, Strings, and Picks

Duane learned to play on an inexpensive Sears Silvertone acoustic that his brother Gregg had bought with money he earned on a paper route. A short while later, Gregg bought a Fender Musicmaster electric guitar. Duane decided that he also wanted to play the electric guitar, so he traded a pile of parts from a wrecked Harley-Davidson 165 motorcycle for a Gibson Les Paul Jr.

By the time that the brothers formed the Allman Joys, Duane was playing a Gibson ES-335 semi-hollowbody electric. With Hour Glass, he played a blonde Fender Telecaster with a Stratocaster neck. The Tele was strung with Fender 150 Rock And Roll strings. According to ZZ Top guitarist Billy Gibbons, Duane purchased his tobacco sunburst '58 Les Paul, which he used throughout his career with the Allman Brothers Band, from (pop singer) Christopher Cross in San

Antonio, Texas. Duane later acquired a Gibson SG, which he preferred for playing slide because its double-cutaway design made it easier for him to access the upper registers. He also used a Fender Stratocaster in the studio. Because he primarily played slide, he liked to keep his guitars set up with low frets and a medium-high action.

Duane enjoyed playing acoustic guitar as much as he enjoyed playing electric slide. Most of the acoustic guitar on *Idlewild South* was played by Duane. He owned a Gibson Heritage and often played a Dobro or National resonator guitar in jam sessions or while relaxing backstage or in his hotel room.

Perhaps the most important part of Allman's slide sound was the glass Coricidin bottle that he wore on his left-hand ring finger. These small, clear medicine bottles have one closed end. Allman often played with the bottle's seam contacting the strings.

Amplifiers, Effects, and Devices

Allman rarely used anything more than a guitar, a distortion box, and an amplifier. His setup with Hour Glass was a Vox Super Beatle amp, an Echoplex, and a tiny fuzz tone that could be attached to the guitar's body. While recording Hour Glass' second record, he swapped the Super Beatle for a Fender Twin Reverb with JBL speakers. This amp remained a favorite of Duane's throughout his days as a studio guitarist at Muscle Shoals Sound Studio.

As a session guitarist, Duane often used a Fuzz Face distortion pedal. He preferred the sound of the Fuzz Face when it was operated with weak batteries. "He would get batteries that were almost worn out because

Allman is best known for his electric slide work, but he often played slide on acoustic guitar as well. Duane played most of the acoustic guitar parts on the Allman Brothers' second album, Idlewild South.

In His Own Words

I heard Ry Cooder playing some time ago and I said, "Man that's for me." I got me a bottle, and I went in the house for about three weeks. I said, "Hey man, we've got to learn the songs, the blues, to play on stage. I love this."
From an interview broadcasted on WQMC

There's a lot of different forms of communication, but music is absolutely the purest one, man. You can't hurt anybody with music. There's nothing that could ever be bad about music, about playing it. It's a wonderful thing, a grace.
From an interview with Ed Shane for the Capricorn promotional album, Duane Allman Dialogues

Music's become so intellectualized. Man, music is fun. It's not supposed to be any heavy, deep intense thing – especially not rock music, man. That's to set you free! Rock 'n' roll will tell you where everything is at.
From Duane Allman Dialogues

What They Say

His playing was incredible. He played great authentic blues, and he phrased like the great black guitar players, playing beautiful melodic segments.
Atlantic VP Jerry Wexler, Guitar Player, May 1973

Duane was pretty shy about stardom. He was just one of the gang, the same dude that hung around with Shepley and shot pool... He used to lean right against the organ, and he hardly ever looked down at his guitar when he played live. He just knew where he was going.
Gregg Allman, Guitar Player, October 1981

Duane... was a great player all the way around, but I think he's probably more famous for being the foremost electric slide player than anything else.
Dickey Betts, Guitar Player, October 1981

the Fuzz Face had a special sound just for so many hours with the batteries at a certain strength," recalled Muscle Shoals guitarist Jimmy Johnson. Duane sometimes played through a Fender Princeton amp on Muscle Shoals sessions, turning the Princeton all the way up and covering it with baffles.

By the time the Allman Brothers Band was formed, Duane had abandoned the use of distortion pedals altogether, preferring the tone he got when he plugged his guitar directly into a 50-watt Marshall powering two 4x12 cabinets. According to Gregg Allman, Duane had tried 100-watt Marshalls, but he liked the sound of the 50-watt heads better.

Discography

Duane's performances with the Allman Joys can be heard on **Early Allman** (Dial), released in 1973. Duane and Gregg made their first recordings for a major label with the band Hour Glass, releasing **Hour Glass** and **Power Of Love** (Liberty). They then worked on a project called 31st of February. Nine outtakes from this session appear on **Duane & Gregg Allman** (Bold).

Duane's finest work was with the Allman Brothers Band. He appeared on three albums with them – **The Allman Brothers Band**, **Idlewild South**, and **At Fillmore East** (all Capricorn). He died before the album **Eat A Peach** was completed, and appears on only three tracks: "Blue Sky," "Little Martha," and "Stand Back." Two posthumous collections were released by Capricorn, **Duane Allman: An Anthology** and **Duane Allman: An Anthology Vol. II**.

Recording Sessions

One of Duane's first session gigs was in 1968 for Wilson Pickett's **Hey Jude** (Atlantic). This led to Duane joining the Muscle Shoals rhythm section. In 1969 he appeared on Aretha Franklin's **This Girl's In Love With You**, **Soul '69**, and **Spirit In The Dark** (all on Atlantic), King Curtis' **Instant Groove** (Atco), Boz Scaggs' **Boz Scaggs** (Atlantic), Clarence Carter's **The Dynamic Clarence Carter** (Atlantic), Arthur Conley's **More Sweet Soul** (Atco), John Hammond's **Southern Fried** (Atlantic), Otis Rush's **Mourning In The Morning** (Cotillion), Barry Goldberg's **Two Jews Blues**, and Johnny Jenkins' **Ton-Ton Macoute!** (Capricorn).

In 1970, he contributed to Ronnie Hawkins' **Ronnie Hawkins** (Cotillion), Laura Nyro's **Christmas And The Beads Of Sweat** (Columbia), Lulu's **New Routes** (Atco) and his first of several recordings with Delaney & Bonnie & Friends, including **To Bonnie From Delaney**, **Motel Shot** and **Delaney & Bonnie Together** (all Atco). Later that year, he teamed with Eric Clapton for the Derek & The Dominos album, **Layla** (Atco).

In 1971, he appeared on Herbie Mann's **Push Push** (Embryo), Ronnie Hawkins' **The Hawk** (Cotillion), Sam Samudio's **Sam – Hard And Heavy** (Atlantic), and Cowboy's **5'll Get You Ten** (Capricorn).

Typical Licks

♩ = 120

E7

These licks, from Allman's "Statesboro Blues" period, show his great control over the slide's intonation, even at high tempos.

♩ = 126

E7

Use your pick and second finger to get the triplets in this lick up to tempo.

♩ = 126

E7

Careful right-hand damping is required to keep the notes in this phrase sounding clear.

Jeff Beck

One of rock guitar's most influential and respected musicians, Beck has been an innovator throughout his career. Steadfastly refusing to follow trends, he continually creates music that sounds fresh and modern. Beck helped invent heavy metal and psychedelia in the '60s, and in the mid-'70s he was one of the pivotal figures in the development of jazz-rock fusion. An inimitable guitarist with an identifiable sound that is truly his own, Beck remains one of the world's most outstanding musical visionaries.

The Player

Influences

In Jeff's early childhood, he sang in the church choir and played violin, 'cello, and piano. None of these instruments held his interest, however. In the liner notes to *Beckology*, Jeff talked about his frustration with practicing piano: "I ripped one of the black keys off. My mother got the idea that I wasn't too keen on it."

A major influence on Beck's career has been Gene Vincent And The Blue Caps. When Jeff turned 13, he decided to build his own electric guitar after seeing a picture of them on a poster for the movie *The Girl Can't Help It,* and their music was also highly influential. Beck has long claimed that Blue Caps guitarist Cliff Gallup is his primary influence, and as recently as 1993 he recorded an album of Gene Vincent covers (*Crazy Legs*) as a tribute to Gallup.

Jeff's older sister listened to many rock 'n' roll records, exposing Jeff to the music of Eddie Cochran, Ricky Nelson (with James Burton on guitar), and Buddy Holly, and when Beck got his first gig playing at a local fairground, he performed Eddie Cochran tunes. Jeff also enjoyed learning to play songs by Hank Marvin And The Shadows, such as their instrumental hit "Apache."

When Beck first heard Booker T. And The MGs, his interest shifted from rock 'n' roll to soul music. A little while later, he discovered blues music and became heavily influenced by blues guitarists, such as Buddy Guy and Otis Rush.

By the time Jeff joined the Tridents in 1963, he had developed a fondness for Les Paul's tricky, sophisticated style and sonic experiments. This inspired Jeff to explore the possibilities of an electric guitar and led to his experiments with feedback and sound effects. Traces of Paul's influence can be heard on "Jeff's Boogie."

More recently, Beck has looked even further afield for inspiration, The Bulgarian Women's Choir and Vietnamese flute music being just two of the sources Jeff has turned to when looking for new musical ideas.

Approach and Style

Beck's approach to the guitar is truly unique. His style incorporates the fluid phrasing of vocals, wind instruments, and harmonica, the percussive staccato of plucked notes, and inventive use of feedback, harmonics, and distortion. The sound of Beck's playing is as

Background

1944 *Jeff Beck is born on June 24 in Surrey, England.*

1952 *His parents enroll him in piano lessons.*

1957 *He builds his first guitar.*

1959 *Jeff joins his first band, the Deltones.*

1963 *Joins the Tridents and makes his recording debut on demos.*

1965 *Beck replaces Eric Clapton in the Yardbirds.*

1966 *The Yardbirds tour the United States, but Beck leaves the group two weeks into the tour.*

1967 *Jeff releases an out-of-character "sing-along" single, "Hi Ho Silver Lining."*

1968 *Forms the Jeff Beck Group with Rod Stewart and Ron Wood, and releases first album,* Truth, *a major success in the U. S. Later Jeff has a serious hot-rod car accident, which puts him out of action for 18 months.*

1969 *Plays guitar on Donovan's hit single "Goo Goo Barabajagal," reaching #12 in the U. K. pop charts.*

1972 *A new line-up of the Jeff Beck Group records* Jeff Beck Group *with Booker T. and the MGs' guitarist Steve Cropper as producer. Later that year, the Jeff Beck Group breaks up and Jeff forms Beck, Bogert, And Appice.*

1976 *Joins the Jan Hammer Group for a world tour and releases* Jeff Beck With The Jan Hammer Group Live.

1975 *Tours the U. S. on a double bill with John McLaughlin and The Mahavishnu Orchestra.*

1978 *Beck tours Japan with jazz bassist Stanley Clarke, keyboardist Tony Hymas, and drummer Simon Phillips.*

1984 *Working with producer Nile Rodgers, Jeff records* Flash. *He is reunited with vocalist Rod Stewart on the single "People Get Ready," and wins his first Grammy for the instrumental "Escape."*

1989 *Teaming up with keyboardist Tony Hymas and drummer Terry Bozzio, Beck records* Jeff Beck's Guitar Shop. *Later he goes on tour with Stevie Ray Vaughan.*

1992 *Beck collaborates with keyboardist Jed Leiber for the soundtrack to Vietnam movie* Frankie's House.

1993 *Beck releases* Crazy Legs, *a tribute to Gene Vincent guitarist Cliff Gallup.*

important as the notes he plays and his phrasing, which is the main reason why his playing is so difficult to imitate.

Several of Beck's signature licks are the direct result of his early influences. His liberal use of pulled-off triplets is reminiscent of Cliff Gallup and Les Paul's playing, and some of his licks are similar to those played by blues harmonica players such as Little Walter.

Beck makes effective use of chromatically ascending octaves and slurred and raked grace notes. His use of the vibrato bar has become an integral facet of his style. He scoops the bar down and rises into notes, plays staccato notes that are accented by upward bar bends, and simulates slide guitar and harmonica with the vibrato.

More of a soloist than a rhythm player, Beck rarely plays conventional barre chords. Instead, he prefers to play single-note lines and double-stops, although he has been known to employ mind-boggling triple-stop bends as well.

Techniques

Jeff employs a variety of complex techniques when playing. The most important aspect of his sound is his use of his fingers and thumb to play the guitar, instead of a pick. Because he plays with his fingers, he has considerable control over dynamics and nuances. He often pulls on the strings to get a percussive snap, and he'll pluck several notes in a chord at once for piano-like note emphasis. Beck likes to play trills on the neck with his right hand, holding a note with his left-hand fingers and tapping a few frets higher than that with his right-hand fingers.

Beck's most recently developed technique is his use of the vibrato bar and harmonics to play melodies. Examples of this technique can be heard on "Where Were You" on *Guitar Shop* and "Vihn's Funeral" on *Frankie's House*. Jeff's guitars are set up so

he can raise or lower notes with the vibrato bar. Sometimes he uses volume swells while utilizing this technique to give notes a soft attack like a wind instrument.

The Hardware
Guitars, Strings, and Picks

Beck started playing on an acoustic guitar with only one string that he borrowed from a friend. When Jeff was 13, he built his first electric guitar. "It was bright yellow with all these wires and knobs," he reminisced. "I used to carry it around without a case so everyone could see it. People just freaked out."

Although there are pictures of Beck playing a rosewood-neck Stratocaster with the Deltones in 1961, one of his first professional-quality guitars was a Fender Esquire that he bought from John Walker of The Walker Brothers. As a member of the Yardbirds, Beck played a variety of guitars, including the Esquire, a Telecaster, and a Fender Jazzmaster. Inspired by seeing Eric Clapton play a Gibson Les Paul with John Mayall's Bluesbreakers, Beck started playing one as well. By the time he formed the Jeff Beck Group, he was using the Les Paul exclusively.

Beck returned to the Stratocaster when he started playing with Beck, Bogert, And Appice in 1972. For the next few years he used both the Strat and the Les Paul, but eventually he abandoned the Les Paul altogether. To this day, the Stratocaster remains the guitar most closely associated with Beck. His current

In the early '70s, Beck pioneered the jazz-rock fusion genre on the best-selling albums Blow By Blow *and* Wired. *His most recent projects have included an authentic rockabilly tribute and an Asian-inspired soundtrack.*

favorites include a Strat with a '62 body. In 1990, Fender introduced the Jeff Beck Signature Strat, which was developed with Jeff's assistance.

Jeff has used a variety of other guitars throughout his career, though. He often uses a stock '54 Telecaster and a Telecaster equipped with two humbucking pickups. In the late '70s, Ibanez made several guitars for him, but he has rarely been seen with them outside of his home. He has also experimented with guitar synthesizers, including the Roland GR-500 in the late '70s and the Roland GR-700 in the mid-'80s. Beck played a pink Jackson Soloist with Tina Turner's name scratched on it for a period during the

Jeff Beck is one of rock's most influential instrumentalists. Using little more than a Strat, Marshall amp, and delay and distortion pedals, he creates a wide variety of tones and timbres.

mid-'80s, including recording sessions and for his *Flash* album. He has also played Gretsch guitars on several occasions. He recorded his solo on "Savoy" with a Gretsch Country Gentleman, and he used a '56 Gretsch Duo-Jet on most of *Crazy Legs* to accurately duplicate Cliff Gallup's tone. Beck rarely plays acoustic guitar, but he used a Gibson J-200 to perform his solo on "Just Another Night" with Mick Jagger.

Jeff's favorite strings are Ernie Ball Hybrid Slinky, which are guage .009, .011, .016, .026, .036, and .046.

He stopped using a guitar pick in 1980, and now plays almost exclusively with his thumb and fingers. The only major exception was *Crazy Legs*, in which he used a thumbpick and metal fingerpicks to duplicate Cliff Gallup's playing style. When Jeff plays slide, he uses a piece of chrome steel tubing.

Amplifiers, Effects, and Devices

For live performance, Beck has used either Vox, Sunn, or Marshall amps. When he first joined the Yardbirds, he played through two Vox AC30s and a Vox Tone Bender fuzz box. Sometimes he also used several Vox Super Beatle amplifiers. By the time he formed the Jeff Beck Group, Beck was using 100-watt Marshall stacks. For a brief period with Beck, Bogert, And Appice, he played through Sunn amps with Univox speakers and used a talk-box device called the Bag. However, he returned to Marshall amps after Beck, Bogert, And Appice's break up and has relied on them ever since.

In the studio, Beck often uses the same amps that he performs with, although lately he has used several amps that he doesn't use live. For *Flash*, Beck recorded with Seymour Duncan Convertible 100 amps. For *Guitar Shop*, he played through Fender Twin Reverb and Fender Princeton amps that were connected in parallel. He used up to

In His Own Words

I don't try to baffle people. If chicks are gonna stand there and go "Huh?" and look at each other, then I'm wasting my time. I want to play notes and chord construction that they'll understand.
Guitar Player, *December 1973*

Emotion rules everything I do. I can switch on automatic and play, but it sounds terrible. I've got to be wound up, in the right mood.
Guitar Player, *October 1980*

I just pick up a guitar, and if I annoy myself within ten minutes, I'll put it down. If I'm not annoying myself, I'll keep going.
Guitar Player, *October 1980*

I shouldn't have done Blow By Blow. I wish I hadn't done any of them – they're just mistakes on record.
On his jazz-rock albums, Guitar Player, *February 1990*

I'm an awkward son of a bitch when it comes to doing the expected.
Guitar Player, *April 1993*

What They Say

Jeff Beck's great to listen to because he takes a chance, and when it comes off it's so emotional... Beck takes a chance every night.
Ritchie Blackmore, Guitar Player, *July 1973*

When he's on, Beck's probably the best there is.
Jimmy Page, Guitar Player, *July 1977*

I began to think of Jeff as probably being the finest guitar player that I'd ever seen. And I've been around... There's something cool and mean about Becky that beats everyone else.
Eric Clapton on playing with Beck at the ARMS concerts, Guitar Player, *July 1985*

It's been a lifelong thing to me, listening to you, man, and for me it's an honor to be out here with you now. And I'm not just being a parrot talking shit. This is the real deal.
Stevie Ray Vaughan on tour with Beck, Guitar Player, *February 1990*

four different Fender amps for the recording of *Crazy Legs*, including a Tremolux combo, a tweed reissue 4x10 Bassman, a Concert amp powering a 2x12 speaker cabinet, and a Twin Reverb.

Frankie's House was recorded without any amplifiers at all. Instead, Beck used a DigiTech GSP-21 multiple effects unit connected directly to the recording console. He has used a limited amount of effects in his career. In 1980, he used an Ibanez booster pedal and a Tycobrahe Paraflanger. For his *Guitar Shop* tour, his only effects were a Rat distortion pedal and a Boss DD-3 digital delay pedal.

Typical Licks

Beck has always played interesting lines. Notice the extensive use of the chromatic passing tones in this blues lick.

Beck's playing often features the suspended 4th note resolving to the major third when playing over dominant seventh chords.

In this phrase Beck uses "keyboard bends" and bounces on the whammy bar to "play" notes.

Discography

Jeff's first recording session, with the Tridents in 1963, was released in 1991 in the **Beckology** boxed set. His work with the Yardbirds appears on **Having A Raveup With The Yardbirds** (1965), **For Your Love** (1965), **Greatest Hits** (1965), and **Over Under Sideways Down** (1966). His singles "Hi Ho Silver Lining" and "Tally Man" followed in '67. With the Jeff Beck Group he recorded **Truth** (1968), **Beck-Ola** (1969), **Rough And Ready** (1971), and **Jeff Beck Group** (1972). With Beck, Bogert, and Appice, he recorded **Beck, Bogert, And Appice** (1972) and **Beck, Bogert, And Appice Live** (1973). Then followed **Blow By Blow** (1974) and **Wired** (1975), **Jeff Beck With The Jan Hammer Group Live** (1976), **There And Back** (1980), and **Flash** (1984). In 1985, he recorded Santo And Johnnie's "Sleepwalk" for the film **Porky's Revenge**, and in 1986, "Wild Thing." "The Train Kept A-Rollin" and "The Stumble" appeared in the movie **Twins** (1988). In 1989, he released **Jeff Beck's Guitar Shop With Terry Bozzio And Tony Hymas.** He collaborated with keyboardist Jed Leiber on the soundtrack to **Frankie's House** (1992) and in 1993 recorded **Crazy Legs** with The Big Town Playboys.

Recording Sessions

Early guest performances include "Jeff's Blues" on **Stevie Winwood and Friends**, Donovan's "Barabajagal," the GTO's **Permanent Damage**, and Screamin' Lord Sutch's **Lord Sutch & Heavy Friends**. In the '70s he played on Stevie Wonder's **Talking Book**, Badger's **White Lady**, Eddie Harris' **Eddie Harris In The U.K.**, Narada Michael Walden's **Garden Of Love Light**, Billy Preston's **Billy Preston**, Upp's **Upp** and **This Way Upp**, Stanley Clarke's **Journey To Love** and **Modern Man**, and the soundtrack to **Sgt. Pepper's Lonely Hearts Club Band**. In 1984 he appeared on Rod Stewart's **Camouflage**, Tina Turner's **Private Dancer**, and Mick Jagger's **She's The Boss**. He reunited with the Yardbirds for **Box Of Frogs**, and with Tim Bogert on Vanilla Fudge's **Mystery**. In the early '90s, he guested on Roger Water's **Amused To Death**, Kate Bush's **The Red Shoes**, Paul Rodgers' **Muddy Water Blues**, Warner Bros' **Stone Free – A Tribute To Jimi Hendrix**, and the soundtrack to **Blue Chips**.

Chuck Berry

Chuck Berry may not have invented rock 'n' roll, but he established the electric guitar as the definitive instrument of the genre. By blending swing and country rhythms with blues guitar playing, Berry innovated a style unlike any heard before. His rhythms and double-stop leads have become a staple of rock 'n' roll guitar playing, and his songs have influenced many popular artists, such as the Beach Boys, the Rolling Stones, and the Beatles. Although he is in his late sixties, Berry still plays with the energy and authority he had as a young man.

The Player

Influences

Chuck was exposed to music at an early age. When he was growing up in St. Louis, Missouri, the local church choir – the Antioch Baptist Church choir – used to practice in his parents' home. Later, Chuck started singing in that same choir. He got his first taste of success as a performer when he sang Jay McShann's "Confessin' The Blues" at a concert arranged by Sumner High School's class of '41. "I realized as I was performing that the audience will respond if you give them what they want," he reminisced in his autobiography.

Berry decided to learn to play guitar while he was attending high school. His favorite music at this time was boogie woogie, blues, and swing. The style that he developed later as a recording artist for Chess records is largely an amalgamation of these styles. One of his first instructional books was Nick Manoloff's *Guitar Book Of Chords*. Later, he studied music theory and harmony at Ludwig's Music in St. Louis.

He was influenced by several blues guitarists, including Muddy Waters, Elmore James, and Tampa Red. He also enjoyed the rhythm-and-blues styles of T-Bone Walker, Lonnie Johnson, and Carl Hogan with Louis Jordan's Tympany Five, as well as Charlie Christian and Django Reinhardt's jazz playing. (A local jazz musician, guitarist Ira Harris, showed Chuck how to play a few jazz licks in the style of Christian.) Hogan's rhythm playing was especially influential on Chuck. "He stuck to the I-IV-V, played mainly quarters and eighths, and played right on the beat," Berry told Tom Wheeler in the March 1988 issue of *Guitar Player*. Berry was also influenced by saxophone players, citing Illinois Jacquet as one of his favorites.

When Berry started playing in clubs, he learned a variety of material to get and keep jobs. The material ranged from blues to pop, such as Harry Belafonte's "Banana Boat Song" and Nat King Cole tunes, to country songs, including "Mountain Dew" and Hank Williams' "Jambalaya." The country influence was very evident on Berry's first single, "Maybellene," as well as on several songs where he played pedal steel.

Approach and Style

Although Chuck Berry once said that he did not recognize any style of his own, most

Background

1926 *Charles Edward Anderson Berry is born in St. Louis, Missouri, on October 18.*

1951 *Berry starts playing guitar at parties.*

1952 *Pianist Johnnie Johnson asks Berry to join his group, featuring Ebby Hardy on drums, for a New Year's Eve gig. Johnson and Hardy later accompany Berry on his first recording session for Chess.*

1955 *Berry records "Maybellene," along with "Wee Wee Hours," "You Can't Catch Me," and "Thirty Days" at Chess Records in Chicago, who release "Maybellene" as a single. By the end of the year, it becomes the #1 R&B song in America.*

1957 *Chuck's first album, After School Session, is released.*

1961 *Berry is incarcerated for transporting a minor across state lines for immoral purposes.*

1964 *He collaborates with Bo Diddley on the album Two Great Guitars.*

1966 *Starts recording for Mercury Records.*

1970 *Berry returns to Chess.*

1972 *He scores his first #1 hit on the Billboard singles chart with the novelty song "My Ding-A-Ling."*

1975 *He records his last album for Chess, Chuck Berry.*

1979 *Berry is imprisoned for tax irregularities.*

1980 *A recording of "Johnny B. Goode" is launched into space on the Voyager spaceship.*

1984 *Awarded a Grammy for Lifetime Achievement.*

1986 *Berry becomes a charter inductee into the Rock & Roll Hall Of Fame.*

1987 *Berry is presented with a star on the Hollywood Walk Of Fame. Hail! Hail! Rock 'n' Roll, a concert/biography film. Chuck also writes Chuck Berry: The Autobiography.*

1990 *He pleads guilty to possession of marijuana and receives a suspended sentence.*

1993 *Berry performs at U. S. President Bill Clinton's inauguration.*

music historians agree that his guitar style was one of the most influential factors that defined the sound of early rock music. Berry's music mixed elements of R&B with country, resulting in what eventually came to be known as rock 'n' roll. His music encompassed many styles – including blues, swing, jazz, and calypso – but it always bore his indistinguishable personality.

The most important aspect of Berry's style is his rhythmic sophistication. Most of his rhythms are syncopated and based on boogie-woogie patterns that were popular during the early '50s. Berry notes that this was a result of his big-band swing influences. His rhythms are often a cross between 4/4 time, eighth notes, downstroke shuffles, and a straight eighth-note rock feel. He likes to change the accents of a shuffle to make the groove swing more. Another common trait of Berry's rhythms is a root-to-fifth bass pattern, which is reminiscent of early country music.

Berry's songs often start with a signature lick, a short solo, or an inventive sound effect, such as his use of an augmented chord to imitate a school bell in "School Days" or the fourth interval he plays on "Maybellene" to mimic a car horn. His solos incorporate liberal use of double-stops and bent notes. One of his most common licks, where a note is bent up a whole step, followed by the same note played on an adjacent string, is similar to a lick that was often played by T-Bone Walker.

Many of Berry's early compositions were influenced by the blues, such as "No Money Down," which is reminiscent of Muddy Waters' "Hoochie Coochie Man." But shortly thereafter his chord progressions deviated slightly from traditional blues progressions and began to display elements of Berry's emerging stylistic variations. For example, instead of playing a V-IV-I change over a verse, he preferred to play V-V-I.

Perhaps because Chuck often plays with pianists (he was heavily influenced by his piano player, Johnnie Johnson), many of his songs are performed in keys such as *B♭* and *E♭*, whereas most guitarists prefer to play in *A* or *E*. Because Chuck primarily uses barre chords and pentatonic box patterns, he does not rely on open strings as much as those guitarists who usually play in *A* or *E*.

Techniques

To fully comprehend Berry's rhythm playing, a guitarist should concentrate on right-hand technique as much as left-hand fingering. To achieve a staccato sound, Berry uses a combination of right-hand muting (resting the heel of his palm against the guitar's bridge), and downstrokes. On faster rhythms, such as the intro to "School Days," he uses a combination of upstrokes and downstrokes. He holds his flatpick between his left-hand thumb and forefinger, picking in the area just above the bridge pickup.

Berry's left-hand rhythm technique incorporates liberal use of double-stops and barre chords. He often uses his left-hand little finger to play alternating bass patterns on the lower strings. These bass patterns have become a signature of Berry's rhythm style.

In addition to bending notes, Berry uses slides and slurs liberally. Many of his songs and solos start with a pattern of descending

With his mixture of swing and country rhythms and blues licks, Chuck Berry was a seminal rock 'n' roll guitarist. His double-stop licks and note-bending phrases have become essential parts of the rock guitarist's vocabulary.

double-stops, where he slurs the chord downward as he moves to the next one. He also tends to slowly bend and release notes several times after picking them, making them sound more like two separate notes than like vibrato. Another favorite technique of his is to utilize hammer-ons and pull-offs sparingly to accent or anticipate a chord.

The Hardware
Guitars, Strings, and Picks

Berry's first guitar was a Kay electric guitar that was sold to him for $30 by Joe Sherman, an R&B performer in St. Louis. Chuck is pictured with an Epiphone archtop electric in early Chess publicity photos, but he claims that he never recorded with that guitar. Prior to his first recording session for Chess, Chuck purchased a blonde Gibson ES-350T archtop electric with two P-90 single-coil pickups from Ludwig's Music in St. Louis. This is the guitar that Berry is seen with in most of his early promotional photos, and it is also the guitar that he used on most of his legendary mid-'50s recordings. Sometime around 1957, he purchased a similar ES-350T, but this guitar was equipped

with two humbucking pickups instead of the single-coils. Berry recollects that this guitar was used on most of the hits that he recorded during the late '50s. He later gave this guitar to his friend, Joe Edwards, and it is now on display at Edwards' restaurant, Blueberry Hill, in St. Louis, Missouri.

Although Berry is seen performing with a Gretsch Chet Atkins 6120 in the movie *Rock, Rock, Rock*, he admits that the guitar was just a prop. He did own a hollowbody Gretsch for a while, but he has expressed a dislike for the guitar's heavier weight compared to his Gibsons. Apparently, he did not use it for live performance or for any significant recordings.

In the '60s, Chuck started playing a Gibson ES-355 semi-hollow electric fitted with two humbucking pickups and a vibrola tailpiece. Because the ES-355's double cutaways provide better access to the upper frets than his early Gibsons, this style of guitar is Chuck's favorite. He still performs with this model today. He also owns a Gibson Lucille model with no f-holes, which is based after B.B. King's ES-355.

For a brief period in the mid '50s, when Chuck was performing at the Cosmopolitan Club in St. Louis, he used a black Gibson Les Paul Custom solidbody. "What made me get the Les Paul was the way it felt," Berry told Tom Wheeler in a March '88 interview for *Guitar Player*. "It had these flat frets, and it was comfortable and seemed to never wear out and it stayed in tune." This was the only time that Berry played a solidbody guitar.

On several of his early singles, such as "Blues For Hawaiians," "Deep Feeling," and "Low Feeling," Berry played a late '30s Gibson Electraharp pedal steel.

Berry got his first big break in 1955, when Muddy Waters suggested he give his demo tape to Leonard Chess at Chess Records in Chicago. By the end of that year, his first single, "Maybellene," reached #1 on the R&B charts.

In His Own Words

Maybellene was a cow in a nursery rhyme that I ran across in the third grade. I was thinking of a freaky name for a girl. I've met three girls with that name since then. Of course, I told them I wrote the tune for them.
Guitar Player, *February 1971*

Music is so much mathematics, it's pathetic. Anything off-beat has to get back on the beat, or the whole thing is going to be out. So with most of my music I keep the basics on 4/4 time and I take the deviations.
Guitar Player, *February 1971*

I didn't know anything about style when I started. I mean, I knew what a style was, but I wasn't aware of having one myself. That sort of thinking was far too technical for me at that time.
Guitar Player, *March 1988*

I didn't give a shit about the fame. Still don't. The only thing I cared about was being able to walk into a restaurant and get served, and that was something I should have had anyway, without the fame.
Guitar Player, *March 1988*

What They Say

If you want to play rock 'n' roll you would end up playing like Chuck, or what you learned from Chuck, because there is very little – actually any – other choice. He's really laid the law down.
Eric Clapton, *from the movie* Hail! Hail! Rock 'n' Roll.

The more you find out about him, the less you know about him. I don't even know if Chuck realizes what he did. Michelangelo probably thought he was third-rate too.
Keith Richards, *from the movie* Hail! Hail! Rock 'n' Roll.

If you tried to give rock 'n' roll another name, you might call it "Chuck Berry."
John Lennon

Amplifiers, Effects, and Devices

One of Berry's first amplifiers was an Epiphone model in a wood cabinet with a cut-out 'E' pattern over the speaker grill. Little is known about the amps Berry used for his early recordings, although he does recall that they were tweed-covered Fenders.

Berry travels to gigs carrying just his guitar. He specifies that two Fender Dual Showman Reverb amplifiers must be provided by the concert promoter. Once at the venue, he plugs straight into the amplifier with no effects other than the amp's built-in reverb. "Tried a wah-wah once," he notes. "Stubbed my toe on it. Forget it."

Typical Licks

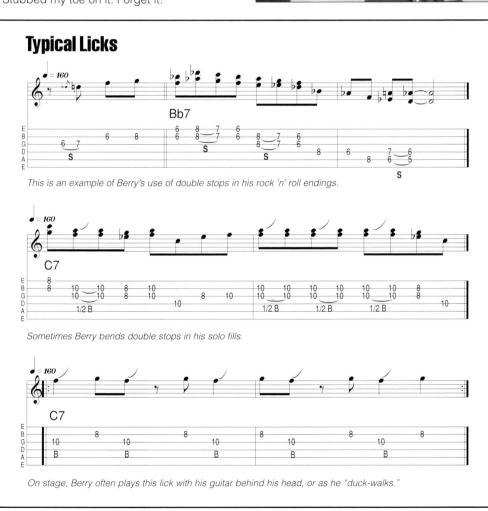

This is an example of Berry's use of double stops in his rock 'n' roll endings.

Sometimes Berry bends double stops in his solo fills.

On stage, Berry often plays this lick with his guitar behind his head, or as he "duck-walks."

Discography

At Muddy Waters' recommendation, Chuck Berry sent a demo tape to Chess Records in Chicago. They were impressed, and on May 21, 1955, Chuck recorded his first single, "Maybellene," at the Chess studios; it was released by them later that summer.

Over the next several years, Chuck released a steady stream of singles, including "Roll Over Beethoven," "School Days," "Rock And Roll Music," "Sweet Little Sixteen," and "Johnny B. Goode," which all charted on Billboard's Hot 100 Singles chart. Berry's first long-playing album, **After School Session**, was released in 1957.

Chess released the following Chuck Berry albums and greatest hits compilations: **One Dozen Berrys** (1958), **Chuck Berry Is On Top** (1959), **Rockin' At The Hops** (1960), **New Juke Box Hits** (1961), **Twist** (1962), **Chuck Berry On Stage** (1963), **Chuck Berry's Greatest Hits** (1964), **Two Great Guitars** (featuring Bo Diddley, 1964), **St. Louis To Liverpool** (1964), **Chuck Berry In London** (1965), **Fresh Berrys** (1966), **Chuck Berry's Golden Decade** (1967), **Back Home** (1970), **San Francisco Dues** (1971), **The London Chuck Berry Sessions** (1972), **Chuck Berry's Golden Decade, Vol. 2** (1973), **Bio** (1973), **Chuck Berry's Golden Decade, Vol. 3** (1974), **Chuck Berry** (1975), **The Great Twenty-Eight** (1982), **Rock 'n' Roll Rarities** (1986), and **More Rock 'n' Roll Rarities** (1986).

The soundtrack to the movie **Hail! Hail! Rock 'n' Roll**, which featured appearances by Eric Clapton, Keith Richards, and Robert Cray, was released in 1987 by MCA records.

Berry's Mercury and Polygram recordings are considered inferior by many, including Berry himself, and are of little interest to any but the most adamant Berry collectors. Most Berry fanatics consider his pre-'65 Chess recordings as his finest work.

Recording Sessions

Berry did not participate on any recording sessions other than those for his own records.

Ritchie Blackmore

With a style influenced as much by Bach as the blues, Ritchie Blackmore introduced classical-music elements to the rock guitarist's vocabulary. His technically advanced playing paved the way for the flamboyant heavy-metal guitar styles of Eddie Van Halen and Yngwie Malmsteen. As a guitarist with Deep Purple and Rainbow, he introduced a new level of sophistication to rock music, while his "Smoke On The Water" riff introduced countless guitarists to the simple joys of heavy-metal guitar.

The Player

Influences

Like many other British adolescents in the '50s, Blackmore was initially attracted to skiffle music, and he joined a band that played covers of Lonnie Donegan songs such as "Rock Island Line." As Blackmore himself recalls: "There were about 20 guitarists involved and none of them could play."

Shortly after he started playing guitar, Ritchie took classical-guitar lessons for about a year. He feels that these lessons were quite important in the development of his playing style as he learned to play with all four left-hand fingers. He later took classical guitar lessons from Big Jim Sullivan, a neighbor of his who worked as a professional session guitarist and gigged with Tom Jones. Sullivan showed him how to play Bach pieces and read music. On his lessons with Sullivan, Blackmore recalled: "He said to me once, 'Whatever type of music you're going to play, you must stick to it; don't be a jack of all trades.' So I decided rock 'n' roll was the thing."

Some of Blackmore's favorite guitarists when he was learning to play included James Burton, Scotty Moore, Hank Marvin, Duane Eddy, and Jimmy Bryant with Speedy West. Blackmore was particularly impressed by Les Paul's flashy guitar playing. Some of his influences during the early days of Deep Purple included jazz guitarist Wes Montgomery, Jimi Hendrix, and Duane Allman with the Allman Brothers Band.

Blackmore has admitted that when Deep Purple was being formed, Jon Lord and he were heavily inspired by Vanilla Fudge's extended, eight-minute songs. Other bands that Ritchie enjoyed during Deep Purple's early years include Pink Floyd and Curved Air. During the late '70s he expressed a fondness for the music of Jethro Tull, Cream, and Procol Harum.

Classical music, however, remains his favorite material. He particularly enjoys medieval, Renaissance, and chamber music, and has a preference for quartets as opposed to orchestras. He has remarked that his classical background was a heavy influence on his songwriting. Inspired by 'cellist Jacqueline Du Pré, he studied 'cello during the late '70s. Although he feels he wasn't a very good 'cellist, and eventually abandoned the instrument, he wrote the Rainbow song "Stargazer" on the 'cello.

Background

1945 *Ritchie Blackmore is born in Weston-Super-Mare, England, on April 14.*

1956 *Ritchie starts playing guitar. Although details of his early amplifiers are unknown, he used to claim in interviews that he ran a 30-watt amplifier through a smashed 3-inch speaker in order to produce a fuzz tone.*

1962 *Becomes a member of Joe Meek's Outlaws and does session work. He becomes a member of Screaming Lord Sutch's band and performs with Jerry Lee Lewis.*

1967 *Forms the band Roundabout with Jon Lord, and releases an album of the same name.*

1968 *Forms Deep Purple with Jon Lord on keyboards, Ian Paice on drums, Rod Evans on vocals, and Nick Simper on bass. The band's debut album,* Shades Of Deep Purple, *is released in the United States. The single "Hush" becomes a hit.*

1968 *Ritchie is rumoured to have released* Supreme Psychedelic Underground, *under the name Hell Preachers, with Jon Lord and Ian Paice.*

1969 *Deep Purple's lineup changes, with vocalist Ian Gillan replacing Rod Evans, and bassist Roger Glover replacing Nick Simper. The band performs with the Royal Philharmonic Orchestra. Ritchie marries German dancer Barbel Hardie.*

1970 In Rock, *a recording of the Royal Philarmonic Orchestra performance, is released.*

1973 *Deep Purple replace lead singer Ian Gillan with unknown 22-year-old David Coverdale and release* Burn *the following year.*

1975 *Blackmore quits Deep Purple and forms Rainbow with vocalist Ronnie James Dio, drummer Cozy Powell, bassist Jimmy Bain, and keyboardist Tony Carey.*

1976 *Blackmore starts playing 'cello. Plays guitar on Adam Faith's* I Survive, *released on Warner Brothers.*

1984 *Rainbow tours Japan with a symphony orchestra. Later that year Rainbow breaks up, and Deep Purple is reunited. The lineup includes Blackmore, Jon Lord, Ian Paice, bassist Roger Glover, and vocalist Ian Gillan. The band releases* Perfect Strangers.

Approach and Style

Blackmore was one of the first rock guitarists to blend blues sensibilities and classical-influenced motifs. His modal and harmonic minor sounds lent a distinctly "European" flavor to his playing that sharply contrasted the pentatonic minor styles favored by American rock and blues guitarists. "I was never sure what I wanted to be," he explained in a '91 *Guitar World* interview. "I found the blues too limiting, too confining. I'd always thought – with all due respect to B. B. King – that you couldn't just play four notes. Classical, on the other hand, was always too disciplined. I was always stuck between the two, stuck in a musical no-man's land."

An accomplished improviser, Blackmore admits that he dislikes to play the same solo twice. His solos make liberal use of pentatonic minor runs, similar to those played by many blues guitarists, but for variety he will add notes such as a ♯4, ♭6, or ♮7 to the scale for variety. These additional notes lend his playing a Dorian flavor. Many of his runs are played entirely in the Phrygian mode, and he will sometimes incorporate a ♭2 in his pentatonic minor runs, which gives the scale a Phrygian slant. For added tension, he'll move entire patterns up and down the neck in half steps. *Am* ostinatos and ascending or descending triplet arpeggios often appear in his solos, lending them a distinct, Bach-influenced classical feel. In the studio he often double-tracks his arpeggio solos with a diatonic third or fifth harmony.

Ritchie claims that he likes to play in the keys of *F♯* and *Dm*, and many of the songs he has written for Deep Purple and Rainbow are in these keys. However, much of his work is also written in the keys of *Am* or *Bm*. His heavy reliance on minor keys is another attribute that lends a classical-influenced flavor to his playing.

Techniques

Without doubt, Blackmore's classical training was the most significant factor in the development of his technique. Some of his classical-influenced traits include playing with all four left-hand fingers, his well-developed left-hand finger vibrato, and his effective use of pedal patterns played on open strings.

Blackmore uses alternate picking to play fast runs and triplets. Sometimes he plays rhythm with his fingers, placing the pick in his mouth. One example of this technique is the introduction to "Smoke On The Water," where he plucks the fifths with his fingers, producing a percussive tone. Although his right-hand technique is quite aggressive, he uses a light touch with his left hand on the fingerboard. He feels that this enables him to play faster.

When he switched to the Stratocaster, Blackmore began making liberal use of the vibrato bar, using it to augment his left-hand vibrato and to create stunning, flamboyant sound effects, such as dropping a note's pitch as much as an octave or shaking notes violently. His vibrato-bar theatrics were inspired by the guitarist in the James Cotton Blues Band and by Jimi Hendrix' techniques. Lately, Ritchie's vibrato-bar technique has become much more conservative, and he uses it during his solos sparingly.

When he plays a Stratocaster, Blackmore doesn't use the middle pickup at all, preferring the tone of the individual neck and bridge pickups. He likes to play with his amplifier turned up all the way, controlling dynamics and cleaning up or overdriving his tone by adjusting the guitar's volume control.

Onstage with Deep Purple and Rainbow, Blackmore was an aggressive, outrageous performer. He says that Screaming Lord Sutch, whom he played with in the early '60s, inspired his stage persona.

The Hardware
Guitars, Strings, and Picks

Blackmore's first guitar was a second-hand Framus Spanish acoustic guitar. He later replaced this with a Hofner solidbody, which he has described as "a great guitar." When Ritchie was 16, he bought a Gibson ES-335, which he used until 1970. He recorded the first three Deep Purple albums with this guitar.

After becoming fascinated with Jimi Hendrix' music, Blackmore decided to put down the Gibson and start playing a Fender Stratocaster, which he has used ever since. Blackmore claims that his first Strat was given to him by Eric Clapton. "I prefer the Stratocaster because it has a more 'attacky' sound," Blackmore told Martin Webb in a '73 *Guitar Player* interview. "A Stratocaster is harder to play than a Gibson, too. You can't race across a Strat's fingerboard so fast. With a Gibson it's so easy to zoom up and down that you end up playing physical shapes rather than really working for an original sound." Blackmore has also mentioned that he developed a preference for the Stratocaster because of the way the guitar sounds when paired with a wah-wah pedal.

Blackmore performs his own modifications on his Stratocasters, such as sanding a concave surface in the fingerboard between the frets, lowering the middle pickup so it is flush with the pickguard, and adjusting the vibrato bar so it can be both pulled up and pushed down. He uses four springs for his vibrato unit. He often replaces the Strat's frets with large Gibson frets and swaps the stock Fender tuning machines for Schaller heads. Blackmore prefers Strats with rosewood fingerboards, feeling that maple necks are too flimsy to handle the abuse that he subjects his guitars to.

Blackmore uses specially made, heavy tortoiseshell picks with squared edges and a point. He endorses Picato strings, gauged .010, .011, .014, .026, .036, and .042.

Amplifiers, Effects, and Devices
Blackmore played through a Vox AC30 on the first three Deep Purple albums. In 1970, he switched to Marshall stacks. "I saw the Marshall setup and liked the way they looked, but the sound was awful," he told Steve Rosen in a '78 *Guitar Player* interview. His amp heads were 200-watt Marshall Majors, which were modified at the Marshall factory. Although Blackmore claims that the amps had extensive tonal modifications, two extra tubes in the output stage, and were boosted to 250 or 300 watts,

Blackmore was one of the first rock guitarists to borrow heavily from classical music. His playing style influenced many guitarists during the '70s and '80s, including Eddie Van Halen, Yngwie Malmsteen, and Vinnie Moore.

In His Own Words

I like leaping around on stage as long as it's done with class.
Guitar Player, *July 1973*

Some nights I feel like I can do anything. Other nights I feel inhibited... If I go on stage and think, "That guy down in the front row thinks I'm an idiot. He thinks I can't play the guitar," I seize up.
Guitar Player, *July 1973*

Actually I don't play in the studio, I have someone else who takes my place. Jim Page comes in.
Guitar Player, *September 1978*

I love to have that freedom of just going onstage and playing whatever I want to play at the time. I'll play the numbers which I'm supposed to play, but in the in-between parts if I'm feeling good I'll play something completely off the wall that I've never ever played in my life.
Guitar Player, *September 1978*

What They Say

Everybody tells me I sound like Ritchie Blackmore, especially guitar players, which is very frustrating because I try to explain to them that I don't play like him at all. But I was very inspired by him in the beginning.
Yngwie Malmsteen, Guitar Player, *March 1984*

I was a fan of Ritchie Blackmore when I first started playing guitar... I read in an interview that he listens to classical music, so I decided to give it a listen, and I bought a Bach and Beethoven record.
Vinnie Moore, Guitar Player, *July 1988*

I picked up a copy of Guitar Player *in England and read where Ritchie Blackmore said to steal from everybody, and he was right!... Every record that I liked became a mini-teacher in a sense. That's a great way to learn; to steal, steal, steal. [laughs]*
Deke Leonard of Welsh rock band Man, Guitar Player, *February 1977*

sources at Marshall say that the only modification to his amps was the addition of a master volume. Blackmore used one stack on stage (one amplifier head with two 4x12 speaker cabinets), and used the same setup in the studio.

Though he expresses a dislike for effects, Blackmore occasionally uses a wah-wah pedal. During his session days and the early days of Deep Purple, he used a Hornby-Kues treble booster. He says that he used this device for added sustain, not for enhancing treble response. Onstage, he often played through a tape echo device that he built from a tape recorder.

Discography

Deep Purple's first three albums, **Shades of Deep Purple** (1968), **Book of Taliesyn** (1969), and **Deep Purple** (1969), are pop-oriented records that are of interest only to those who are curious to explore Blackmore's early guitar style. The band's next record, **Concerto For Group And Orchestra** (1970), signifies Deep Purple's transformation into a classical-influenced heavy metal group and it shows a few signs of Blackmore's emerging style.

Blackmore's style had fully matured by the time Deep Purple released **In Rock** (1970). **Fireball** (1971), **Machine Head** (1972), the live album **Made In Japan** (1972), **Who Do We Think We Are?** (1973), **Burn** (1974), and **Stormbringer** (1974) all contain examples of Blackmore's finest playing.

His early albums with Rainbow, **Ritchie Blackmore's Rainbow** (1975), **Rainbow Rising** (1976), **On Stage** (1977), and **Long Live Rock 'n' Roll** (1978) continue to showcase his fiery playing. With the replacement of vocalist Ronnie James Dio with Graham Bonnet, Rainbow toned down its approach and pursued pop hits. The albums **Down To Earth** (1979), **Difficult To Cure** (1981), **Straight Between The Eyes** (1982), and **Bent Out Of Shape** (1983) are of little interest to fans of Blackmore's playing.

Blackmore's efforts with the reformed Deep Purple, **Perfect Strangers** (1984), **The House Of Blue Light** (1987), **Slaves And Masters** (1990), and **The Battle Rages On** (1993), are a mixed bag. His playing is still commendable, but the material is not as compelling as that from Deep Purple's early-'70s prime.

Recording Sessions

Although Blackmore participated on many sessions during the '60s, little of his work has been documented or can be verified. Anyone interested in his early playing should search for Screaming Lord Sutch's **Hands Of Jack The Ripper**, and the **Green Bullfrog** album, which features guitarists Albert Lee and Big Jim Sullivan, as well as future Deep Purple members Ian Paice and Roger Glover.

Typical Licks

♩ = 132

C7

```
E|----------------8----------------------------------------|
B|------8--------11--11------11--10--8----------------------|
G|--10--------B---B-----------------11--10--8----8---8----~~|
D|--B------------------------------------C---10--C---10-----|
E|----------------------------------------------------------|
```

This is Blackmore at his finest, a fast, triplet-based blues-scale lick with an added sixth note.

♩ = 160

A7

```
E|----------------------------------------------------------|
B|----------------------------------------------------------|
G|--7--5------8--5------7--5------8--5------7--5--7--8--7--5---7--5--7--8--7--5-----|
D|-------7----------7----------7----------7-------------------7-------------------7|
E|----P-------P---------P-------P---------P-------P---------P---------P-------------|
```

Blackmore is the master of fast hammer-ons and pull-offs in repeated sequences.

♩ = 76

E7

```
E|--------------------------------------------------------------|
B|--9--10--9---------------8----8--8--8--7--7--7-----------------|
G|---------9---7----(7)---8--9-----------------9--9--9--7--9--9-9|
D|--H------P-------(B)-----S----------------------------B--------|
E|--------------------------------------------------------------|
```
1 1/2

This lick starts with minor pentatonics played staccato and ends with lazy, fluid vibrato.

Eric Clapton

Eric Clapton was a leading exponent of the '60s British blues revival. As a member of the Yardbirds, John Mayall's Bluesbreakers, Cream, and Blind Faith, and as a solo artist, he introduced the blues to thousands. Although he has sustained many ups and downs in his life, he has turned his personal turmoil into inspiration and has remained a leading guitar hero throughout his musical career. Today, Clapton is considered the greatest white blues guitarist by countless music fans.

The Player

Influences

Clapton started playing the guitar at 14. He was entirely self-taught, learning most of his licks off of records. His first influences were rock 'n' roll guitarists, such as Chuck Berry and Buddy Holly. When Eric enrolled at the Kingston College Of Art in London, he was introduced to the blues by other students and became highly interested in the early Delta-blues styles. His early blues influences include Big Bill Broonzy, Muddy Waters, Charlie Patton, Tampa Red, and Blind Willie Johnson, who was one of the biggest influences on Clapton's slide playing. Clapton later developed an interest in contemporary blues artists such as Buddy Guy, Otis Rush, B.B. King, Albert King, and Freddie King.

The blues artist who had the most impact on Clapton, though, was Robert Johnson. Johnson's *King Of The Delta Blues Singers,* (Volumes 1 and 2), are Clapton's favorites. "Both of the Robert Johnson albums actually cover all of my desires musically," he says. "Every angle of expression and every emotion is expressed on both of those albums." Eric has covered Johnson songs throughout his career, including "Ramblin' On My Mind" (his first recorded lead vocal), "Crossroads," which he recorded with Cream, and "Walkin' Blues," from his *Unplugged* appearance.

Other albums that Eric enjoyed during his early playing years include *Blind Willie Johnson – His Story, Ray Charles Live At Newport,* B.B. King's *Live At The Regal, The Best Of Muddy Waters, Howlin' Wolf,* Jimmy Reed's *Rockin' With Reed,* Chuck Berry's *One Dozen Berrys,* and *Freddie King Sings.*

During the '70s, Clapton strayed briefly from his blues roots and became interested in country and reggae. J.J. Cale was one of his strongest influences during this time, and Clapton recorded several Cale tunes, including "After Midnight" and "Cocaine."

Approach and Style

Clapton's playing style emphasizes emotion over flashy displays of speed. Like the blues guitarists that influenced him, he plays primarily in pentatonic minor scales. He admits that many of his licks are derived from Albert, B.B., and Freddie King. However, he has added his own idiosyncrasies to develop a style that is truly his own.

The most distinctive element of Clapton's style is his note-bending and vibrato

Background

1945 *Eric Patrick Clapton is born in Ripley, Surrey, England, on March 30.*

1962 *He starts attending the Kingston College of Art, where he discovers blues music.*

1963 *Eric forms his first band, the Roosters. In October he replaces Top Topham in the Yardbirds.*

1964 *The Yardbirds record* Five Live Yardbirds.

1965 *Clapton leaves the Yardbirds to concentrate on the blues. He later joins John Mayall's Bluesbreakers.*

1966 *Leaves the Bluesbreakers to form Cream with Ginger Baker on drums and Jack Bruce on bass.*

1969 *Cream disbands. Eric joins Blind Faith, then becomes a member of Delaney & Bonnie & Friends.*

1970 *Derek And The Dominos record* Layla And Other Assorted Love Songs. *Later that year, Clapton releases his first record as a solo artist,* Eric Clapton.

1973 *After a two-year break, performs with Rick Grech, Steve Winwood, and Ron Wood in the Palpitations.*

1974 *Kicks heroin addiction. Starts working with Carl Radle. Records* 461 Ocean Boulevard.

1979 *Marries George Harrison's ex-wife Patti. Tours with Muddy Waters, then forms an all-English band with guitarist Albert Lee, bassist Dave Markee, drummer Henry Spinetti, and keyboardist Chris Stainton.*

1983 *He appears at the ARMS (Action Research in Multiple Sclerosis) shows benefiting Ronnie Lane.*

1988 *Divorced by Patti Harrison.*

1989 *Clapton is awarded a Living Legend Award at the first International Rock Awards.*

1991 *Conor, the four-year-old son of Clapton and Italian actress Lori del Santo, falls to his death on March 20. Later that year, Clapton tours with George Harrison.*

1992 *Tours with Elton John. Writes the score for the movie* Rush. *Makes an appearance on MTV's* Unplugged.

1993 *Cream reunites at a Rock And Roll Hall Of Fame induction ceremony. Clapton wins six Grammys for his* Unplugged *album.*

1994 *Releases well-received album* From The Cradle.

techniques. He frequently bends notes in whole- or half-step intervals, adds vibrato to the bent note, and holds the bend for two or more beats. Sometimes his bends are slow and deliberate, taking a while to reach the final pitch.

When playing slide, Clapton generally prefers to use an open-*A* tuning (*E, A, E, A, C#, E,* low to high), though he has often recorded with open *G* (*D, G, D, G, B, D,* low to high), which is the same as open *A*, only a whole-step lower. The only exception is "Tell The Truth," which Clapton recorded with Derek And The Dominos in open *E* (*E, B, E, G#, B, E,* low to high).

Tone is a crucial element of Clapton's style. With the Bluesbreakers and Cream, he often played solos with the guitar set to the neck pickup and with the tone control turned all the way down. This fluid, singing tone was nicknamed "woman tone" by Clapton fans. With Derek And The Dominos, his tone was more biting and stinging, reminiscent of Buddy Guy. He achieved this tone by using the bridge pickup on his Stratocaster. His current tone is a cross between the two. His favorite setting for lead is the middle position on the Stratocaster's pickup selector, although he often uses the bridge/middle and neck/middle settings as well.

Techniques

Clapton's playing technique is noteworthy for its economy of motion. He plays within typical pentatonic "box" patterns, but will use techniques such as string skipping, note bending, and interval jumps to add variety. To ease transitions between patterns, he often plays duplicate notes on adjacent strings. Unlike most blues players, he likes to use open strings in his lead lines, damping the strings with his right-hand fingers to keep them from ringing out too long.

When playing electric, he plays almost exclusively with a flatpick, holding the pick between his thumb and first finger. On acoustic guitar, however, he prefers to fingerpick using a flatpick and his fingers.

The Hardware

Guitars, Strings, and Picks

Eric received his first guitar, a semi-hollow Kay electric, as a gift from his grandparents. He experimented with different guitars in his early playing years, including a Gibson ES-335, and a Fender Telecaster, Jazzmaster, and Jaguar. During his brief stint in the Yardbirds, he played a Telecaster. By the time he joined John Mayall's Bluesbreakers, he was using a late-'50s Gibson Les Paul Standard. His use of this created a big demand for Les Pauls from that era, driving up their price considerably. With Cream he switched to an SG-shaped early-'60s Les Paul.

Although Clapton used a variety of guitars throughout his early career, the guitar that is most closely associated with him is the Fender Stratocaster. He started playing the Strat in 1969 when he became a member of Delaney & Bonnie. His most famous Strat, nicknamed "Blackie," was made of parts from three different Strats that Clapton bought in the U.S. In 1988, Fender made Eric several custom Strats, which became the basis for the Eric Clapton signature model. The signature Strats are Clapton's current favorite for live performance.

At various times in his career, he has performed or recorded with a Gibson ES-335, a Gibson Firebird, a Fender Telecaster Custom, a Roland GR-505, and a Gibson Byrdland, and he still takes a 1958 Gibson Explorer and a 1960 Les Paul Standard on the road with him.

Clapton owns several Martin acoustic guitars, his favorite being a D-28. His other acoustic instruments include a Santa Cruz, a wood-body Dobro with a Martin neck, and a Zemaitis 12-string. For live performance he often uses a Gibson Chet Atkins electric nylon-string guitar.

Eric prefers heavy Fender or Ernie Ball picks. His strings are also made by Ernie Ball, gauged .010, .013, .017, .026, .036, .046. When playing slide he likes to use a medium-weight glass tube.

Clapton first came to the public's attention as a member of the Yardbirds. Although he was a member of the band for only a few months, he was already considered a legendary player by the time he quit.

Amplifiers, Effects, and Devices

Clapton's first amplifier was a Vox which he used throughout his stint with the Yardbirds. When he joined John Mayall's Bluesbreakers, he switched to a 45-watt Marshall "1962" 2x12 combo. He also used this amp on sessions with the Beatles. Eric was still using Marshalls when he joined Cream, but now he was playing through two 100-watt heads and four 4x12 speaker cabinets. At this time he also used a Leslie cabinet in the studio.

In the early '70s, Clapton started using Fender Dual Showman amps. A little while later, he switched to Music Man 130 series combos and 150 series heads. He used the Music Man amps until 1984, when he switched to Marshall JCM 800 50-watt heads.

Clapton often plays through tiny amps in the studio. "Layla" was allegedly recorded

Few recording artists have done more to popularize the blues than Eric Clapton. From his first recordings with the Yardbirds to his recent blues tribute From The Cradle, *he has always expressed a deep love for blues music.*

using an old tweed-covered Fender Champ and his slide performance on "Motherless Children" was played through a Pignose practice amp.

Currently, Clapton prefers Soldano 100 amps for live performance. In the studio he uses a variety of amplifiers, including '57 and '89 Fender Twins, a Music Man HD-130 2x10 combo, Fender Champs, Gibson Rangers, and various Marshalls.

Clapton avoided effects for most of his early career, preferring to plug the guitar directly into the amp. By the time he joined Cream, he started using a limited amount of effects – most notably, the Vox wah that he played through on "White Room." After Cream, he stopped using effects until the early '80s, when he began using an Ibanez UE405 multiple effects unit. While working on *Behind The Sun*, he became fascinated with Steve Lukather's effects rack, and he had Bob Bradshaw configure a system for him. It included an Ibanez harmonics delay, a dbx

In His Own Words

Most people say that I'm not playing blues guitar anymore, and I beg to differ, because it's the only thing I can play... So whether or not I'm playing blues guitar anymore isn't the point, but whether I'm playing it good or bad.
Guitar Player, *March 1968*

The only planning I do is about a minute before I play. I never sit down and work it out note for note.
Guitar Player, *June 1970*

As a rule, I actually prefer to play rhythm or let whoever else I'm playing with take the stage. But there are times when I just can't resist joining in.
Guitar Player, *August 1976*

I don't deliberately change the solos, but I think of devices, or ways of playing the solo, to make it more interesting. I went through a period of trying to minimize everything – take shorter solos – and it was very badly received.
Guitar Player, *July 1985*

Since I got into my forties, the pressure has... been lifted off a great deal. I don't feel I have to prove anything... I feel a lot less inhibited.
Guitar Player, *August 1988*

What They Say

He no longer has anything to do with my style – you know, at one time we were blues. And he was better. I think he can play blues better than I can because he studies it and is loyal to it.
Jeff Beck, Guitar Player, *October 1980*

I first heard Eric sometime in the '60s, playing the blues. He's an individualist... one of a kind. Eric is very versatile; he can play anything he wants to play. But he plays blues with the feeling – you know it's the blues when he plays it.
B. B. King, Guitar Player, *July 1985*

The first time I saw him, I couldn't believe it... He was just like a thunderbolt out of the sky.
John Etheridge, Guitar Player, *July 1985*

160 compressor, a Roland SDE-3000 digital delay, a Tri-Stereo chorus, Boss CE-1 chorus and HM-2 Heavy Metal pedals, and a Dunlop Crybaby wah-wah. He also started using a Roland GR-700 guitar synthesizer.

In the '90s, Clapton's rack system consisted of a Samson wireless unit, a Drawmer Vac/Tube compressor, a Yamaha SPX90 multi-effects unit, the Tri-Stereo chorus, a t. c. electronics 2290 multi-effects unit, a Dynacord CLS 222, a Yamaha GEP60 guitar effects processor, the Roland SDE-3000, a t. c. electronics 1210 spatial expander, an Ernie Ball volume pedal, and a Crybaby wah-wah.

Discography

Clapton has appeared on dozens of records since he started recording with the Yardbirds in 1963. For an overview of his career up until 1988, the **Crossroads** box set is a great place to start.

With the Yardbirds: **Five Live Yardbirds** (1964) and **For Your Love** (1965), which features him on seven of the 11 tracks. With John Mayall's Bluesbreakers: **Bluesbreakers** (1965). With Cream: **Fresh Cream** (1966), **Disraeli Gears** (1967), **Wheels Of Fire** (1968), **Goodbye** (1969). **Live Cream** and **Live Cream Volume II** were released after the band broke up, but both contain fine examples of Clapton's playing. With Blind Faith: **Blind Faith** (1969). With Derek And The Dominos: **Layla And Other Assorted Love Songs** (1970), and **Derek And The Dominos In Concert** (1971).

As a solo artist: **Eric Clapton** (1970), **461 Ocean Boulevard** (1974) (including his cover of "I Shot the Sheriff"), **There's One In Every Crowd** (1974), **E.C. Was Here** (1975), **No Reason To Cry** (1976), **Slowhand** (1977), **Backless** (1978), the live album **Just One Night** (1980), **Timepieces** (1982), **Money And Cigarettes** (1983), **Backtracking** (1984), **Behind The Sun** (1985), **August** (1986), **Journeyman** (1989), **24 Nights** (1991) (a live album recorded during his appearances at London's Albert Hall), **Unplugged** (1992), and **From The Cradle** (1994).

Clapton has also recorded soundtracks to several movies, including **Rush** and **Lethal Weapon I** and **II**.

Recording Sessions

Clapton has appeared as a guest on many recordings since the mid '60s. Some of his more notable sessions include the Beatles' "While My Guitar Gently Weeps," "Good To Me As I Am To You" on Aretha Franklin's **Lady Soul**, the **London Howlin' Wolf Sessions** album, George Harrison's **All Things Must Pass**, Freddie King's **Burglar** and **Freddie King (1934–1976)**, and Buddy Guy and Junior Wells **Play The Blues**. Among his '90s sessions is a cover of "Stone Free" for Warner Bros.' **Stone Free: A Tribute To Jimi Hendrix**.

Typical Licks

From the last two bars of a blues, here is a good example of one of Eric's blues turnarounds.

Clapton always shines playing simple rhythms with great feel, even at high tempos.

In the last four bars of a slow blues, Clapton hits 9th-chord tones and just the right "blues" notes.

Ry Cooder

Ry Cooder is the most highly regarded living slide guitarist. He has explored a wide variety of musical styles, including folk, blues, Hawaiian, Tex-Mex (Norteño), Okinawan, Indian, and African music, developing his own distinctive style along the way. Cooder has inspired a diverse array of artists, including Duane Allman and the Rolling Stones. A highly expressive musician, Cooder has participated on countless sessions and has composed soundtracks to several films.

The Player

Influences

One of Cooder's earliest musical influences was the Spanish classical guitarist, Vicente Gomez. However, Ry's interest in that style of music waned when he became familiar with folk music. He listened to Woody Guthrie and Leadbelly 78s and enjoyed the music of Burl Ives and Josh White. For a while, he aspired to play Merle Travis-style country guitar, but he soon found the style too limited for his taste. He also played banjo.

Ry attended many shows at the Ash Grove, a folk club in his hometown of Los Angeles, where he witnessed performances by Doc Watson, Sleepy John Estes, Jesse Fuller, Skip James, Mississippi John Hurt, and Reverend Gary Davis. Occasionally, he encouraged the performers to give him lessons, and for a brief period he received instruction from Davis.

As a result of the shows he saw and the lessons he took from performers, the teenage Cooder began increasingly to favor blues and old jazz music. Joseph Spence, the Bahamian blues guitarist who Cooder

called "one of my all-time great inspirations," introduced him to open tunings. During his high-school years, Ry mastered Arthur "Blind" Blake's open-tuned fingerstyle songs such as "Police Dog Blues." Then John Fahey introduced Cooder to slide guitar, and he soon became an expert in the history of slide guitar. To this day, one of Cooder's biggest slide influences is Blind Willie Johnson. He also became fascinated with Robert Johnson's slide work. Cooder's other favorite blues guitarists include Charlie Patton and Bukka White.

Cooder's primary electric-guitar influences are Curtis Mayfield and Pops Staples. "Curtis Mayfield – that's the way I like to hear guitar," Cooder told Steve Fishell in a 1980 *Guitar Player* interview. "It made me wonder how in the world he did 'People Get Ready,' with the Impressions and Jerry Butler's stuff like 'He Don't Love You (Like I Love You).' I stole licks from all of those things. That's the sound I like – all pulsation and midrange, delicate and feathery. He plays so smooth and pretty and very gracefully with a sense of style, really warm and vibrant."

Ry enjoys many varieties of American ethnic music, such as Hawaiian slack-key guitar and Norteño (Tex-Mex). He is also a

Background

1947 *Ryland Peter Cooder is born in Santa Monica, California, on March 15.*

1951 *Ry starts learning to play the guitar.*

1962 *Cooder begins playing in Los Angeles clubs with Jackie DeShannon.*

1965 *He forms Rising Sons with Taj Mahal.*

1966 *Ry Cooder works with Captain Beefheart on his debut album, Safe As Milk.*

1967 *Taj Mahal's first release is notable for Ry's brilliant mandolin playing.*

1969 *After working on the Rolling Stones album Let It Bleed, and despite being recommended as replacement for guitarist Brian Jones, Cooder does not stay with the band, due to personal differences.*

1970 *Cooder releases his first solo album, Ry Cooder.*

1975 *He has established an enviable reputation in the music business as a first class session man, appearing on many albums.*

1977 *Cooder tours with the Chicken Skin Review, a group that combines Tex-Mex musicians and gospel singers.*

1980 *He travels to Hawaii to record Bloodlines with Okinawan artist Shoukichi Kina.*

1983 *Cooder backs up Duane Eddy on a series of comeback shows.*

1985 *Cooder scores the soundtrack to the film Paris, Texas.*

1986 *Cooder scores the soundtrack for Crossroads, featuring Steve Vai as the "devil" guitar player.*

1991 *Cooder, Nick Lowe, John Hiatt, and Jim Keltner form the band Little Village.*

1992 *Ry returns to Hawaii to collaborate with the three sons of the late and renowned slack-key player, Gabby Pahinui.*

1993 *Cooder wins a Grammy for his collaboration with Vishwa Mohan Bhatt on A Meeting By The River.*

1994 *Cooder and Mali guitarist Ali Farka Toure release Talking Timbuktu.*

supporter of music from all over the world, and has collaborated with artists such as Hawaii's Gabby Pahinui, Okinawa's Shoukichi Kina, India's Vishwa Mohan Bhatt, and Mali's Ali Farka Touré.

Approach and Style

Cooder plays with a minimalist approach that emphasizes phrasing and complex variations of tone and texture. His playing sounds somewhat primitive, but closer examination of his performance reveals his excellent command of emotion, subtlety, and variety.

Although Ry used to fret notes on the neck with his left hand, he now only plays slide guitar. Trying to make his slide playing sound like a vocal part, he has developed a highly accurate sense of intonation and an expressive vibrato style. His style is quite complex, making effective use of microtonal inflections and dramatic timbral shifts.

Ry plays in a variety of open tunings. His favorites are open G (D, G, D, G, B, D, low to high) and open D (D, A, D, F♯, A, D, low to high). He rarely plays above the 12th fret. "Anything above that is trick," he explains. "It's goofy, it's showmanship – it's irritating, almost."

Techniques

Instead of using a pick, Cooder prefers the complexity and tonal control of playing with his right-hand fingers. He modifies the sound by picking with his fingertips for a soft tone, snapping the strings aggressively with his nails for a sharp, staccato tone, or using his nail and finger at the same time. Ry also uses his right-hand fingers to mute strings when he shifts slide positions. He plays with his right hand near the bridge, feeling that added string tension in this area gives his playing more accuracy. In general, he plays with a hard attack, although he will often play lightly for dynamic variety.

Cooder wears the slide on his left hand's little finger. He mutes behind the slide with his other three fingers, although occasionally he doesn't mute at all, preferring the overtones generated by an unmuted string. He usually plays on no more than one or two strings at a time, preferring single-note lines to chords. Unlike most other slide players, who move the slide perpendicular to the string to generate vibrato, Cooder moves the slide in an arc, pivoting on the treble side of the strings and with wider movement on the bass strings. When he is playing a stock Stratocaster, he prefers to use the middle pickup for slide.

The Hardware
Guitars, Strings, and Picks

Ry received his first guitar, a Silvertone tenor, as a gift when he was four years old. He played this guitar until he was given a 6-string Martin 00-18 when he was ten. Since then he has owned and collected a wide variety of guitars and stringed instruments.

Some of the acoustic guitars Ry has played include a Martin D-45, a 1956 Martin 000-18, a Takamine archtop prototype that was built for him in the late '70s, a Takamine flat-top acoustic-electric, a custom-built Lloyd Baggs cutaway flat-top with a scalloped fingerboard, a 1930 Gibson L-5, and a '30s Gibson Roy Smeck Radio Grande.

Cooder has owned a number of electric guitars as well, but generally prefers Fender Stratocasters. "Somebody gave me a Strat a long time ago," he told *Guitar Player*. "I came to like the chunky, fat sound, especially for bottleneck. I like their sound, but not always. Strats are sometimes strong-sounding with a good high end, but never the real high end and never the real low bass. I'm always lacking the broadness."

His current main Stratocaster features an Oahu pickup that he took out of a lap steel, and a Teisco Del Rey pickup at the neck position. He also plays several custom electric guitars made by Danny Ferrington. In the early '70s he played a '66 Strat with flatwound medium-gauge strings and a Gibson ES-335. His main electric in the early '80s was a '64 Strat with a Lake Placid Blue finish, rosewood neck, and a National lap steel pickup placed near the bridge. At this time he was also playing a '50s Strat with a maple neck and Red Rhodes Velvet Hammer pickups.

Cooder used an early '60s Fender Bass VI 6-string bass tuned to open D to record "Little Sister," "If Things Could Talk," and

A master of touch and emotion, Cooder has composed and performed music for several movie soundtracks and guested on records by Eric Clapton and the Rolling Stones. His playing style emphasizes phrasing and complex variations of tone and texture.

"Jesus On The Mainline." His other electric guitars include a Teisco Del Rey "for wang-bar, beautiful, sad, ballad songs," a Gretsch 6120 Chet Atkins, and a Danelectro Longhorn. He also owns several acoustic stringed instruments, including a Gibson F-4 mandolin, a Mexican Bajo Sexto, two tiples, an Orpheus tenor guitar, and Gibson mandolas and mandocellos.

Ry makes his own glass slides. He has made them out of vinegar, sherry, and wine bottles, and he also has some made from bottles of Fighting Cock Kentucky Bourbon and Old 101. His current favorite, cut from a Bo Joseph amaretto bottle, is 2¾ inches long, tapering in width from 1½-1¼ inches. He used to like straight and heavy bottlenecks, but now he prefers ones with a tapered shape.

One of the most acclaimed slide guitarists, Ry Cooder has a deceptively simple style that is influenced by several American and ethnic musical styles, including folk, blues, Hawaiian, Norteño, African, Indian, and Okinawan music.

Cooder's electric guitar strings are a heavy set gauged from .012 to .052. For acoustic guitar, he likes to use a light top/medium bass set.

Amplifiers, Effects, and Devices

Cooder's current live amplification setup is a rather complex affair that comprises a mixture of simple guitar amplifiers and studio-quality processing. "My setup is the product of years and tremendous sums of money buying gear," he explains. His main tone source is a '50s Gibson GA-20 tweed amplifier. This is run into a '70s Hiwatt 100-watt Custom Slave amplifier head, which is used primarily to boost the Gibson's volume to levels necessary to play in larger halls. The tone is processed with a preamp from an early-'70s solid-state Neve recording module, a '60s API parametric equalizer, an Audio Design Compex Limiter, and an Alesis Midiverb, which is used for reverb. He uses two speaker cabinets – one containing a single 15-inch speaker, and the other housing two 12-inch speakers. In the studio, he usually records with only the Gibson GA-20.

"Old amps sound great," he told Jas Obrecht in a 1992 *Guitar Player* interview. "But you don't really know what they sound like because the output stages were low-power and the speakers were crappy. The front end of these old amps tells a story that's never told, unless you do what I do, which is to send it through this expanding trip."

Ry generally does not use any effects, though sometimes he will run his guitar through an early-'60s Rickenbacker "oil-can" reverb unit. "It's crude and inefficient," he comments. "The oil-can reverb not only slaps the note, it sloshes it around. It's very vague but spatial. This one has the illusion of a chamber-like sound that really is interesting."

In the early '80s, his system consisted of an Ashly SC-40 preamp, an early-'60s

In His Own Words

Bottleneck is unique in that it has the same quality as the human voice, because it's not limited to the fret. What Blind Willie Johnson did that was real striking was to play melodies with the bottleneck just as he would sing them.
Guitar Player, *March 1971*

The style that I've been working on for the last ten years has come to be a kind of a Joseph Spence/slack key/Mexican/gospel style – it's nothing more than that.
Guitar Player, *March 1980*

The performance, the quality, the musicianship – I'm in control of that. I cannot imagine a third party masterminding this thing – not to say that it wouldn't work or couldn't be done. If I have to stop and listen to somebody talk in the middle of getting a song that's painstakingly worked out, I'd probably shoot them.
Guitar Player, *March 1988*

Tunings are very useful for everybody. Talk about unlocking! It releases all the harmonics and the tonality that's in the instrument. A little kid can pick up a guitar that's tuned in a chord, lay his finger down, and have I-IV-V in five seconds.
Guitar Player, *November 1992*

What They Say

Ry's fantastic. I love him as a player and as a person. He's got such a different approach, and when he describes things – music or guitars – it makes it magical.
Duane Eddy, Guitar Player, *June 1984*

I had been working with Ry on Crossroads, *and he inspired me. I'd be playing all these notes, and Ry would sit down and start tapping his foot and playing these grooves – and I felt embarrassed. God, man, this guy knows where the beat is! This guy's got serious soul.*
Steve Vai, Guitar Player, *October 1986*

blonde Fender Bassman amp head, and a Yamaha monitor cabinet with a horn and JBL 15-inch speaker. Sometimes he toured with a Howard amp, which was given to him by Duane Eddy. This amp is a high-fidelity unit that was made from a converted Dynaco home stereo amplifier and featured a 15-inch JBL speaker. During this period, Cooder's effects included a Dan Armstrong Purple Peaker equalizer, a Boss Chorus pedal, a studio-quality compressor, and a digital delay unit. He also liked to use a late-'50s tweed 4x10 Fender Bassman for live performance, and a Fender Princeton for work in the studio.

Typical Licks

Tuning to open D, Cooder plays a lot of licks in a three-fret box either side of the 12th fret.

Play this slow, moody intro with reverb and tremolo to evoke blues from the deep South.

Cooder is acknowledged as the master of accurate slide intonation. Pitching these sixteenth notes will show you why.

Discography

Cooder's solo albums include: **Ry Cooder** (1970), **Into The Purple Valley** (1971), **Boomer's Story** (1973), **Paradise And Lunch** (1974), **Chicken Skin Music** (1976), the live album **Show Time** (1977), **Jazz** (1978), **Bop Till You Drop** (1979), **Borderline** (1980), **Why Don't You Try Me Tonight?** (1986), **The Slide Area** (1982), and **Get Rhythm** (1987). He has also written and performed on the following soundtracks: **The Long Riders** (1980), **The Border** (1981), **Blue City** (1986), **Blue Collar** (MCA), **Southern Comfort** (1981), **Alamo Bay** (1985), **Paris, Texas** (1985), **Crossroads** (1986), **Johnny Handsome** (1989), and **Trespass** (1992).

Recording Sessions

Cooder made his recording debut with Taj Mahal's band in 1967 on **Taj Mahal**. He was then hired by Columbia Records to do session work with artists such as Paul Revere, Harpers Bizarre, and the Everly Brothers. His early sessions include the Rolling Stones' **Jamming With Edward** and "Sister Morphine" on **Sticky Fingers**, Randy Newman's "Let's Burn Down The Cornfield" on **12 Songs**, and "Forty Four Blues" and "How Many More Years" on **Little Feat**. He also wrote the scores for the films **Performance** and **Candy**, and appeared on **Safe As Milk** by Captain Beefheart's Magic Band.

His guest appearances in the '70s include **Maria Muldaur**, and Arlo Guthrie's **Last Of The Brooklyn Cowboys** and **Running Down The Road**. He also collaborated with Gabby Pahinui on **The Gabby Pahinui Hawaiian Band**, primarily playing mandolin and tiple.

In the '80s, Cooder appeared on Shoukichi Kina's **Bloodlines**, Eric Clapton's **Money And Cigarettes**, Duane Eddy's **Duane Eddy**, and John Hiatt's **Bring The Family**, with Nick Lowe, John Hiatt, and Jim Keltner. His '90s guest appearances include John Lee Hooker's **Mr. Lucky** and **Peace To The Neighborhood** by Pops Staples. In 1991, he teamed up again with the **Bring The Family** lineup to record **Little Village**. In 1993 he collaborated with Indian guitarist Vishwa Mohan Bhatt on **A Meeting By The River** and in 1994 with Malian guitarist Ali Farka Touré on **Talking Timbuktu**.

Robert Cray

Robert Cray was one of the leading forces behind the resurgence of the blues during the mid '80s. With a style that combines urban-blues influences with soul and R&B sensibilities, Cray developed a form of the blues that appeals to rock and pop fans as well as traditional blues enthusiasts. Cray has inspired a new generation of blues musicians and has been a significant force in the genre's continued development. As a guitarist, he has forged a distinctive sound that has influenced many aspiring blues musicians.

The Player

Influences

Like most guitarists who started playing as teenagers in the '60s, Cray was inspired to pick up the guitar after hearing the Beatles. His early influences included rock artists such as Jimi Hendrix, Eric Clapton, and Steve Cropper. He also enjoyed listening to records by Miles Davis and Ray Charles that his parents owned, as well as the music of Bobby Bland, Sam Cooke, and B.B. King.

Hendrix was Cray's first significant guitar influence. In high school, Cray played in a rock band called One Way Street that did covers of Hendrix tunes such as "Purple Haze" and "Wind Cries Mary." Rock and soul music remained his primary influences until he graduated from high school.

When he was 18, Cray became interested in the blues after a friend of his, Bobby Murray, played him some records by Buddy Guy, old B.B. King, and Magic Sam. Later he discovered Albert King, Little Milton, Otis Rush, Jimmy Reed, and Hubert Sumlin. "I would say the blues music or musicians I learned from were the most important influence," Cray told Dan Forte in a 1987 *Guitar Player* interview. "But I listened to a lot of Eric Clapton stuff, too, and Jimi Hendrix. I listen to music all the time, but I guess the things I learned most from were blues records and musicians."

At the same time, Cray developed an appreciation for soul and R&B artists, such as Curtis Mayfield, Bobby Womack, Aaron Neville, and Bobby Purify. Cray's early bands played covers of James Brown, Junior Parker, and Sam and Dave songs. He admits that Steve Cropper and Teenie Hodges were two of his biggest rhythm guitar influences.

Albert Collins was a pivotal artist in the development of Cray's style. Cray saw several shows by Collins, including a 1969 appearance at a rock festival and a performance at Cray's high school graduation party in 1971. He attempted to copy Collins' licks, not realizing at the time that Collins used a non-standard tuning. From 1976 to 1978, Cray's band opened for Collins frequently, and Collins often hired the group to back him up as well.

Gospel music has also had a deep impact on Cray's music and playing. Some of his favorite gospel artists include the Five Blind Boys and the Dixie Hummingbirds.

Cray's more recent influences include

Background

1953 *Robert Cray is born on August 1 in Columbus, Georgia.*

1965 *Cray begins playing guitar.*

1969 *Cray meets bass player Richard Cousins at a jam session in Tacoma, the start of their long professional relationship.*

1974 *He forms Robert Cray Band.*

1976 *The Robert Cray Band becomes a popular attraction on the Pacific Northwest tavern circuit.*

1977 *Cray appears as a bass player with Otis Day & The Knights in the movie* Animal House. *His band makes an appearance at the San Francisco Blues Festival.*

1978 *Concludes a two-year stint backing bluesman Albert Collins on all of his shows across the Northwest.*

1980 *The Robert Cray Band releases its first record,* Who's Been Talking, *on Tomato Records. The record fails to sell as the record company folds.*

1983 *The band release* Bad Influence, *which includes the songs "Phone Booth" and "Bad Influence" that were covered later by Albert King and Eric Clapton respectively.*

1984 *Cray wins four W. C. Handy National Blues Awards: Contemporary Artist, Contemporary Album (*Bad Influence*), Song, and Single Of The Year ("Phone Booth").*

1985 *Cray's album* False Accusations *soars to #1 on the British independent album chart within one month of its release.*

1986 *Strong Persuader, Cray's first recording for Mercury Records, becomes his biggest hit album and is the first Top 20 U.S. blues album since Bobby Bland's 1972 release* Call On Me. *Cray wins several W. C. Handy National Blues Awards, including Entertainer of the Year.*

1987 *Cray wins his first Grammy award for Best Traditional Blues Recording, which he shared with Albert Collins and Johnny Copeland for their* Showdown *album.*

1989 *Cray guests on John Lee Hooker's album,* The Healer, *and Eric Clapton's* Journeyman. *He also guests on Eric Clapton's sell-out gigs in London's Royal Albert Hall.*

blues guitarists Charlie Baty of Little Charlie & The Nightcats, Jimmie Vaughan, Ronnie Earl, and Texas-guitarist Alan Haynes. He also enjoys Brazilian music, country, and jazz. "Blues and country are pretty similar," Cray told *Guitar Player*. "I might want to do a country thing sometime, just because I like it. [Cray producer/co-writer] Dennis Walker usually writes in country bag. So Dennis presents something, and we just take it around and turn it into blues. It's really easy to make the music go either way."

Approach and Style

Cray's style combines elements of Albert Collins' staccato attack with the fluid, melodic phrasing of R&B guitarists such as Bobby Womack, Curtis Mayfield and Steve Cropper. Like most blues guitarists, his playing is rooted in pentatonic minor scales. Some of Cray's signature licks employ minor triads and angular note clusters similar to those played by Otis Rush.

Many songs on Cray's early records stayed well within the boundaries of standard 12-bar blues I-IV-V chord progressions. As his career developed, however, he often wrote songs in minor keys with chord progressions that are similar to pop music.

To take his music even further beyond the constraints of traditional blues music, he would add unconventional melodic and rhythmic surprises, or he would make ample use of major seventh and suspended chords. This is a direct reflection of Cray's rock, jazz, gospel, soul, and R&B influences.

In true blues fashion, Cray never memorizes or works out any of his solos in advance. He prefers to capture the emotion and freshness of a spontaneous approach. In the studio, he tries to record most of his solos within three takes.

Emphasizing tone and texture more than flashy licks, Cray's playing style is especially economical. He prefers to play sparse, lyrical lines with a clean, biting tone, and a fast, stinging vibrato. He rarely uses the distorted or overdriven tones that are favored by most modern blues guitarists. "When I used to play Gibsons I had a rounder sound," Cray told Art Thompson in a 1993 *Guitar Player* interview. "I was looking for the sound I heard from [Buddy Guy's brother] Phillip Guy. Eventually I got a Strat. Its brightness made a big difference. I always went for a clean sound from the amplifier, and I never was able to find a sound that would fatten up a Strat without using effects."

Techniques

Cray primarily plays with a flatpick, although he sometimes pops strings with his right-hand thumb and first finger, an idea that he picked up from playing with Albert Collins. In combination with his clean tone, this gives Cray's playing a staccato feel with a sharp attack and little sustain.

He has a well-developed vibrato technique with great control over speed. He

Although Cray is best known for his albums with the Robert Cray Band, he has collaborated with several other blues guitarists, including many of his biggest influences, such as Eric Clapton, John Lee Hooker, and Albert Collins.

varies between a slow, wide vibrato and a fast, shimmering vibrato, depending on the effect that he wants to convey. He generates a stunning vibrato effect on chords by pulling down on two or three strings at a time and shaking them around.

Note-bending is an essential blues guitar technique, and Cray has developed an accurate bending style. His bends range from subtle half-step bends to dramatic bends that extend nearly two whole steps, although he generally does not exceed a whole step. Cray also makes liberal use of hammer-ons, pull-offs, slides, and slurs.

Although Cray usually tunes his guitar in standard tuning, on several tracks on his *Bad Influence* album he used a *Dm* tuning that he learned from Albert Collins. He has also experimented with open *G* tuning on several occasions.

Cray prefers to use the "in-between" (middle-and-neck or middle-and-bridge) pickup positions on his Strat, but towards the end of a solo he may switch to middle or rear pickup settings for tonal variation.

The Hardware
Guitars, Strings, and Picks

Cray's first guitar was an inexpensive Harmony model he bought along with a Kalamazoo amp. After playing this guitar for five years, he got what he considers his first good guitar, a Gibson SG Standard, in 1970. By the time Cray recorded his debut album in 1979, he was playing a non-stereo Gibson ES-345 semi-hollow electric.

Since the '80s, Cray has primarily played Fender Stratocasters. For a while, he played a '64 non-tremolo Strat with a rosewood neck and an extra toggle switch that provided neck/middle and bridge/middle pickup combinations. "That Strat just felt real comfortable in my hands," he recalled to Tim Kaihatsu in a 1986 *Guitar Player* interview. "I liked the sound of it more and more, and pretty soon it was my main guitar." He also played a red Japanese-made '50s Fender Strat reissue with low impedance pickups, several different American Standard Strats with maple necks, and a maple-neck '58 Strat, also without a tremolo unit. Cray modified the '58 by adding a five-position pickup selector switch.

In the late '80s, Fender's Custom Shop started producing the special-order Robert Cray signature Strat, which is Cray's current main guitar. Designed to combine the best attributes of Cray's '58 and '64 Strats, it has an Inca-silver finish and a rosewood fingerboard. The electronics are stock, except that the middle pickup features reverse winding and polarity to eliminate noise when the "in-between" pickup settings are used. Cray usually replaces the small, stock Fender frets on his Strats with jumbo frets.

Cray also plays a Steel Deville built by

James Trussart of Paris, a Telecaster-shaped hollow guitar made of sheet steel with a bolt running through the body that can be tension-adjusted with an Allen wrench. This guitar has a rosewood neck and two Joe Barden pickups. "I can get a good dobro sound with it," Cray comments. He takes a nylon-string acoustic guitar on the road to practice playing. He does not record or perform with an acoustic guitar, although he once played a dobro tuned to open *G* on an unreleased cover of a Howlin' Wolf song.

Cray uses heavy-gauge, blue Dunlop Tortex picks and D'Addario strings gauged .011, .013, .018, .028, .036, and .046.

Amplifiers, Effects, and Devices

Cray's favorite amplifier is a blackface Fender Super Reverb from the mid '60s. "I like to use the Super for everything," he told *Guitar Player*. "I'd been using a Fender with two 12-inch speakers, but I just wasn't getting the sound I wanted. Then I heard [San Francisco blues guitarist] Tim Kaihatsu using a Strat with a Super. When I played through his rig, I like the sound of those four 10s." Cray bought his amp from a music store in Sparks, Nevada, that specializes in used equipment. He usually sets the Super's volume to five, the treble and middle on ten, the bass at four, and the reverb on three. The amp's bright switch is on.

For live performance, Cray plays through a Super Reverb and a recent reissue of a Fender Twin Reverb. "I added the Twin because I wanted more depth," he explains. "The new Twin really makes my old ones sound like they're out of wind." He also uses both of these amps for his studio work, miking both of them at once and

With a distinctive, percussive tone and R&B-based songs, Robert Cray was one of the most popular new blues guitarists to emerge during the '80s. His Strong Persuader *is one of the top-selling blues albums.*

In His Own Words

I love blues, but there's a whole lot more going on in what we do – gospel, soul, R&B, whatever you want to call it. The blues label used to make me mad, but now it doesn't really matter what they call it, as long as they like it and listen to it.
Guitar Player, *February 1986*

I feel comfortable with just the guitar, the amp, and getting different sounds by the way I use my fingers. I learned so much from Albert Collins about phrasing and attack. He just knows how to get that tough, mean sound.
Guitar Player, *February 1986*

All the songs aren't based around just the guitar. I like to play rhythm sometimes, maybe not even take a solo in the song. But what we're trying to get across is basically the story to the song; the music's just the accompaniment.
Guitar Player, *May 1987*

We don't feel like we have to change anything now. If we want to do blues, we can do blues; if we want to get funky, we get funky.
Guitar Player, *May 1987*

What They Say

Robert might be a lot further along now if he was into hard rock and jive stage stunts, and sometimes I try to get him to push his show a little harder. But what Robert is about is being a musician.
Cray bassist Richard Cousins, Guitar Player, *February 1986*

If you like the blues and you don't like Robert Cray, then something's wrong with you.
Jimmie Vaughan, Guitar Player, *July 1986*

I really like playing with Robert. He's remarkable, and having him around always pushes me. You don't have time to warm up or anything because it's there for him and you'd better be ready.
Eric Clapton, Guitar World, *June 1991*

I did one of his songs because the groove fits and that's what I look for.
Albert King, Guitar World, *July 1991*

blending their tones. Cray played his solo on "Playin' In The Dirt" through a small Yamaha amp with a 10-inch speaker.

Cray doesn't like to use any effects during live performance other than the reverb and tremolo on the amplifier. When using the amp's tremolo, he prefers a slow vibrato effect, and he adjusts the tremolo's intensity control to suit the song. In the studio, he sometimes processes his guitar with a stereo chorus and digital delay. The song "Right Next Door (Because Of Me)" from *Strong Persuader* features Cray's sole use of flanging, which was added to his guitar track during mixing.

Typical Licks

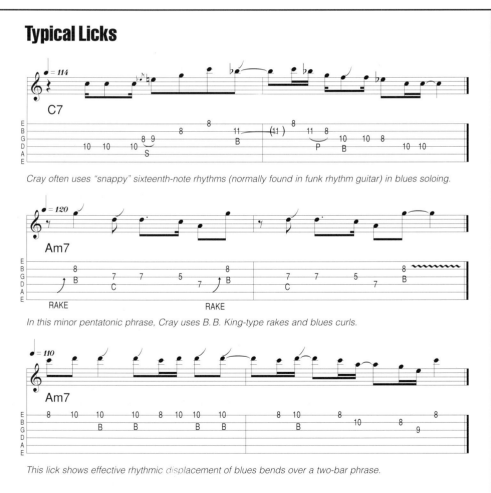

Cray often uses "snappy" sixteenth-note rhythms (normally found in funk rhythm guitar) in blues soloing.

In this minor pentatonic phrase, Cray uses B. B. King-type rakes and blues curls.

This lick shows effective rhythmic displacement of blues bends over a two-bar phrase.

Discography

All of Cray's albums contain fine examples of his playing. His records include: **Who's Been Talking** (1980), **Bad Influence** (1983), **False Accusations** (1985), **Strong Persuader** (1986), **Don't Be Afraid Of The Dark** (1988), **Midnight Stroll** (1990), **Too Many Cooks** (1991), and **I Was Warned** (1992).

In 1985, he collaborated with Albert Collins and Johnny Copeland for the superb album **Showdown**.

Recording Sessions

Cray has guested on Eric Clapton's **Journeyman** (1990) and John Lee Hooker's **Mr. Lucky** (1991) and **Boom Boom** (1992). His songs have been recorded by Eric Clapton and Albert King.

Duane Eddy

Duane Eddy's guitar-driven instrumental hits helped bring the guitar to the forefront of rock 'n' roll music. Playing melodies on the bass strings of his guitar, Eddy developed a simple, uncomplicated style that inspired many guitarists to play. His trademark twangy tone, characterized by generous amounts of reverb and tremolo, is one of the most identifiable sounds to emerge from the '50s. Eddy had more instrumental hits than any other rock guitarist and has sold more than 60 million records worldwide.

The Player

Influences

Duane started playing guitar at the age of five, when he was taught a few basic chords by his father. One of the first tunes Duane learned to play was "Wildwood Flower." While growing up in New York, he listened to country music that was broadcast by local radio stations, as well as stations as far away as West Virginia, Cincinnati, and Nashville. His first influences were singing cowboys Roy Rogers and Gene Autry, who played guitar in their movies.

When Eddy was a teenager, he formed a country band that played country hits and rockabilly songs. His early influences include Chet Atkins, Merle Travis, Grady Martin, Les Paul, and steel-guitarist Jerry Byrd. In the mid-'50s, he developed a taste for jazz and enjoyed the playing of Barney Kessel, Howard Roberts, and Django Reinhardt. Later he became interested in the blues, with B.B. King becoming a personal favorite, and in the late '50s he recorded a version of King's "Three-30-Blues". He also had several non-guitar influences, including trumpet player Louis Armstrong.

Duane never had any formal music instruction and has never learned to read music, but when he was 17 he took lessons from Jimmy Wyble for a brief period. Al Casey, a member of Eddy's band since the mid-'50s, also showed Duane how to play a variety of licks. Eddy's producer, Lee Hazelwood, gave him the idea to play melodies on the guitar's bass strings. Duane practiced the style for a few months before he recorded his first instrumental hits.

Approach and Style

Most of Eddy's early songs were simple riffs played over a standard I-IV-V chord progression. He usually picked single-note lines for the melodies and played driving double-stop rhythms. Many of his biggest hits, such as "Rebel Rouser" and "Detour", were simple major scale-based melodies played on the guitar's bottom four strings. This approach was a suggestion of Eddy's producer Lee Hazelwood, and Eddy felt that the low-string melodies recorded better than melodies played higher on the guitar. "Also, I wanted to do something different," he told Dan Forte in a 1984 *Guitar Player* interview. "Sometimes it's harder to do the simple things than it is to do the tricky stuff."

Background

1938 *Duane Eddy is born in Corning, New York, on April 26.*

1943 *Duane starts playing guitar.*

1948 *He performs the instrumental "Missouri Waltz" on a lap steel for a local radio broadcast.*

1953 *Duane is given his first electric guitar, a Gibson Les Paul, as a birthday present. He starts gigging in local roadhouses as the guitarist in Al Casey's band.*

1956 *Eddy and partner Jimmy "Dell" Delbridge press their first single, a demo of "Soda Fountain Girl" and "I Want Some Lovin' Baby." Duane trades his 1952 Les Paul Gold Top for a Gretsch 6120.*

1957 *Eddy cuts the track "Ramrod" in an attempt to secure a record deal.*

1958 *Jamie Records release Eddy's single "Movin' N' Groovin'," which peaks at #70 on the singles chart. He records the hits "Rebel Rouser," "Detour," and "Cannonball." After a live performance of "Ramrod" on the Dick Clark Show, Duane's original recording is released to advance orders of 150,000 copies.*

1959 *Over the next five years, Eddy tours with Chuck Berry, Bill Haley, Richie Valens and Eddie Cochran.*

1960 *He is voted the World's Top Music Personality in the U.K.'s New Musical Express poll, winning more votes than runners-up Elvis Presley and Frank Sinatra.*

1963 *Releases his last major hit, "Boss Guitar."*

1975 *Eddy gives a command performance to Princess Anne at London's Cambridge Hall.*

1977 *He records "You Are My Sunshine," featuring unlisted vocal performances by Waylon Jennings and Willie Nelson.*

1983 *Duane stages a comeback tour.*

1986 *Eddy guests on a recording of Henry Mancini's "Peter Gunn," performed by the Art Of Noise. The single wins a Grammy for Best Rock Instrumental.*

1987 *Capitol Records releases Duane Eddy, his first U.S. release in more than 20 years.*

1989 *Duane tours with the Everly Brothers.*

As his career progressed, this style became Eddy's predominant approach to playing the guitar. He also liked to use pentatonic minor scales, most notably on his cover version of B. B. King's "Three-30-Blues." Most of the time he played in "open" position, below the fifth fret and making liberal use of open strings.

To add variety to the melodies, Eddy often modulated up or down in pitch on subsequent verses. A good example of this can be heard on "Rebel Rouser," which starts in F, modulates up a half-step to F#, modulates up another half-step to G, and ends in G#.

Eddy's biggest deviation from his usual approach appears on the song "Trambone." For this recording, he imitated the playing style of Chet Atkins, fingerpicking the melody while playing an alternating bass line on the lower strings with a thumbpick. The song also features brief chord melody interludes unlike anything Eddy ever recorded before.

Duane's playing style is sparse and uncomplicated. He rarely improvised leads or fills, feeling that space is more effective in getting a listener's attention than flashy playing. "On 'You Are My Sunshine' I was so tempted to put in some fills and do some things on my solo," he explained to *Guitar Player*. "I held myself back because sometimes leaving a hole is more effective than filling it."

Techniques

Much of Eddy's distinctive tone can be attributed to his right-hand technique. He usually picked between the pickups or near the neck, preferring the round tone to the more percussive tone of picking near the bridge. He used the guitar's bridge pickup on the majority of his songs, although he occasionally also used both pickups at once. He likes to use the neck pickup when he's playing blues or in the guitar's high register.

Eddy's vibrato-bar technique was another integral part of his distinctive sound. He would use the bar to execute exaggerated bends or to add subtle vibrato to chords. His control of pitch was quite accurate, and he frequently would raise a note up to pitch from a whole-step below by depressing the bar before he hit the string.

After nearly two decades without a major hit record in the United States, Eddy staged a comeback tour in the mid-'80s. On separate legs of the tour, guitarists Ry Cooder and Albert Lee played in his backup band.

The Hardware

Guitars, Strings, and Picks

Duane's first instrument was a Martin acoustic guitar that belonged to his father. Eventually he was given a Kay acoustic guitar, and for his ninth birthday he received a lap steel as a present from his aunt. He played those guitars until he received a Les Paul for his fifteenth birthday. When he was 18, he traded the Les Paul for a Gretsch 6120 Chet Atkins with DeArmond pickups and a Bigsby tailpiece. Eddy used this guitar to record all of his early hits.

During the early '60s, Guild made the Duane Eddy model, which is similar to his Gretsch and features a Bigsby tailpiece and DeArmond pickups. After getting the Guild,

Heavily influencing surf-guitar bands such as the Ventures and the Chantays in the '60s, Duane Eddy pioneered the rock 'n' roll guitar-instrumental genre in the late '50s. His simple, melodic style inspired many young guitarists.

Duane used the Gretsch exclusively for recording and performed live with the Guild.

Eddy rarely used any guitars other than the Gretsch or the Guild. There are a few exceptions, including a black, single cutaway Danelectro six-string bass that he used to record "Because They're Young" and "Kommotion," a copperburst Danelectro Longhorn six-string bass that he played on "Tiger Love And Turnip Greens," and a Danelectro 12-string Bellzouki that he used to record a cover of Buck Owens' "Buckaroo." Duane also played a Howard doubleneck, made by Tom Howard McCormick of Phoenix and featuring a guitar neck and a 6-string bass neck, which he occasionally used onstage. In '86, Duane used a green Gretsch Country Club to record a new version of "Peter Gunn" with the Art Of Noise. Although he was often photographed holding a Papazian classical guitar, Duane rarely recorded or performed with anything other than an electric guitar.

He uses a set of medium-gauge strings with a wound *G* string. In the late '70s he was using Gretsch Chet Atkins strings. His current string gauges are .011, .017, .020 (wound), .034, .044, and .054. He prefers a small mandolin-style pick, although sometimes he uses a thumbpick when he plays Atkins/Travis-style fingerpicked songs.

Amplifiers, Effects, and Devices

On Eddy's early recordings, he used a Magnatone that was modified by Buddy Wheeler and Dick Wilson. Its 15-inch Jensen speaker was replaced with a 15-inch JBL speaker and a tweeter, and the output power was boosted to 100 watts. He used a DeArmond tremolo unit with the Magnatone. In the late '50s, he replaced the Magnatone with a Howard amp custom made for him by Tom Howard McCormick in Phoenix. It is currently owned by Ry Cooder. During the

In His Own Words

"Twangy" was a corny name that got stuck on it in the early days as a gimmick. I really don't know what "twangy" means.
Guitar Player, *February 1978*

Surf music was just like watching a son grow up. Those groups were branching out and going in a slightly different direction from what I was doing. Studio players tell me they used to get scores with instructions to "play Duane Eddy."
Guitar Player, *June 1984*

The important thing is to play with some authority – not sound wimpy... When you're playing an instrumental, it's got to start somewhere and end somewhere, and it's got to say something.
Guitar Player, *June 1984*

Though what I do has been put down as being simple and even dumb... I'll continue on with my style. I like to keep an open mind, but I'm not going to start playing hot licks and work up a lot of complicated stuff just to dazzle everybody and prove that I can do it.
Guitar Player, *June 1984*

What They Say

When I was playing at home, I used to stick tremolo on the amp and play Duane Eddy numbers on the bass. He was about the greatest influence on me.
John Entwistle, Guitar Player, *November 1975*

"Have Twangy Guitar, Will Travel" was the first album I ever bought. What a sound! That clean Gretsch tone. I still play licks I stole from him.
Duke Robillard, Musician, *November 1991*

It's certainly my opinion that he stood at the crossroads of rock 'n' roll and transformed things by putting the musicians up front. Duane came along and was a real musician out front. It really all started for me in rock 'n' roll with Duane Eddy.
John Fogerty, Musician, *November 1991*

late '70s, Eddy used a Stramp amplifier and JBL speakers. During the '80s, he started using solid-state Fender Showman amps.

To get his distinctive "twangy" tone, Duane sets his amp's treble control almost all the way up, turns down the bass, and adjusts the midrange wherever he thinks it sounds the best.

Eddy uses liberal amounts of tremolo, echo, and reverb. On his early recordings, his reverb "unit" was a large 2,100-gallon water tank with a speaker and a microphone placed inside. The single-repeat, slapback echo effects were generated with an Ampex 401 tape recorder.

Typical Licks

To capture the real "Eddy" sound, tune your guitar down a tone and play this lick with lots of reverb.

This lick runs down the first position of a blues scale into a typical open-position "twang" phrase.

Eddy combined blues and country licks with special effects, such as tremolo, to create his own recognizable style.

Discography

Eddy recorded dozens of singles and albums during his career. For an overview, Rhino Records' **Twang Thang** is an ideal place to start. Sire's **The Vintage Years** also includes many of Eddy's biggest hits.

All of Eddy's original albums are out of print. He recorded the following albums for the Jamie label: **Have "Twangy" Guitar Will Travel**, **Especially For You**, **The "Twang's" The "Thang"**, **Duane Eddy Plays Songs Of Our Heritage**, **$1,000,000 Worth Of Twang**, **Girls, Girls, Girls**, **$1,000,000 Worth Of Twang Vol. II**, **Twistin' With Duane Eddy**, **Duane Eddy In Person**, **Surfing With Duane Eddy**, and **Duane Eddy's 16 Greatest Hits**.

RCA released **Twistin' And Twangin'**, **Twangy Guitar – Slinky Strings**, **Dance With The Guitar Man**, **Twang A Country Song**, **Twangin' Up A Storm**, **Lonely Guitar**, **Water Skiing**, **Twangin' The Golden Hits**, **Twangsville**, and **The Best Of Duane Eddy**.

Colpix Records released **Duane A Go Go** and **Duane Does Bob Dylan**, and Reprise released **The Biggest Twang Of Them All** and **The Roaring Twangies**.

In the '70s, Duane recorded two singles, "Play Me Like You Play Your Guitar" (1975), and "You Are My Sunshine" (1977). Britain's GTO label released the album **Guitar Man** in 1975. Eddy made his U.S. recording comeback in 1987 when Capitol released **Duane Eddy**.

Recording Sessions

Duane has appeared on only a handful of recording sessions other than his own in his career. In 1958, he played guitar on "Have Love, Will Travel," a single by the Sharps, who were Eddy's labelmates at Jamie and who performed backup vocals on many of his singles. That same year Duane also played guitar on several Sanford Clark recordings and Donnie Owens' "Need You." In 1959 he played rhythm guitar on Ray Sharpe's "Linda Lu."

During the '60s, Eddy guested on Nancy Sinatra's "These Boots Are Made For Walkin'" and B.J. Thomas' "Rock And Roll Lullaby." In 1986, he teamed up with The Art Of Noise to record a cover of his version of Henry Mancini's "Peter Gunn." This single won a Grammy for Best Rock Instrumental.

The Edge

Entirely self-taught – he has never learned to read music – The Edge is one of the most original players to emerge from the early-'80s post-punk movement. As a member of the Irish band U2, the Edge developed a stripped-down minimalist style that makes effective use of single notes, double stops, effects, and textures, instead of engaging in flashy displays of technique. His distinctive rhythm style has been widely imitated, yet few are able to equal his character and sophistication.

The Player

Influences

The Edge started playing guitar when he was nine, but he didn't become serious about it until he was 15, when he formed a band at school that eventually became U2.

Unlike most aspiring guitarists in the mid-'70s, the Edge wasn't interested in copying the licks and riffs of rock guitar heroes. "We were pretty disillusioned with a lot of the music that was coming out in the mid-'70s," he told *Guitar Player* in 1985. "There seemed to be a lot of ground that had already been covered." He learned a few Rory Gallagher licks and played a lot of cover versions of songs before U2 was formed, but once the band was together, they concentrated on creating their own sound.

His inspirations during U2's early years were Lou Reed, David Bowie, and Talking Heads and early punk-rock bands, such as the Jam, the Patti Smith Group, Richard Hell And The Voidoids, and Television. "Their music was so new and different," he told *Guitar Player*. "It made us excited and enthusiastic. As a would-be guitar player, I was struck by the fact that all these bands

had a really well-defined sound that was like no one else's. When we first started putting material together, that was always in my mind: 'We have to find out what we have to offer, what we can do that's different.'"

Neil Young, Tom Verlaine of Television, and John McGeoch of Magazine, were a few of The Edge's favorite guitarists. However, he was more inspired by their distinctive, identifiable tones and approach to the instrument rather than by the specific notes that they played. He has also mentioned Steve Howe of Yes as an influence, primarily for his employment of natural harmonics. The Edge's primary goal has always been to create new sounds and to create music that communicated with the audience.

Some of the recent guitar players that the Edge enjoys include Johnny Marr and Peter Buck of R.E.M. "I'm not a fan of the million-miles-per-second guitar player," he said in a 1988 *Rolling Stone* interview. "That's more a form of athletics than anything else."

Approach and Style

The Edge has developed a distinctive minimalist approach with an economic rhythm style that emphasizes single-note lines, double stops, and tritones rather than

Background

1961 *Dave Evans is born on August 8 in East London, England. Although he took piano lessons as a child, he did not stick with it long enough for him to understand most basic music-theory concepts.*

1970 *Evans starts playing a Spanish guitar.*

1976 *U2 is formed, comprising the Edge on guitar, Bono on vocals, Adam Clayton on bass, and Larry Mullen Jr. on drums.*

1978 *The band win a talent contest, sponsored by the Guinness brewery.*

1979 *The band's first EP, U2:3, tops the Irish charts, helping the band get a contract with Island records.*

1980 *U2 releases their first album, Boy.*

1982 *U2 are voted fifth best group and their album October is voted fourth best album in the U.K. U2 kick off their U.S. tour in New Orleans.*

1983 *U2 reaches new success with the release of War. The album climbs to #1 on the U.K. charts and sells over a million copies worldwide. The band's next U.S. tour establishes them as a major concert draw. U2 is named as band of the year by the Rolling Stone critics' poll.*

1984 *The band starts working with Brian Eno and Daniel Lanois on the recording of their fifth album, The Unforgettable Fire.*

1985 *U2 performs at Live Aid and launch their own record label, Mother Records.*

1987 *The band releases The Joshua Tree, which goes to the top of the U.S. charts for nine weeks. The album produces two #1 singles – "With Or Without You" and "I Still Haven't Found What I'm Looking For." The band also make the cover of Time magazine.*

1988 *U2 wins two Grammy awards.*

1989 *The Joshua Tree becomes the industry's first million-selling CD.*

1992 *The band's massive multi-media Zoo TV tour attracts more than two million fans.*

full chords. He prefers to voice major chords with the root and a fifth, adding octaves for greater body, and tends to use a lot of simple minor chord voicings. He dislikes major thirds and almost never plays this interval.

The Edge rarely plays solos, and when he does they are usually brief, melodic passages, or extensions of his rhythm part. "Our music needed more than just one-string solos of the blues variety," he told *Guitar Player*. "That sort of thing didn't work, and it also didn't interest me very much, because it was being done so well by other people."

Most of the Edge's guitar parts are created by experimentation. He admits that he rarely practices, preferring to approach the guitar as if for the first time. He writes his guitar parts by improvising ideas without any pre-conceived notions of what the final part will sound like. If he has trouble coming up with a part that satisfies him, he often finds inspiration by changing the guitar's tuning.

One of the most recognizable facets of the Edge's style, particularly on early U2

records, is his rhythmic use of a digital delay. Some of his approaches include setting the delay to generate percussive counter-rhythms or to repeat short phrases. Examples of his rhythmic use of a delay can be heard on "Wire" and "A Sort Of Homecoming."

The Edge's playing, particularly his more recent work, is also characterized by a wide range of textures. He uses droning strings, slide, E-Bow and feedback to create a loose, ambient atmosphere, yet his tone can also be metallic and percussive. He often layers parts in the studio to create expansive, full arrangements, but sometimes he prefers sparse single lines.

Techniques

Since so much of the Edge's playing is rhythm-based, his right hand does most of the work. He holds his pick "backwards," with the sharp point facing away from the strings, and tends to pick in the center area between the neck and bridge pickups. On U2's early records, he relied mostly on downstrokes, giving his rhythm lines a choppy feel. "I Will Follow" is a prime example of this approach, where his downstrokes emphasize the melody line played on the *B* string while he lets the *E* string drone on an open note.

For inspiration, the Edge often changes the guitar's tuning. One of his favorite unconventional tunings is *F, A, D, D, G, D* (low to high), which he used on "The Unforgettable Fire." He also uses a lap steel that he tunes to a minor chord with the first and fourth, second and fifth, and third and sixth strings tuned an octave apart.

Another source of The Edge's inspiration, particularly on U2's first five records, was his delay unit. He would often set the delay

A member of the band U2, the Edge developed a minimalist style that emphasizes tone, texture, and simple melodic lines. He is one the most original guitarists to emerge from the early-'80s post-punk movement.

between 50 and 400 milliseconds, damp the strings – either with his hands or a piece of gaffer's tape – and play percussive, muted quarter-note patterns while the delay generated a counter rhythm. He has a very accurate sense of time, partially aided by playing in time to the delay's rhythm.

The Edge's left-hand technique is based on a minimalist approach. His left hand usually stays in a stationary position, holding a chord or note pattern while he skips strings with his right hand. He rarely bends strings, but uses a lot of vibrato. The Edge frequently uses natural harmonics for tonal variation. "For me, harmonics are approaching the most pure sound available to a guitarist," he said in a *Guitar Player* interview. "I love it. It's one of the nicest sounds you can take from a guitar. I've taken it a step further with various different tunings and treatments." In general, he uses a clean tone, although lately he has experimented with effects and distortion a greater amount.

When he plays slide, he wears the slide on his left-hand middle finger and he doesn't damp behind the slide, preferring the over-tones generated by the open strings. Unlike most guitarists, he plays slide on both lap steel and on conventional guitar. He keeps his lap steel tuned to various open tunings, but he uses standard tuning when playing slide on the guitar.

The Hardware
Guitars, Strings, and Picks

The Edge's first guitar was a battered, inexpensive Spanish guitar that he borrowed from his brother. "It took me five years to learn how to tune it," he told *Rolling Stone*. When he was 14, his mother gave him a better guitar.

The Edge currently uses a variety of guitars, but his main instrument is a white '73

Les Paul Custom. He also plays several Fender Stratocasters, including an '89 Eric Clapton signature model and a '68 Strat, a '76 Rickenbacker 12-string electric, a Gibson doubleneck electric, a Gibson ES-330, a 1945 Epiphone lap steel, a '60s Gretsch White Falcon, and assorted other Gretsch electric archtops. His primary acoustic guitar is a Washburn Festival outfitted with a Bill Lawrence soundhole pickup and a Photon MIDI pickup. In the mid-'80s, he also played a Gibson Explorer and a Fender Telecaster.

He uses German-made picks that have dimples in the surface. He strikes the strings with the dimples, enjoying the raspy top end that this produces. The Edge prefers the tone of heavy strings, and he feels that they stay in tune better. His current strings are made by Rotosound, gauged .011 to .048. In

Whereas the Edge's early work often emphasized single-note lines, drones, and rhythmic echo patterns, his recent playing style relies on highly processed, thick electronic textures, and inventive chords.

the mid-'80s he used Superwound Selectras gauged from .011 to .052. He plays slide with a piece of chrome-plated tubing.

Amplifiers, Effects and Devices

Throughout U2's career, the Edge has played through Vox AC30 amplifiers. He currently uses four of them onstage, along with two Randall combos. He plugs his Washburn acoustic into an AC30 with no effects.

The Edge relies heavily on effects for creating his sound. "I tend to use effects that don't change the tone of the guitar," he told *Rolling Stone* in 1988. "I don't like phasing or flanging or anything like that. I like echo. I like reverb." He has changed his attitude somewhat since then, proven by the heavily distorted and processed guitar sound on the intro to *Achtung Baby*'s "Mysterious Ways."

On the Zoo TV tour, the Edge used a custom Bradshaw effect rack system outfitted with an AMS digital delay, two Yamaha SPX90s, a Yamaha GP50 guitar-effects processor, a t. c. electronics 2290 multi effects unit, an Eventide H3000 Harmonizer, two Korg A3 multi-effect processors, an Infinite Sustain box, a Photon MIDI converter, and a Roland SDE-3000. His wireless unit is a Sony UHF WRR37 system. The Edge's floor pedals include a Mosfet preamp, Boss SD-1 distortion, Turbo Overdrive, and Graphic EQ pedals, an MXR compressor, a couple of t. c. electronics preamps, a Crybaby wah-wah, and a DigiTech Whammy pedal. He also uses an E-Bow, a hand-held sustain device.

In the mid-'80s, he used a Boss SCC-700 effects center, which controlled a Korg SDD-3000 digital delay, an MXR Pitch Transposer, two Electro-Harmonix Memory Man Deluxe echos, and a Yamaha R1000 Digital Reverb. He ran his effects through a Mesa/Boogie MK-IIC amp.

Because effects are an integral part of the Edge's sound, he usually records to tape

In His Own Words

What do I find challenging? Tearing up the rule book and saying, "Okay, given that this is my instrument, what can I do with it that no-one else has done before?"
Guitar Player, *June 1985*

Whenever I start working on a song, I immediately try to forget everything, to empty my hands and head of anything that may be hanging over from another song or album. I try to approach it like, "This is the first time I've ever played a guitar. What am I going to do?"
Guitar Player, *June 1985*

My parts come generally out of exploration; they come from improvisation and accident. My strength is seeing them when they come out and capitalizing on them.
Guitar Player, *June 1985*

I don't feel that attached to my instruments. It's almost like I'm going to dominate them in some sort of way. I don't feel like they're a part of me; they stand between me and something new.
Guitar Player, *June 1985*

If there's anything that's good about my playing it's because I'm me, I'm different. If somebody is going to sound like me, they really haven't understood me very well. I'm more interested in what Joe Bloggs down the road in this garage band is doing than, say, what the new Jeff Beck album is like.
Guitar Player, *June 1985*

What They Say

I remember B. B. King one night said he thought The Edge was one of the greatest rhythm-guitar players alive.
Steve Cropper, Guitar Player, *July 1994*

The Edge has got a deep pocket. He can play guitar and piano at the same time too, which is a pretty bitchin' trick.
Stone Gossard, Guitar Player, *July 1994*

with his complete processed sound, instead of adding effects during the mixing stage. "The treatment is as much a part of the sound as the playing or the guitar tone itself," he explained to *Guitar Player*. "When you're being creative in the studio or writing, the most important thing is being inspired by your equipment."

Typical Licks

The Edge often uses an echo unit to produce trails of rhythmic high notes over a rock groove.

A "ripple texture" guitar part, using a compressed, clean sound with reverb, echo, and chorus.

Octaves played in sixteenth notes are one of the main ingredients in the Edge's innovative style.

Discography

All of U2's albums on Island contain noteworthy performances by The Edge. No compilations have been released to date. U2's albums include: **Boy** *(1980),* **October** *(1981),* **War** *(1983),* **Under A Blood Red Sky** *(1983),* **The Unforgettable Fire** *(1984),* **Wide Awake In America** *(1985),* **The Joshua Tree** *(1987),* **Rattle And Hum** *(1988),* **Achtung Baby** *(1991), and* **Zooropa** *(1993).*

Recording Sessions

The Edge has guested on few records during his recording career. His most notable sessions include Jah Wobble's **Snake Charmer** *(1983) and his collaboration with guitarist Michael Brook on the soundtrack to* **Captive** *(1987). Along with the other members of U2, he backed Robbie Robertson on his 1987 solo album,* **Robbie Robertson**.

In 1990 the Edge wrote the score to a stage production of A Clockwork Orange, *but a soundtrack album has not been released.*

Robert Fripp

With a style that is a compelling mixture of tone, technique, texture, and technology, Robert Fripp was one of the first true modern guitarists. During the "progressive" rock movement of the late '60s, he forged an entirely new voice, more "electronic" than "electric," and greatly broadened the boundaries of rock, opening up a wider palette of experimentation with sound and styles. Whether as a member of King Crimson, a solo artist, a session player, or a collaborator, Fripp has always challenged conventional notions of rock guitar.

The Player

Influences

Fripp started playing guitar when he was 11 years old. Although he is naturally left-handed, he decided to learn to play in the conventional right-handed manner. At this time, he mostly listened to rock 'n' roll, and particularly enjoyed the early Chuck Berry, and Scotty Moore's playing with Elvis Presley.

He taught himself to play the guitar by practicing on his own for about three months, then he started taking music-theory lessons from a piano teacher at the School Of Music at Corse Mellon for about one year. His first true guitar teacher was Don Strike, a '30s-style player who Fripp started studying with after he stopped taking lessons at Corse Mellon. Fripp studied with Strike for two years, learning Nick Lucas- and Eddie Lang-style playing on acoustic guitar. Fripp has since credited Strike with helping him to develop his cross-picking technique. One of his favorite guitarists during this period was Django Reinhardt.

Next, Fripp bought a flamenco guitar and decided to learn about fingerstyle playing and how to play classical guitar.

His primary influences at this time were modern and classical music. He also took ten lessons from Tony Alton, a jazz guitarist who taught Fripp about scales, chords, playing technique, and solos.

During the '60s, Fripp enjoyed listening to Jimi Hendrix, although he admits that he was more inspired by his music than his guitar playing. He also enjoyed Eric Clapton's playing during his stint in the Bluesbreakers. Fripp appreciated Jeff Beck's talent, saying his playing was "good fun," but he wasn't particularly influenced by Beck either. "I've never really listened to guitarists, because they've never really interested me," Fripp explained to Steve Rosen in a 1974 *Guitar Player* interview. "In fact I think guitar is a pretty feeble instrument. Virtually nothing intrigues me about the guitar."

Fripp's major influences are classical and jazz music. Some of his favorite classical pieces include Bartok's string quartets, Stravinsky's *Le Sacre du Printemps (The Rite Of Spring)*, Dvôrák's *New World Symphony*, and he has expressed an affinity for the music of Ornette Coleman, Charlie Parker, Miles Davis, Tony Williams, the Mahavishnu Orchestra, and Weather Report. The Beatles' *Sgt. Pepper's Lonely Hearts Club Band* was

Background

1946 *Robert Fripp is born in Wimborne, Dorset, on May 16.*

1957 *Starts playing guitar.*

1960 *Starts playing in groups.*

1964 *Takes a steady gig playing at the Majestic Hotel, replacing future Police guitarist and collaboration partner, Andy Summers.*

1968 *Makes his first recorded appearance on* The Cheerful Insanity Of Giles, Giles, And Fripp.

1969 *Fripp forms King Crimson.*

1972 *While working with Brian Eno, Fripp is introduced to a tape loop system, which he later dubs "Frippertronics."*

1974 *King Crimson disbands. Fripp retires from the music business for three years.*

1976 *The Young Persons' Guide To King Crimson, a compilation of the band's work, is released.*

1977 *Fripp guests on records by Peter Gabriel, David Bowie, Blondie, and the Roches. He starts working on his first solo album.*

1980 *Fripp forms the League Of Gentlemen.*

1981 *A new version of King Crimson is formed, featuring Fripp, guitarist Adrian Belew, drummer Bill Bruford, and bassist Tony Levin.*

1984 *King Crimson disbands once again. Fripp begins conducting a series of guitar seminars called Guitar Craft.*

1988 *Fripp starts working on* Sunday All Over The World, *featuring his wife, Toyah Wilcox, on vocals.*

1991 *He compiles* Frame By Frame, *a four-CD box set of King Crimson material.*

1993 *Fripp records and tours with David Sylvian.*

1994 *A new version of King Crimson is formed, featuring the 1981 lineup, plus Stick player Trey Gunn and drummer Pat Mastelotto.*

a pivotal influence on him as a musician and composer, and Fripp has also expressed an interest in Frank Zappa's work.

More recently, Fripp has become interested in the music of various world cultures, particularly Balinese gamelan music and the Bulgarian women's choir.

Approach and Style

Fripp's style is mainly characterized by his scalar playing, making extensive use of scale modes. He uses a variety of scales, such as the diatonic major scale based on the Dorian mode, whole-tone scales, and octatonic scales. He likes to explore exotic scales, such as Super Locrian and Oriental.

His music is often polyphonic and polymetrical, making use of several odd meters which overlap to create complex, shifting patterns. His single-note lines are usually comprised of pointillistic percussive arpeggio patterns or linear sustained modal melodies with whole-tone/tritonic tonal structures. He frequently relies on the latter approach when using his Frippertronics system. He rarely bends strings or uses vibrato, preferring to vary timbres by the way he picks the notes or with effects devices.

Fripp is particularly adept at conveying emotions and producing a wide variety of textures and tone colors with his guitar. He creates sounds that are dissonant, violent, and savage, and performs solos that are melodic, subtle, and harmonically pleasing. His albums boast an astonishing array of timbres, which are all the more amazing in that few of the tones sound anything like those produced by other guitarists.

In the early '80s, Fripp developed what he calls the new standard tuning (C, G, D, A, E, G, low to high), which he feels offers guitarists a more rational system of playing. He also thinks that this system provides better-sounding chords and single notes.

One of the seminal figures in the development of progressive rock during the late '60s, Fripp eschewed the rock guitarist's blues-based vocabulary and greatly broadened the perspective of rock guitar.

Techniques

Fripp has developed a highly disciplined approach to playing that was inspired by his classical-guitar instruction. Realizing that no one had established a proper playing technique for steel-string and electric guitars such as the one developed for classical guitar, Fripp created his own approach. Like a classical guitarist, Fripp never plays standing up, and he is meticulous about his posture and arm and hand positions.

Fripp emphasizes the importance of proper hand positioning for the most effective playing. He feels that the left-hand thumb should be held straight and placed at the center of the back of the guitar's neck. The left hand should be arched so that only the fingertips touch the string, and the left elbow should be held near the body to prevent fatigue. The left hand exercises considerable economy of motion, with the fingers maintaining pressure on the strings as notes ascend up the neck. The fingers are not released until it is necessary to play a lower note. Fripp grasps his pick between his thumb and forefinger, with the thumb held straight. His picking action is generated from the wrist, with the elbow positioning the hand above the proper strings. He lets his right hand float above the strings without resting on the guitar, unless he wants to damp or mute strings.

With his well-developed alternate picking technique, Fripp performs dazzling displays of speed with remarkable accuracy. When picking in this manner, he holds the pick vertical to the strings. If he is using only downstrokes, he holds the pick at a 30- to 45-degree angle relative to the string. He notes that, unlike most guitarists, he uses the same picking technique whether he is playing acoustic or electric guitar. When he plays acoustic guitar, Fripp prefers to pick notes directly over the soundhole.

The Hardware
Guitars, Strings, and Picks

Fripp's first guitar was an Egmund Freres acoustic, which he started playing when he was 11. He acquired his first electric guitar, a Hofner President, when he was 14. In 1963, he started using a Gibson ES-345 semi-hollowbody electric.

In 1968, while playing with Giles, Giles, And Fripp, he bought his first Les Paul. This model remains his favorite electric, though his current Les Pauls have been heavily modified with the addition of several switches and Kahler vibrato units. He also uses a Tokai Les Paul copy that features a built-in hexaphonic guitar synthesizer pickup, a Kahler tremolo, and a coil-tap and phase-reverse switch for each pickup.

Fripp has also played Fender Strats periodically during his career. Some of the Strats he has owned include a '63, a '66, and a '57 sunburst given to him by Robin Trower.

Though Fripp established his reputation as an electric-guitar player, he has used acoustic guitars throughout his career. Early

Fripp has developed a highly disciplined playing approach to the steel-string and electric guitar that emphasizes proper posture and hand positions, alternate picking techniques, and his "new standard tuning."

favorites include a Gibson J-45, a Yamaha, a pre-war Milner, a Gibson tenor, and a Takamine. When he started the Guitar Craft seminars, he found the Ovation Legend 1867 most suited to his playing technique, and he recommended this guitar to his students.

Fripp prefers light-gauge triangular tortoise-shell picks. In the mid-'70s, he was using John Alvie Turner light-gauge strings. To accommodate his new standard tuning, he uses a set of strings gauged .012, .015, .023, .032, .047, .060 (high to low) on his acoustic guitars.

Amplifiers, Effects, and Devices
Fripp's first amp was a six-watt Watkins with an 8-inch speaker. Since then he has experimented with various makes and models, such as Hiwatt and Fender, but generally he prefers solid-state Roland JC-120 Jazz Chorus amps and tube Marshalls. The Roland is used for his clean tones, and the Marshall is used for distorted tones. "Virtually any valve [tube] amp will do when I'm working with fuzz sustain," he explains. "The JC-120s are appalling for fuzz sustain."

The Frippertronics system has gone through various configurations during Fripp's career. His main echo sources have been either two Revox tape recorders or two Electro-Harmonix 16-Second Digital Delays. The system has also included a harmonizer and a Roland Space Echo.

His pedalboard contains an Ibanez digital delay and various volume, wah-wah, and fuzz pedals, including Electro-Harmonix Big Muffs and Foxey Ladys, as well as a Burns Buzzaround, and a Colorsound unit.

He has often experimented with guitar synthesizers, most notably in the '80s with King Crimson and during his collaborations

In His Own Words
I don't feel myself to be a jazz guitarist, a classical guitarist, or a rock guitarist. I don't feel capable of playing in any of those idioms, which is why I felt it necessary to create, if you like, my own idiom.
Guitar Player, *May 1974*

I suggest that guitar playing, in one sense, can be a way of uniting the body with the personality, with the soul and the spirit. Working in a band is a good way of making magic. What affects my playing more than anything is my state of mind.
Guitar Player, *May 1974*

Some of the supposedly best players are remarkably insensitive. They don't even listen to themselves, let alone other people. But you see, one has to be able to divide one's attention in order to listen to other players, as well as oneself.
Guitar Player, *January 1986*

Some people make music their god. I don't. But music is a very remarkable opportunity. It's a tangible way of dealing with the intangible. It's a practical, down-to-earth way of developing a relationship with the inevitable.
Guitar Player, *January 1986*

What They Say
There have been players like Robert Fripp and myself who started in the '80s with guitar synthesizers, and kept that up and kept going forward, and I think more and more people are developing things like that.
Adrian Belew, The Guitar Magazine, *November 1994*

I can do certain things on guitar that he can't do, and he can do certain things that I can't do. He's very disciplined, self contained, and precise. He's very supportive of my style of playing and my lyrics. Coming from Robert, who I've always admired and thought a lot of, that means a lot to me.
Adrian Belew, Guitar Player, *June 1982.*

with Andy Summers. He prefers Roland guitar synthesizers, and has played both the GR-300 and GR-700 systems. "I don't think the guitar synthesizer has reached the point yet where it has become a new instrument," he told Tom Mulhern in a 1986 *Guitar Player* interview. "The electric guitar was originally an acoustic guitar that became louder. But because it became louder, it became another instrument. It's a different instrument with a different vocabulary, different bodies of technique, different music, a different lifestyle of the person playing it. The synthesizer guitar has not yet reached that level of individuality, though it's on the way."

Discography

Fripp made his recording debut with the group Giles, Giles, And Fripp on **The Cheerful Insanity Of Giles, Giles, And Fripp** *(1968). He appears on all of the King Crimson albums, including:* **In The Court Of The Crimson King** *(1969),* **In The Wake Of Poseidon** *(1970),* **Lizard** *(1970),* **Island** *(1971),* **Earthbound** *(1972),* **Larks' Tongues In Aspic** *(1973),* **Starless And Bible Black** *(1974),* **Red** *(1974),* **USA** *(1975),* **Discipline** *(1981),* **Beat** *(1982), and* **Three Of A Perfect Pair** *(1984).*

His solo work includes: **Exposure** *(1979),* **God Save The Queen/Under Heavy Manners** *(1981),* **Let The Power Fall** *(1981), and* **Network** *(1984).*

He was a primary collaborator with the League Of Gentlemen in **The League Of Gentlemen** *(1981) and* **God Save The King** *(1985).*

Working with students from his Guitar Craft seminars, Fripp formed the League Of Crafty Guitarists, and released the following albums: **Robert Fripp And The League Of Crafty Guitarists Live** *(1986),* **How I Became A Professional Guitarist** *(1988),* **Live II** *(1990),* **and Show Of Hands** *(1991). He formed a "conventional" rock band with his wife, singer Toyah Wilcox, and in 1991 released the album* **Sunday All Over The World***.*

Recording Sessions

Fripp's projects with Brian Eno include: **No Pussyfooting** *(1973),* **Evening Star** *(1975),* **Here Come The Warm Jets** *(1973),* **Another Green World** *(1975), and* **Before And After Science** *(1977). He guested on two albums by Van der Graaf Generator,* **H To He Who Am The Only One** *(1970), and* **Pawn Hearts** *(1970), Colin Scott's* **Colin Scott** *(1971), Peter Hammill's* **Fool's Mate** *(1972), Peter Gabriel's* **Peter Gabriel** *(1977), David Bowie's* **Heroes** *(1977) and* **Scary Monsters** *(1980), Blondie's* **Parallel Lines** *(1978), Talking Heads'* **Fear Of Music** *(1979), Daryl Hall's* **Sacred Songs** *(1980), the Roches'* **The Roches** *(1980), and the Flying Lizards'* **Fourth Wall** *(1981). He collaborated with Andy Summers on* **I Advanced Masked** *(1982), and* **Bewitched** *(1984), guested on David Sylvian's* **Alchemy – An Index Of Possibilities** *(1985), and* **Gone To Earth** *(1986), and collaborated with Sylvian on* **The First Day** *(1993).*

Typical Licks

Fripp uses "infinite" sustain to play "violin-type" rock solos. Interestingly, this minor lick includes both the flat and sharp fifth.

On synth guitar, Fripp uses the minor third, flat fifth, and flat ninth over an E major drone.

Fripp dramatically increases tension by sustaining the major third over a "minor" rock groove.

Cliff Gallup

Cliff Gallup was one of the most outstanding and innovative guitarists of the rockabilly genre. His leads displayed a wild rock 'n' roll abandon and jazzy sophistication that few guitarists since have been able to match. Although he recorded and toured as a member of Gene Vincent And The Blue Caps for less than a year, he left an indelible impression on many guitarists, including Jeff Beck, Jimmy Page, and Albert Lee.

The Player

Influences

Gallup started playing guitar when he was eight years old. Two of his uncles were musicians – one played fiddle and the other played banjo. "He used to sit and watch them play when he was just a little guy," recalls Gallup's widow, Doris. Although Cliff probably received a few playing tips from his uncles, he was mainly a self-taught player who learned by listening to records, the radio, and other musicians. "Everything he played was strictly by ear," says Doris. "He didn't read music. He didn't know one note from another when it comes to reading it on paper. All he had to do was listen to a song one time and he had it in his mind."

Gallup started playing electric guitar when he was 12. Shortly thereafter, he started playing with bands. He practiced and gigged often. When he met Gene Vincent, Gallup was playing in the Virginians, which was the staff band at radio station WCMS in Norfolk, Virginia. Gallup was only 26, but he was already quite an experienced musician. This may

explain why his chops were so advanced for a relatively young player.

There weren't very many rock 'n' roll guitarists around in the mid-'50s to imitate, so Gallup developed a style of his own. His style was primarily influenced by country and pop players, such as Chet Atkins and Les Paul. He also drew inspiration from mainstream jazz guitarists and the music of Elvis Presley and Carl Perkins. "I kind of thought Les Paul was the going thing in my younger years," he told Dan Forte in a *Guitar Player* interview. "I used to listen to a lot of Atkins stuff when he first started. I played a little bit of everything, I guess."

After he quit touring and recording with Vincent, Gallup played with local bands and worked on the staff of a local radio station, where he backed up several country artists and recorded commercials. "He played a lot of gospel music," Doris Gallup comments about Cliff's later years. "All kinds of people used to call him up and beg him to teach them chords. He would play for anybody who came over and asked him to play. People would call him up and ask him to sit in. He would play with them and he wouldn't charge them anything. A lot of times he played seven nights a week."

Background

1930 *Cliff Gallup is born.*

1938 *Gallup starts playing music.*

1942 *He gets his first electric guitar.*

1956 *Cliff becomes a member of Gene Vincent And The Blue Caps. Tired of constant touring, he quits the band late that summer. In October, he records with Vincent one more time before quitting the band for good.*

1966 *Gallup records a solo album,* Straight Down The Middle.

1988 *Gallup suffers a massive heart attack on October 10 and passes away at the age of 58.*

Approach and Style

Gallup's style is best described as a combination of country and jazz with a lot of rock 'n' roll energy. Gallup frequently utilized jazzy single-note lines in his rhythm work and solos. Sometimes he played sax-like motifs that complemented Vincent's vocals. Like many jazz players, Gallup utilized octave jumps and chromatic lines. His first solo on "Race With The Devil" is a fine example of these approaches.

Gallup also liked to play double stops. On "Cruisin'" he played a jazzy, slurred *G*, *C9*, *D7* double-stop pattern on the second and third strings. For the solo, he employed a dissonant, minor-second double stop lick that was often played by country guitarists.

Unlike most early rock 'n' roll guitarists who usually played only major, minor, and seventh chords, Gallup liked to use jazz-chord voicings. The 6add9 chord was one of his favorites, and he would often use it to end songs. He also liked to conclude songs with a major 7 chord.

Gallup often relied on Travis- or Atkins-style picking, a style that was common in country music during the mid-'50s. It involves simultaneously playing a bass line on the bottom three strings while plucking out melodies on the upper three strings. A good example of this style can be heard on Vincent's recording of "Be-Bop-A-Lula" and Gallup's solo on "Red Bluejeans And A Ponytail."

According to Gallup, most of the solos that he recorded with Gene Vincent were created spontaneously in the studio. On early Gene Vincent sessions, producer Ken Nelson had hired Nashville studio guitarists Grady Martin and Hank "Sugarfoot" Garland to back up Vincent in case the Blue Caps didn't work out. However, after hearing Gallup flawlessly execute his first take for "Race With The Devil," Nelson realized that the backup musicians weren't necessary.

Techniques

Much of the intricacy of Gallup's flashy playing style can be attributed to his right-hand technique. He used a combination of a flatpick and fingerpicks, holding the flatpick between his thumb and forefinger and wearing the fingerpicks on his second and third fingers. He also used a hybrid of Atkins- or Travis-style picking and traditional flatpicking techniques. His use of the flatpick allowed Gallup to execute lightning-fast runs that would be impossible or very difficult to play with a thumbpick in the manner that they were used by most Travis-picking stylists. Gallup utilized each of his right-hand fingers, resting his little finger on his Bigsby vibrato bar.

Gallup's use of the vibrato bar was especially innovative for his time. Like most players, he used the bar to apply vibrato to chords, but he often would depress the bar before striking a note and then raise the note to pitch, similar to pedal-steel playing techniques. An example of this can be heard in the middle of the first solo on "Bluejean Bop."

Perhaps a direct result of his Les Paul influences, Gallup used hammer-ons and pull-offs to increase his playing speed. Many of his solos – particularly those on "Race With The Devil" and "Cruisin'" – feature fast pulled-off triplet figures. Gallup made effective use of raked and slurred grace notes that gave his leads a distinctive, jazz-like sophistication. Sometimes he would slide up and down the strings as much as an octave. Gallup bent notes only occasionally, and he never bent them more than a whole step, which was probably as much due to the heavy-gauge strings he used as to his non-blues background.

The Hardware

Guitars, Strings, and Picks

Details about Gallup's first guitar are unknown. Although Gallup himself was not certain, he said that he obtained his first electric guitar from the Sears & Roebuck catalog sometime in the early '40s.

When Gallup joined Gene Vincent and his Blue Caps in 1956, he acquired a brand-new Gretsch Duo-Jet with a black finish, and fitted with single-coil DeArmond pickups, and a fixed-arm Bigsby vibrato unit. This is the guitar that Gallup used on all of his recordings with Vincent. Although many rumors have since circulated about the Duo-Jet being

One of the most influential and innovative rockabilly guitarists (seen here with the Blue Caps, top left), Gallup's playing can be heard on such classics as "Race With the Devil" and "Be-Bop-A-Lula".

stolen at one of Vincent's shows, Doris Gallup still owns the guitar.

After quitting Vincent's band, Gallup bought a hollowbody, double-cutaway Gretsch Country Gentleman fitted with humbucking Filtertron pickups. This is the guitar that he used for the rest of his playing career. He also owned a Gibson Everly Brothers acoustic that he set up with nylon strings.

Gallup wore two metal National finger-picks on his second and third right-hand fingers, and held a large, thin triangular flatpick between his thumb and forefinger. His Duo-Jet was strung with medium-gauge flat-wound strings.

Amplifiers, Effects, and Devices

Although the guitars that Gallup used are well-documented in a handful of photos, details about which amplifiers he used are not as well known. In a *Guitar Player* interview, Gallup mentioned that he used an amp that belonged to Grady Martin when recording at Owen Bradley's studio in Nashville. Although he was not certain, Gallup thought that the amp was a Standel. This is highly likely, since Martin did use a Standel amp at this time, and Standel amps were very popular with country-music studio guitarists. This amp probably had a single 15-inch speaker.

For live performance, Gallup used a tweed-covered Fender amp, most likely a

Although Gallup (second from the right) played with Gene Vincent's Blue Caps for less than a year, he recorded 35 songs with the band before he decided to abandon his career as a professional musician.

In His Own Words

Like most musicians, you listen to a lot of people – pick up a lick here, a lick there. Pretty soon you originate some kind of a style.
Guitar Player, *December 1983*

When we first came together with that style of music, why, it just wasn't around. I mean, it wasn't patterned behind anybody that I know of. It all just got started.
Guitar Player, *December 1983*

I never played a Fender. Don't like Fenders. Well, it's not that I don't like them. It's just that some people like Fords, some people like Chevrolets.
Guitar Player, *December 1983*

What They Say

The best influence I had was trying to copy the solos by Cliff Gallup on Gene Vincent records. It was a good exercise trying to learn his solos because he used a lot of guitar, as opposed to copying blues solos which often hang around two or three notes and go for effect.
Albert Lee, Guitar Player, *May 1981*

Gallup was easily the most sophisticated of any of the players of that period.
Dave Edmunds, Guitar Player, *September 1983*

He was one of the most experimental, wild, end-of-the-world players. Some of that stuff on the Gene Vincent And The Blue Caps *album holds up even today. Futuristic style. Wild, ridiculous runs all over the place.*
Jeff Beck, Guitar Player, *December, 1985*

One of my dreams was to meet Cliff and see if there was anything to be tapped from that period that would be useful to me in order to pass on the music.
Jeff Beck, Guitar Player, *April 1993*

He'd listen to a song once and play it. He could do anything – country, pop, gospel. He loved music. I always told him it was his first love.
Doris Gallup, Guitar Player, *April 1993*

Twin. This was confirmed in a recent interview with Doris Gallup, who says that she gave the amplifier to Cliff's best friend after he passed away.

On the early Gene Vincent records, Gallup's guitar was often processed with reverb and slapback echo. Since neither of these effects were available as amplifier features or portable units at that time, the effects were produced by expensive pieces of studio gear and special recording techniques. In the late '50s, Gallup built his first two echo units from old tape recorders. These echo units were not used on any Vincent recordings.

Discography

Gallup played on only the first two Gene Vincent albums, **Bluejean Bop** *and* **Gene Vincent And The Blue Caps**. *He recorded 35 songs with Gene Vincent: "Ain't She Sweet," "B-I-Bickey Bi Bo Bo Go," "Be-Bop-A-Lula," "Bluejean Bop," "Blues Stay Away From Me," "Bop Street," "Crazy Legs," "Cruisin'," "Five Days, Five Days," "Five Feet Of Lovin'," "Cat Man," "Double Talkin' Baby," "Gonna Back Up Baby," "Hold Me, Hug Me, Rock Me," "I Flipped," "Important Words," "I Sure Miss You," "Jezebel," "Jump Back, Honey Jump Back," "Jumps, Giggles & Shouts," "Peg O' My Heart," "Pink Thunderbird," "Pretty Pretty Baby," "Race With The Devil," "Red Bluejeans & A Ponytail," "Teenage Partner," "Unchained Melody," "Up A Lazy River," "Waltz Of The Wind," "Wedding Bells (Are Breaking Up That Old Gang Of Mine)," "Well I Knocked Bim Bam," "Who Slapped John?," "Woman Love," "You Better Believe," and "You Told A Fib." All of these songs were recorded at Owen Bradley's studio in Nashville between May 4 and October 18, 1956.*

All of Gallup's playing with Vincent can be heard on EMI's **The Gene Vincent Box Set: Complete Capitol And Columbia Recordings 1956-1964**. *Nine of the 21 tracks on Capitol's CD* **Gene Vincent – The Capitol Collector's Series** *feature Gallup.*

In 1966, Gallup recorded a self-produced album called **Straight Down The Middle** *with a group called the Four C's. This album is especially rare, as only 500 copies were originally pressed. Some of the material was reissued on the out-of-print Magnum Force album* **The Legendary Guitarists Of Gene Vincent**.

Recording Sessions

Although Gallup was quite active as a guitarist in Norfolk, Virginia, studios after he quit Vincent's band, he did not participate in any significant or high-profile recording sessions.

Typical Licks

Gallup had great technique, even at breakneck tempos. Here is an example of one of his earliest and most copied rock 'n' roll licks.

Gallup used double stops featuring the thirteenth and sharp ninth in blues curls.

This lick shows Gallup playing the Dorian mode over a dominant chord.

Dave Gilmour

Emerging out of Britain's late-'60s psychedelic movement with the band Pink Floyd, David Gilmour has remained one of rock's most effective and distinctive sonic architects. With an understated yet emotional style, he tends to play guitar parts that support the song, rather than drawing attention to his technical skills. His soaring, blues-based leads and folk-inspired acoustic rhythms are deceptively simple, but few players can match the conviction of his performance. Gilmour remains one of the most distinctive rock guitarists.

The Player

Influences

David Gilmour began playing guitar at 14 when he borrowed one from a neighbor. He has no formal musical training, and he largely taught himself to play by listening to records.

His early influences were folk and blues guitarists, such as Leadbelly and Howlin' Wolf. Bob Dylan was one of his favorite performers, and he also enjoyed rock 'n' roll, citing Bill Haley as one of his early favorites. In the '60s, Gilmour enjoyed the playing styles of B. B. King, Hank Marvin, Peter Green, Eric Clapton, Jeff Beck, and Jimi Hendrix.

Gilmour became friends with Syd Barrett, whom he later replaced in Pink Floyd, at the Cambridge High School for Boys. The two practiced guitar together and learned to play blues and songs by the Beatles and Rolling Stones. They also occasionally played shows together as a duo. After Barrett left Cambridge to attend Camberwell Art School in London, Gilmour formed a rhythm-and-blues cover band called Joker's Wild.

Ever since joining Pink Floyd, Gilmour has paid little attention to contemporary guitarists. "Eddie Van Halen has done a few things that

I like a lot," he mentioned in a *Guitar World* interview. "But for the most part that kind of thing doesn't interest me. There hasn't been anyone recently that I've been turned on by."

Approach and Style

Gilmour's style is often described as simple and economical, but his highly emotional and melodic phrasing and powerful tone have earned him a reputation as one of rock's finest stylists. One of his stylistic signatures is his use of quarter-note triplet arpeggios, which give his leads a lyrical quality. His other stylistic traits include effective use of silence and melodic repetition.

Traces of Dave's folk and blues influences can be heard in Pink Floyd's music. Some of his rhythms and riffs have a loose Delta-blues feel, and he often uses pentatonic minor blues scales in his solos. But he will add non-blues touches, such as ending rhythm patterns with bitonal chords or inserting a ♭2 into his blues licks. He wrenches blues-like emotion out of his playing with powerful bent notes and soulful vibrato.

For his rhythm accompaniments, Gilmour liberally uses open-string voicings, minor chords, and minor tonalities that give the music a folk feel. However, he often plays Dorian-

Background

1944 *David Gilmour is born in Cambridge, England, on March 6.*

1958 *Gilmour learns to play guitar on a Spanish acoustic that he borrowed from a next-door neighbor. His parents give him a Pete Seeger instructional record, Pete Seeger Teaches Guitar, which helps him to progress more rapidly.*

1968 *Gilmour becomes a member of Pink Floyd, joining Syd Barrett on guitar, Roger Waters on bass, Richard Wright on keyboards, and Nick Mason on drums. Gilmour makes his first recorded appearance on A Saucerful Of Secrets.*

1970 *Syd Barrett – who has now left Pink Floyd – mounts EXTRAVAGANZA '70 at London's Olympia Stadium, at which Gilmour plays bass.*

1973 *Pink Floyd records Dark Side Of The Moon, the band's most successful record ever. It remains on the Billboard Top 200 chart for another 14 years.*

1976 *A giant inflatable pig being photographed for Pink Floyd's album Animals breaks free and drifts into London Airport's flight path.*

1978 *Gilmour releases his first solo album, David Gilmour. He also sponsors demo tapes of an unknown singer, Kate Bush.*

1979 *Pink Floyd releases The Wall and performs a monumental series of elaborately staged concerts.*

1982 *He admits that members of Pink Floyd "don't not get along, but are working partners."*

1984 *Gilmour records his second solo album, About Face.*

1985 *Roger Waters quits Pink Floyd, making the future of the band uncertain.*

1987 *Pink Floyd makes its comeback with A Momentary Lapse Of Reason and a world tour.*

1986 *Gilmour leads a band in a benefit gig at London's Royal Albert Hall in support of Columbian earthquake victims.*

1994 *Pink Floyd releases The Division Bell, and embark on another world tour.*

based i-IV progressions and added 9ths (especially in his soloing and chording) that add a moody, somber emotion to his songs.

Although Gilmour lacks any formal musical training, he has a well-developed awareness of the relationships between chords and scales, most evident in his effective use of diatonic triads, such as those on *The Wall's* "Run Like Hell." His use of double-stops and arpeggios often invoke a jazzy sophistication rare among rock guitarists.

Techniques

Gilmour is more concerned with tone, note-bending, and vibrato than playing fast lines. In general, his tone is clean and undistorted with emphasized highs providing enhanced articulation. To convey the percussive nuances of his picking technique, he prefers the clarity and definition of the Strat's bridge pickup. He rarely uses the other pickups.

Gilmour holds his pick with his thumb and first finger and picks between the middle and neck pickup. He tends to use alternate picking patterns and utilizes left-hand hammer-ons to add speed to his playing. To create harmonic "squeals," he will deaden the string with his right-hand thumb immediately after picking the note. On an acoustic guitar he will alternate between using a pick if he is strumming chords or his fingers if he is picking single-note lines or playing fingerpicked patterns. Sometimes he attaches a capo to the neck.

Gilmour's vibrato and note-bending technique is particularly refined, and his mastery of these techniques is the source of much of the emotion in his playing. He generates vibrato either with his fingers or with his Strat's vibrato bar. He often waits a moment before he adds vibrato to a picked note. His vibrato is slow, subtle, and narrow, unlike the fast and exaggerated vibrato favored by many rock players. Gilmour has developed a highly accurate note-bending technique.

He occasionally utilizes compound bends where he will stop at two different notes while bending up, or he will use bend and release techniques. His bends range from understated quarter-step bends to exaggerated two-and-a-half step bends. He produces the latter by supporting the bend with three fingers and anchoring his thumb on the top edge of the guitar's fingerboard. He often employs natural harmonics and feedback as well.

Many guitarists play slide on a standard electric guitar in a standing position, but Gilmour prefers to play slide on a lap steel. "I always had a fondness for pedal steels and lap steels," he told *Guitar World* in a 1994 interview. "I guess it's because I could never come to grips with standard bottleneck playing." On rare occasions, he will use a slide on a standard guitar, but he will hold the slide in his right hand and touch the strings while fretting notes "to make spaceship noises." He uses a standard solid chrome bar and damps with the edge of his right hand as well as damping behind the bar with his left hand. He picks with a flatpick and his fingers. He uses two different tunings on his lap steels – E minor (*E, B, E, G, B, E,* low to high) and open G (*D, G, D, G, B, E,* low to high).

He also sometimes uses alternate tunings on standard guitar. He used a dropped-*D* tuning (*D, A, D, G, B, E,* low to high) on "Run Like Hell" (*The Wall*) and *D, A, D, G, A, D* (low to high) on "Poles Apart" (*The Division Bell*). On "Hey You" (*The Wall*) he used a "Nashville strung" guitar, which involves replacing the bottom four strings (*E, A, D, G*) with thinner strings tuned up an octave above usual (the bottom *E* is tuned up two octaves higher).

Effects have also become important elements in Gilmour's playing technique. He likes to use a digital delay to turn simple quarter-note patterns into intricate-sounding double-picked lines. He achieves this effect by setting the delay to echo three-quarters of

a beat apart. He also used a DigiTech Whammy pedal to achieve an octave bend on "Marooned" (*The Division Bell*).

The Hardware
Guitars, Strings, and Picks

Gilmour learned to play on a nylon-string Spanish guitar, and his first instrument was an arch-top acoustic guitar with f-holes, which he put a pickup on. Later, he owned a Burns Sonnet, which he has described as an awful guitar, and a Hofner Club 60.

For his 21st birthday, Dave's parents gave him a Fender Telecaster that they bought on a trip to the United States. He considers this his first good guitar. It was lost a year later by the airlines during his first trip to the U.S.

Gilmour has a sharp, biting, clean tone that emphasizes the nuances of his picking and note-bending technique. He prefers Fender guitars, generally playing either a Stratocaster or Telecaster, both in the studio and onstage.

Fender Stratocasters with maple necks are Dave's favorite guitars. His main guitar is a red '84 vintage series '57 Strat reissue with EMG SA pickups, EXG expander, and SPC mid boost. He shortens its tremolo arm by cutting it in half, and uses either three or four tremolo springs. He owns several other Strats, including a black one from the early '70s, a '63 sunburst, a '57 Lake Placid Blue Strat originally made for Homer Haynes of Homer and Jethro, and a '54 Strat (serial number 0001) with a white finish, gold-anodized pickguard, and gold-plated hardware.

Gilmour has a large collection of vintage instruments, including a variety of early-'50s Fender Broadcasters, a '61 sunburst Telecaster Custom, a '55 Gibson Les Paul, a '57 Les Paul custom with three humbucking pickups, a National Resoglas electric, and a transparent lucite Dan Armstrong electric. He also has several Gretsch electrics, including a Silver Jet, Duo-Jet, Roc Jet, 6120 Chet Atkins hollowbody, 6121 Chet Atkins solidbody, White Falcon, and White Penguin. Some of the oddities in his collection include a Vox organ guitar and a headless, short-scale, custom-made electric by Roger Giffin.

Gilmour prefers to play slide on lap steels, and he owns several. His main slide guitar is a Japanese-made Jensen lap steel with Fender pickups. He also owns a '30s Rickenbacker lap steel, a '50s Fender double-neck pedal steel, and a Smith Melobar, a lap steel that can be worn like a standard guitar and played standing up.

He owns several acoustic guitars, and usually records with a Martin D-35 or D-18. His other favorites include a Gibson J-200, a mid-'60s Gibson Everly Brothers, a wood-body Dobro resonator guitar, a Washburn acoustic-electric, and an Ovation Custom Legend.

On his electric guitars, Gilmour uses GHS Boomers (.010, .012, .016, .024, .034, .044). He plays with a Jim Dunlop .88 gauge Tortex pick.

Amplifiers, Effects, and Devices

In the early days of Pink Floyd, Dave used a 50-watt Selmer amp with four 12-inch speakers. He then switched to an H&H amp with a built-in vibrato unit, before discovering Hiwatt amplifiers, which remain his favorite. On stage, he tends to use two 100-watt Hiwatt stacks, with Celestion-loaded Marshall 4x12 cabinets on the bottom and Fane Crescendo-loaded WEM 4x12 cabinets on the top.

Her also likes Fender amps, and his stage setup includes two Fender '59 4x10 Bassman reissues. On his 1984 solo tour, he played through a pair of Fender Twin Reverbs with two 4x12 cabinets instead of his Hiwatt stacks, and he often uses the Twin Reverbs or a Fender Princeton in the studio. His other amps include a Mesa Boogie head used as an overdrive unit, and a Gallien-Krueger GK 250ML to record.

He utilizes various effects to add texture to his sound, a favorite being a rotating speaker. Until recently, he used 200-watt Yamaha rotating speaker units, but now favors a Maestro

Gilmour's playing style is a combination of his folk, blues, and psychedelic rock influences. His soaring, emotion-filled guitar solos have been the highlight of many Pink Floyd classics, including "Comfortably Numb" and "Money."

In His Own Words

My fingers weren't designed to go very quickly. Any trick or device I can buy to make me sound more technically proficient is fine with me.
Musician, *August 1992*

I've thought of parts that I can't play. If I can't play it, I'll get someone else to.
Musician, *August 1992*

The guitar just happens to be the instrument I can best express my feelings on.
Guitar World, *February 1993*

Basically, I'm a person who's stuck within certain limitations, and I have to work within them.
Guitar Player, *May 1979*

In the studio, I can go in and get a guitar and an amplifier to sound perfect – to me. And then the next day, I just turn the mains on and don't touch anything else at all and it sounds completely different. And you hate it. You wind up going for a different guitar, different everything.
Guitar Player, *November 1984*

What They Say

You can give him a ukulele and he'll make it sound like a Stradivarius. He's truly got the best set of hands with which I've ever worked.
Producer Bob Ezrin, Guitar World, *February 1993*

David Gilmour is a great player. You know the lead in "Comfortably Numb"? It's such a great solo... It sounds so good, it's got this weird tone to it.
Slash, The Guitar Magazine, *November 1991*

I was sitting in a pub when in walked Dave Gilmour and said, "I've just got the gig with Floyd and I'm getting £25 a week!" I thought to myself, you better make the best of the money because without Syd Barrett the band's going nowhere. Boy was I wrong!
John Etheridge, musician, 1994

Rover unit. He used a Binson Echorec, a primitive delay unit with a built-in wire recorder, on most of the early Pink Floyd albums, including *Dark Side Of The Moon*, and briefly used a Boss DD-2 Digital Delay pedal. He favors stomp boxes, and has used a variety of effects, including an MXR Phase 90, Electro-Harmonix Electric Mistress flanger, and Big Muff distortion, Orange treble and bass booster, Dallas-Arbiter Fuzz Face, and Boss HM-2 Heavy Metal and DM-2 Digital Metalizer distortion units.

His current floor effects setup consists of a DigiTech Whammy pedal, Boss CS-2 compressor, CE-2 Chorus, and DM-2 pedals, an Ibanez Tube Screamer overdrive, a Rat II distortion pedal, a t. c. electronics line driver, a Big Muff, an Ernie Ball volume pedal, and a pair of modified Boss GE-7 graphic EQs. His rack contains a Mesa Boogie Studio .22 preamp, a mid-'70s Alembic F2-B bass preamp modified with an extra tube for more drive, a Summit Audio F100 EQ, a t. c. electronics 2290 multi-effects unit, a Lexicon PCM-70, and an MXR delay system designed by Pete Cornish. His pedal board was made by Custom Audio Electronics. He also uses a hand-held E-Bow sustain device. He uses many of these effects in the studio, and sometimes records direct with a Zoom 9030 multi-effects unit, a Sansamp, or a Scholz Rockman.

Discography

Gilmour has played on all of Pink Floyd's albums recorded since 1968. He appears on the following Pink Floyd albums: **A Saucerful Of Secrets** (1968), **Piper At The Gates Of Dawn** (1968), **Ummagumma** (1969), **Atom Heart Mother** (1970), **Meddle** (1971), **Obscured By Clouds** (1972), **Dark Side Of The Moon** (1973), **Wish You Were Here** (1975), **Animals** (1977), **The Wall** (1979), **The Final Cut** (1983), **Momentary Lapse Of Reason** (1987), and **The Division Bell** (1994).

Gilmour has also recorded two solo albums – **David Gilmour** (1978) and **About Face** (1984).

Recording Sessions

Gilmour has guested on several albums, including Syd Barrett's **The Madcap Laughs**, Roy Harper's **HQ**, and Paul Rodgers' **Muddy Water Blues – A Tribute To Muddy Waters**, where he is featured on the song "Standing Around Crying". He has also played on albums by Kate Bush, Wings, Bryan Ferry, Dream Academy, and Supertramp.

Typical Licks

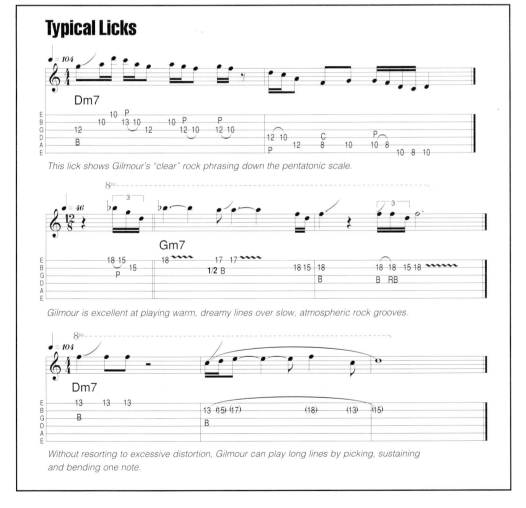

This lick shows Gilmour's "clear" rock phrasing down the pentatonic scale.

Gilmour is excellent at playing warm, dreamy lines over slow, atmospheric rock grooves.

Without resorting to excessive distortion, Gilmour can play long lines by picking, sustaining and bending one note.

Buddy Guy

Buddy Guy is one of the finest second-generation Chicago blues guitarists. He established himself as a first-rate blues musician by backing up Muddy Waters on several of Waters' most influential Chess albums. Guy's wild performance antics and flamboyant guitar playing style has influenced several rock and blues guitarists, most notably Jimi Hendrix, Jeff Beck, Eric Clapton, and Stevie Ray Vaughan. Guy may be one of the most important players in establishing the link between the blues and rock music.

The Player

Influences

Before Buddy Guy learned to play guitar, he listened to gospel vocalists, such as Lou Rawls with the Pilgrim Travelers and Sam Cooke with the Soul Stirrers. Guy tried to sing gospel himself for a while, but he never felt that he advanced to the level that he could perform it in public.

Buddy got his first guitar when he was 13, and taught himself how to play. One of the first songs he learned was John Lee Hooker's "Boogie Chillen'." Guy never had any formal musical training. "I'd worn *B♭* out before I found out what it was," he said in a *Guitar Player* interview.

When Buddy was growing up, he listened to radio broadcasts from WLSC in Nashville, which exposed him to Chicago blues artists Muddy Waters and Little Walter, and Texas artists Lightnin' Hopkins and T-Bone Walker. He also used to watch local blues musicians in New Orleans night clubs. "Every time I got a chance to see a guitar player, it was like a teacher," Buddy recalls.

Guitar Slim, who played at the Dew Drop Inn in New Orleans, was a huge influence on Buddy, but more for his stage antics than playing. Buddy stole many performing ideas from Guitar Slim, such as using a 150-foot guitar cord and walking into the audience or outside the club while playing. Earl King and Lightnin' Slim were also big influences on Guy at this time. "Lightnin' Slim was the first time I'd ever seen an electric guitar," he told *Guitar Player*.

While living in Louisiana, Buddy learned to play Jimmy Reed songs, "The Things I Used To Do" by Guitar Slim, and B. B. King licks. He also became proficient at playing country blues, although he rarely exposed this side of his playing until later on in his career. Guy eventually got gigs playing with Big Poppa Tilley, Lightnin' Slim, Lazy Lester, and Slim Harpo, before moving to Chicago in 1957. While playing in Louisiana clubs, he learned to play a variety of material, including rock 'n' roll, gospel, and country and western as well as the blues. "That's what made who Buddy Guy is today," he said in *Guitar Player*.

The Chicago blues scene had a huge impact on Guy. Here he was exposed to players such as Otis Rush, Magic Sam, Muddy Waters, Howlin' Wolf, Little Walter, Junior Wells, and Sonny Boy Williamson.

Background

1936 *George Guy is born on July 30 in Lettsworth, Louisiana.*

1949 *Buddy starts playing an acoustic guitar.*

1953 *Guy plays gigs with Lightnin' Slim, Lazy Lester, and Slim Harpo.*

1957 *Buddy moves to Chicago.*

1958 *Wins the Battle Of The Blues competition at the Blue Flame Club and starts recording for Cobra Records, with whom he went on to cut several influential singles.*

1960 *Buddy becomes a house musician at Chess Records.*

1963 *Guy and his band back Muddy Waters and Howlin' Wolf on* Folk Festival Of The Blues.

1965 *Buddy travels to England for the first time specifically to see T-Bone Walker play.*

1968 *Buddy releases his first solo album,* A Man & The Blues.

1970 *He goes on tour as an opening act for the Rolling Stones. He also appears briefly with Muddy Waters in the film* Chicago Blues.

1971 *Buddy is voted in the top five in the U.K.'s New Musical Express' Guitarist Poll behind Eric Clapton and Jimi Hendrix.*

1972 *The album* Buddy Guy and Junior Wells Play The Blues, *co-produced with Eric Clapton, is released.*

1987 *Buddy is extensively profiled in the PBS documentary,* Rainin' In My Heart.

1989 *Buddy is invited to collaborate on Clapton's* Journeyman *album.*

1991 *Guy releases* Damn Right I've Got The Blues. *Eric Clapton, Mark Knopfler and Jeff Beck all make guest appearances. He feels that it is the first album that truly displays his playing style and personality.*

Using the wild performance stunts he learned from watching Guitar Slim, Guy won the "Battle Of The Blues" competition at the Blue Flame Club, which helped him to gain the respect of many of Chicago's finest musicians. Guy eventually worked with many of these musicians, and, most importantly, he landed a gig with Muddy Waters, who had a profound effect on Guy's music and career.

In a recent interview, Guy mentioned that his favorite records were anything by Muddy Waters and B.B. King's "Sweet Little Angel."

Although Guy has been playing blues music for more than four decades, he also enjoys the music of contemporary blues guitarists, such as Eric Clapton and Stevie Ray Vaughan, as much as he appreciates that of his early influences.

Approach and Style

Like most traditional blues artists, Guy plays in a style that is firmly rooted in pentatonic minor scales and I-IV-V chord progressions. But even when his playing remains well within these boundaries, he retains a distinctive, identifiable sound.

Guy frequently uses major and minor chords for his rhythm playing, but his chord voicings sometimes differ from standard fingerings. For example, he usually plays an A chord in the conventional manner by holding down the second-fret of the D, G, and B strings, but he will also add a high A played on the fifth fret of the high E string. He often throws in ninth, sixth, and diminished seventh chords for variety, and he will sometimes play 7sus4, 7♭9, minor 6, and eleventh chords. Many of Guy's rhythms consist of double-stop "walking bass" or "boogie woogie" patterns played on the bass strings. He has an elastic sense of time, rushing or laying back against the beat as he sees fit.

Guy primarily sticks to conventional box patterns when playing solos. For example,

when playing in the key of A, he will generally play in the fifth-, twelfth-, and seventeenth-position patterns on the neck. One of his signature licks is a repeating double-stop pattern consisting of a constant note played on the higher string and a hammer-on figure played on the lower string. He usually hammers a minor third interval when playing this lick.

Perhaps the most distinctive feature of Buddy Guy's playing style is his string-bending technique. His bends are especially wide, aggressive, and exaggerated, and sometimes they will reach as high as a major third. "I'll make the little E kiss the big E," he explained to *Guitar Player* about his bending technique. Not all of Guy's bends are this exaggerated, though. Usually he bends notes a whole step or a half step, and sometimes he will bend double-stops.

Techniques

Guy plays with an aggressive attack, keeping his right hand stiff and picking hard. He holds his pick with his thumb, forefinger, and middle finger, but he often curls the pick up into his palm and plays with just his fingers, pulling and snapping the strings. When he hits a string, he will often strike the adjacent, muted strings on either side as well, producing a percussive triplet effect.

Guy's left-hand technique is equally aggressive, especially his string bends. He bends strings with his third finger, but he does not use his other fingers to support the bend. This is particularly surprising, since his bends often extend from one edge of the fingerboard to the other. Guy also has a well-developed left-hand vibrato, which ranges from a subtle shimmer to a wide, fast quiver. He uses one finger for vibrato as well.

Guy has invented a few special tricks that have been imitated by several blues guitarists. One of these techniques is to bend a note and slowly release it while using a

staccato pick attack, producing a stuttering effect with each picked note sounding at a different microtonal interval. He also frequently uses legato slides, slipping between different notes or even chords for as much as a full measure without picking a note. Guy's fast triplet pull-off patterns have been imitated by many rock guitarists, such as Jimmy Page and Jeff Beck. While playing live, Guy also likes to use a drumstick to play his guitar, striking rhythms with the stick in his right hand and fretting chords with his left hand.

Although Guy admits that he never plays slide live or on record, he sometimes practices slide guitar at home. "When I came to Chicago I had a slide," he told *Guitar Player*, "I saw them guys play that slide, man – Muddy, Elmore James, Earl Hooker, and all these people – and I said, 'Ain't no sense in me even tryin',' the way they was playin' that slide."

Although Guy has been recording since the '50s, he feels that 1991's Damn Right I've Got The Blues *was the first time that he had the opportunity to make a record that showed his true personality as a blues artist.*

The Hardware

Guitars, Strings, and Picks

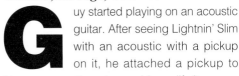

Guy started playing on an acoustic guitar. After seeing Lightnin' Slim with an acoustic with a pickup on it, he attached a pickup to his own acoustic so he could amplify it.

When Guy was gigging around Louisiana, he was playing a Fender Stratocaster. He had wanted a Strat ever since he saw Guitar Slim playing one in a Louisiana club. Just before leaving Baton Rouge, Louisiana for Chicago, Guy acquired a Gibson Les Paul that was given to him by a friend, but he had it for only a few weeks before it was stolen. "That's like joining the union in Chicago," Guy remarks.

He acquired another Stratocaster after his Les Paul was stolen, and the Strat has

In the late '50s Buddy Guy moved to Chicago, where he landed gigs backing up legendary blues performers such as Muddy Waters. Guy became a legend himself and has influenced many blues and rock guitarists.

remained his primary guitar ever since then. "I found out that if I dropped it or it fell, it stayed in one piece," he told *Guitar Player*. "That made me love it more than anything else." Guy has owned several different Strats throughout his career, and he currently plays several Buddy Guy signature Stratocasters made for him by Fender's Custom Shop.

Guy has also played several different Guild guitars during his career. He signed an endorsement contract with Guild in 1967 and started playing a semi-hollow Starfire 4. He has also played Guild's Nightingale and Bluesbird models, as well as a Guild 12-string acoustic.

Guy uses light-gauge rounded triangular Gibson picks and light-gauge Ernie Ball strings (.009, .011, .012, .026, .032, .042).

Amplifiers, Effects, and Devices

Guy played through a variety of different amps when he was starting out in Louisiana clubs, but he has no recollection of specific types. When he established himself as a guitarist in Chicago in the late '50s, he bought a Fender 4x10 Bassman. This is the amp the he used on all of his early Cobra and Chess recording sessions. The Bassman, which Guy still owns, is adorned with red covering.

When Guy started endorsing Guild instruments in the late '60s, he played through a Guild Thunderbird amplifier with two 15-inch speakers for a brief period. During the '80s, he started playing through Marshall JCM 800 model 2210 amplifier heads and Marshall 1982A 4x12 cabinets with high-output Celestion speakers. "I've been in love with Marshall amplifiers ever since Eric [Clapton] started coming over here with them," he told Dan Forte in *Guitar Player*. "If people would have listened to me, they would have had Marshall stacks in 1958." He used the Marshall amps up until recently, when he switched to Fender 4x10 Bassman reissues.

In His Own Words

You can't learn the blues out of a book, you've got to soak in it. It's got to be in your soul.
Guitar Player, *March 1970*

A lot of stuff you see me do onstage, I've never done it before. Everything I do onstage comes to me right then. I just have this good feeling about blues music and what I'm doing, and I feel like I should try it, man.
Guitar Player, *April 1990*

Whenever you hear me play, man, there's always a part of Muddy Waters, Howlin' Wolf, Little Walter, T-Bone Walker, and all those great musicians. Everybody comes out in me.
Guitar Player, *June 1993*

When I learned how to play guitar, I couldn't look up and see a Prince or a Eric or a Beck or a Keith, makin' all this money playin' the guitar. You just had to love this thing to play it.
Guitar Player, *November 1994*

What They Say

He's by far and without a doubt the best guitar player alive. I don't know what it is – it doesn't stand up in a recording studio, you couldn't put him on a hit record – but if you see him in person, the way he plays is beyond anyone.
Eric Clapton, Musician

Part of my reason for forming Cream was, I... had this kind of mad idea about leading a blues band and being the English Buddy Guy. I wanted to be Buddy Guy with a composing bass player.
Eric Clapton, Guitar World, *June 1991*

What he does is just plain raw. I don't mean without finesse. I mean raw, like raw can be real gentle as easily as it can be bare wires.
Stevie Ray Vaughan, Guitar World, *July 1991*

He is not only a good guitarist, he's a good person. His head has never ballooned and to be so talented and not let that happen is so good.
B. B. King, Guitar World, *July 1991*

Guy's tone settings are straightforward – he turns up every control except for the bass. "I like a lot of treble, and then I control the different sounds from my guitar," he said in *Guitar Player*.

Like most blues guitarists, Guy is not a big fan of effects. As he has explained, "Whenever they come out with a new effect, I try to figure out a way to do it with just Buddy Guy." He occasionally uses a Jim Dunlop Cry Baby wah-wah pedal and a Boss octave divider. These effects can be heard on Buddy's recordings of "She's A Superstar" and "Country Man" from *Feels Like Rain*.

Discography

Buddy's first recordings were the singles "Sit And Cry (The Blues)"/"Try To Quit You Baby" and "This Is The End"/"You Sure Can't Do," recorded for Cobra but released by the Artistic subsidiary. They are available, with other early Buddy Guy recordings, on **The Cobra Records Story** *box set.*

Guy's first solo recording was **A Man & The Blues** *(Vanguard) released in 1968. Subsequent solo albums include:* **This Is Buddy Guy** *(Vanguard),* **Hold That Plane!** *(Vanguard),* **I Was Walking Through The Woods** *(Chess),* **Left My Blues In San Francisco** *(Chess),* **Buddy Guy** *(Chess),* **First Time I Met The Blues** *(Chess Japan),* **In The Beginning** *(Red Lightnin'),* **Hot And Cool** *(Vanguard),* **Got To Use Your Head** *(Blues Ball),* **The Dollar Done Fell** *(JSP),* **DJ Play My Blues** *(JSP),* **Ten Blue Fingers** *(JSP),* **Breaking Out** *(JSP),* **Buddy And Philip Guy** *(JSP),* **Live At The Checkerboard Lounge** *(JSP),* **Stone Crazy!** *(Alligator),* **The Complete Chess Studio Sessions** *(Chess), and* **My Time After Awhile** *(Vanguard). He considers his most recent releases on the Silvertone label,* **Damn Right I've Got The Blues**, **Feels Like Rain**, *and* **Slippin' In**, *to be the albums that display his true talents and personality.*

Recording Sessions

As a staff guitarist at Chess Records during the '60s, Guy recorded with nearly every artist on the label, including John Lee Hooker, Howlin' Wolf, Muddy Waters, Sonny Boy Williamson, Koko Taylor, and Little Walter. Many of these performances can be heard on Chess anthologies **The Blues, Volume 1**, **The Blues Volume 2**, **Chicago Blues Anthology**, **Chess Blues Rarities**, **The Golden Age Of Chicago Blues**, **The First Time I Met The Blues**, *and* **The Second Time I Met The Blues**.

Buddy recorded several albums as a duo with Junior Wells, including: **Buddy Guy & Junior Wells Play The Blues**, **Buddy And The Juniors**, **Drinkin' TNT, Smokin' Dynamite**, **The Original Blues Brothers**, **Going Back**, **Live In Montreux**, *and* **Atlantic Blues: Chicago**. *He also appears on several of Junior Wells' solo albums, including* **Hoodoo Man Blues**, **Southside Blues Jam**, **It's My Life, Baby**, **Chicago/The Blues/ Today, Vol. 1**, **Coming At You**, *and* **Live Recording**.

Typical Licks

This slow blues turnaround lick shows Guy's intricate phrasing in triplet time.

This catchy blues phrase is played over the ninth and tenth bars in a 12-bar blues.

Another great lick with a hint of Hendrix shows how contemporary Guy has always been.

Jimi Hendrix

Perhaps the most influential rock guitarist ever, Jimi Hendrix innovated many of the playing techniques and equipment applications used by guitarists today. An intensely creative musician, he was a skillful songwriter, a turbulent performer, and an imaginative arranger. Hendrix' impact was universal – shaping the development of modern hard rock, changing recording techniques, and encouraging new musical instrument and equipment designs. He remains the consummate guitar hero.

The Player

Influences

Hendrix often admitted to being influenced by a very diverse range of musical styles. His father and mother were both musicians – his father played saxophone and spoons, his mother played keyboard. At an early age, Jimi listened to his father's extensive record collection, which consisted primarily of blues and R&B. He enjoyed the music of country-blues guitarist Robert Johnson, and urban-blues artists, such as B. B. King, Albert King, Muddy Waters, Albert Collins, Elmore James, and Howlin' Wolf. Undoubtedly, Hendrix was deeply affected by the blues and R&B artists that he toured with early in his performing career. In the '60s, he became inspired by Buddy Guy's musicianship and showmanship, and would often attend Guy's shows. The blues became an integral part of the music that Hendrix performed, although he took his own music far beyond the genre.

Hendrix also enjoyed many of the current popular artists, particularly instrumentalists. He later recalled that as a high-school student he especially liked "Sleepwalk" by Santo & Johnny, "Cathy's Clown" by the Everly Brothers, Eddie Cochran's "Summertime Blues," and Henry Mancini's "Peter Gunn Theme." He also appreciated the work of singer-songwriters – Bob Dylan was a particular favorite – and he honed his own song and lyric-writing skills to match his talents as a guitarist and singer. Hendrix also loved jazz. Members of his early bands recall that he was as comfortable playing jazz solos as he was performing rock and R&B.

In addition, Jimi had many non-guitar influences. Early in his career, he aspired to imitate the sound of horn instruments. In interviews conducted shortly before he died, Jimi often talked about his interest in flamenco music. He also listened frequently to classical music, and cited Bach, Strauss, and Wagner as his favorites.

Approach and Style

Although Hendrix' guitar playing was truly ground-breaking, it remained deeply rooted in the blues and R&B styles that influenced him. His solos were based largely around the pentatonic minor scale favored by most blues musicians. Hendrix, however, had a strong sense of melody, and he would often break free of the pentatonic scale with melodic signatures. He was not a reserved or calculated

Background

1942 *James Marshall Hendrix is born on November 27, in Seattle, Washington.*

1955 *Starts playing guitar after receiving an inexpensive acoustic as a gift from his father.*

1959 *Enlists in the U.S. Army and becomes a paratrooper in the 101st Airborne Division – the "Screaming Eagles." During his 26 months of service, he meets future Band of Gypsies bassist Billy Cox.*

1962 *Hendrix injures his back and foot on his 26th jump. He returns to Seattle and joins Bobby Taylor And The Vancouvers.*

1963-64 *Tours the southern United States with several artists, including Little Richard, Ike and Tina Turner, The Supremes, B. B. King and Jackie Wilson.*

1965 *Hendrix purchases his first Stratocaster. He moves to New York City and forms his own band, Jimmy James and the Blue Flames.*

1966 *Jimi is discovered by Chas Chandler at New York's Cafe Wha? He moves to England and forms the Jimi Hendrix Experience, with bass player Noel Redding and drummer Mitch Mitchell. The band's first single, "Hey Joe," is released in the U.K. and becomes an immediate success.*

1967 *The first album by the Jimi Hendrix Experience, Are You Experienced?, is released. The Experience makes its U.S. debut at the Monterey Pop Festival, June 16-18.*

1968 *The Experience drifts apart late in the year. Hendrix forms the Band of Gypsies, with Buddy Miles on drums and Billy Cox on bass.*

1969 *Hendrix plays the final set at the Woodstock festival.*

1970 *An Experience reunion is planned, but doesn't materialize. On September 16, Hendrix plays with ex-Animals' singer Eric Burdon and War at Ronnie Scott's jazz club in London, his last public appearance. Two days later, Hendrix dies. The pathologist's report states that his death was the result of vomit inhalation due to barbiturate poisoning. He is buried at Greenwood cemetery, Seattle, on October 1.*

player, as his several different live versions of any particular song shows. He played with wild abandon, resisting repetition, and experimenting and creating new arrangements whenever he performed.

Hendrix' rhythm playing encompassed the influence of artists such as Curtis Mayfield and Wes Montgomery, and was far more advanced than that of most rock players of his day. His melodic rhythm style often sounded like a combination of rhythm and lead, perhaps as a result of the sparse instrumentation of the trio formats he played in. He would weave melodies into chord structures, stroke unison octaves, and slide and bend individual notes seductively. He preferred to play chords with his right-hand thumb draped over the fingerboard, and fretting as many as three strings at once.

Hendrix had extremely large hands, which enabled him to create voicings that many guitarists find difficult to perform. He also possessed exceptional dexterity, and was able to manipulate the guitar's tremolo bar and controls while he played.

Techniques

To say that Hendrix revolutionized electric-guitar technique would be an understatement. He ventured beyond the guitar's fretboard and utilized every inch of the instrument – plucking strings at the headstock, hitting the back of the neck, detuning strings, scraping the pick against the strings, and manipulating the guitars controls and toggle switch.

He also counted his amplifiers and special-effects hardware as his instruments. Playing at excessive volume, he would use distortion and feedback to sustain individual notes and chords. He generated sound effects through liberal use of the guitar's tremolo bar, creating dive-bomb rumbles and piercing screams. His wild showmanship was also part of his technique. He often destroyed his

guitars and amps, and played the guitar with his teeth, between his legs, and even behind his back or head.

Perhaps the most identifiable facet of Hendrix' technique is his liberal use of effects. He made the fuzz pedal an integral part of his tone, and in the studio used many custom boxes that emphasized different frequencies. His wah-wah technique, as heard on later records and live performances, often imitated vocals with uncanny precision.

Although Hendrix is known for his aggressive whammy-bar technique, he also frequently employed a soft touch, wavering chords lightly and coaxing individual notes into feedback. He was a master at controlling feedback, and could often play entire melodic passages with fedback notes alone. He used many slide-type effects on both studio and live recordings, but he did not use a traditional slide, preferring instead to use one of the rings on his fingers or a microphone stand to achieve the effect.

Although Eddie Van Halen is often credited with pioneering the use of two-handed tapping, Hendrix also used this technique frequently – sometimes as subtle percussive effect to embellish chords, and at other times to trill individual notes.

The Hardware
Guitars, Strings, and Picks

For Jimi's 12th birthday, his father traded an old saxophone in exchange for Jimi's first guitar, an inexpensive used acoustic. Later, his dad bought him an inexpensive electric. Jimi's first serious guitar was an Epiphone electric that he received when he was 15. Photos of Hendrix taken in 1964, when he was a member of Curtis Knight and The Squires, show him playing a Fender Duo Sonic.

However, no guitar is more closely associated with Jimi than the Fender Stratocaster – indeed, the Strat's longevity and continued success has been largely attributed to him. Although a southpaw, he played a right-handed model, putting the strings on in reverse order, turning the nut around, and wearing the guitar "upside down" so the controls and tremolo bar were on the guitar's top half instead of the bottom. He preferred rosewood necks, but switched to maple-neck Strats towards the end of his career.

Influenced by the "head-cutting" antics of blues guitarists, Hendrix was a flamboyant performer, and often played guitar behind his head or back, between his legs, and even with his teeth or tongue.

Despite rumors to the contrary, Jimi rarely modified his Strats, though he often adjusted the tremolo so he could raise and lower pitch and bent the tremolo bar closer to the guitar's body so he could tap individual strings with it. Hardware aside, many of his guitars featured hand-painted designs, some reputedly painted by Jimi himself. He often saved parts from guitars he smashed in performance, and reassembled them into new guitars.

As Hendrix became more successful, he purchased many instruments. Although he rarely performed with anything other than a Strat, he occasionally played several other instruments live and in the studio, including Gibson Flying V and Les Paul electrics; Gibson Dove, Martin D-45, and Guild 12-string acoustics; and Hagstrom 8-string basses.

Jimi tuned his guitar down a half-step to

Although Jimi Hendrix' career lasted a brief three years, from the release of Are You Experienced? *in 1967 to his death in 1970 at the age of 28, he remains one of rock's most influential guitarists.*

E♭ and preferred Fender Rock 'n' Roll light gauge strings (.010, .013, .015, .026, .032, .038). Buddy Miles, who owns several of Jimi's guitars, has allegedly said that Jimi used heavy strings on the bottom *E*, medium gauge strings on the *A* and *D*, a Hawaiian *G* string, a light *B*, and a super-light high *E*. Hendrix used medium-gauge picks that he bought from Manny's Music in New York City.

Amplifiers, Effects, and Devices

Before Jimi went to England, he used tiny combo amps for his club gigs. As he started playing larger venues, however, his requirements changed, so he switched to Marshall amplifiers. In live performance, he would use up to three stacks, consisting of three 100 or 200-watt "plexi" heads with six Marshall 4x12 speaker cabinets equipped with Rola Celestion speakers. Because Hendrix often destroyed his equipment as part of his show, he carried boxes of replacement speakers and between 12 to 18 amp heads with him on the road. Some of his 100-watt heads were modified by Long Island technician Tony Frank to provide 137 watts of output.

After the Monterey Pop Festival, Jimi regularly began using Sunn equipment to fulfil a five-year endorsement contract with Sunn. He used five Coliseum P.A. amps with 10 Sunn 100-F cabinets equipped with two JBL D-130 F speakers. Dissatisfied with the sound, though, his association with Sunn lasted only 14 months. He then tried Orange amps for a few live gigs, while occasionally using a Fender Twin Reverb in the studio.

Hendrix pioneered the concept of chaining several effects pedals together and using them all at the same time. He was partial to the Dallas-Arbiter Fuzz Face (a distortion unit), Univox Uni-Vibe (an electronic tremolo/vibrato device), and Vox wah-wah pedals. But he abused his pedals as much as he abused his guitars and amps, and often

In His Own Words

Our music is like that jar of candy over there. Everything's all mixed up.
Vancouver Free Press, *April 1968*

I feel guilty when people say that I'm the greatest guitarist on the scene. What's good or bad doesn't matter to me; what does matter is feeling and not feeling.
Hit Parader, *January 1969*

I'd like to get something together, like with Handel, and Bach, and Muddy Waters, flamenco type of thing. If I could get that sound, I'd be happy.
Guitar Player, *September 1975*

Most of my writing was a clash between fantasy and reality. I felt you had to use fantasy to illuminate some aspects of reality. Even the Bible does that. You have to give people something to dream on.
Record Mirror, *October 1970*

What They Say

A lot of what made Jimi distinctive was his touch and his confidence. And his touch was not just felt in his playing, but in his perspective on everything. He seemed to be reaching for more.
Stevie Ray Vaughan, Guitar Player, *May 1980*

I'm still really sad about his not being here, because I need somebody around that I can believe in. I don't believe in anybody else.
Jeff Beck, Guitar Player, *October 1980*

Hendrix was an amazing innovator as a guitarist. He stood out there like a black rock warrior. He was the ultimate role model.
Nile Rodgers, Guitar Player, *December 1993*

Jimi's music transcends time and space. I don't think it will ever go out of fashion.
Hendrix' producer/engineer Eddie Kramer,
Guitar Player, *December 1993*

smashed them by placing his full weight on the box. Although he survived his first tour with only three Fuzz Faces, he later toured with two-dozen fuzz boxes, a dozen Uni-Vibes, and two dozen wah-wah pedals.

Some of Hendrix' effects were custom-built for him by Roger Mayer, notably the Octavia – a frequency doubler pedal that generates a duplicate signal one octave higher than the original. It can be heard on Hendrix' solo on "The Wind Cries Mary." He also played a Maestro Fuzz-Tone, Leslie rotating speakers, and a talk-box unit called The Bag. Despite rumors, he apparently never used Electro-Harmonix effects or an Echoplex.

Typical Licks

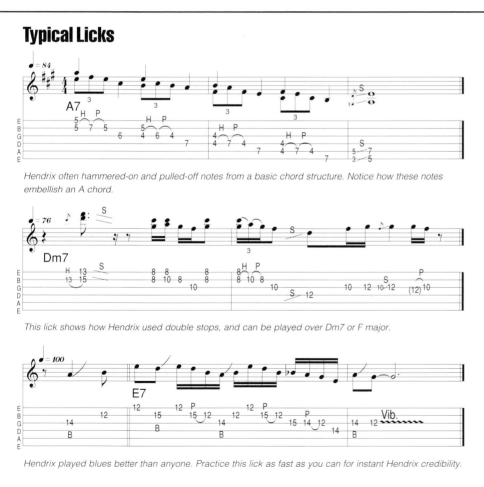

Hendrix often hammered-on and pulled-off notes from a basic chord structure. Notice how these notes embellish an A chord.

This lick shows how Hendrix used double stops, and can be played over Dm7 or F major.

Hendrix played blues better than anyone. Practice this lick as fast as you can for instant Hendrix credibility.

Discography

*Although hundreds of bootlegs and posthumous collections of Hendrix material exist, most of these are either repackaged compilations of material culled from various pre-existing sources or dubious forgeries which may not be Hendrix at all. The live-performance bootlegs range in quality from very good to awful, and most are of little interest to anyone but the most ardent Hendrix fan. Surprisingly, only five albums were officially released during Hendrix' lifetime. These are: **Are you Experienced?** (1967), **Axis: Bold As Love** (1968), **Electric Ladyland** (1968), **Smash Hits** (1969), and **Band Of Gypsies** (1970). The first three were recently remastered and repackaged for CD by Hendrix' latter-day producer, Alan Douglas.*

*Authorized posthumous releases include **Rainbow Bridge** (1971), **The Cry Of Love** (1971), **Hendrix In The West** (1972), **War Heroes** (1972), **Soundtrack From The Film Jimi Hendrix** (1973), **Crash Landing** (1975), **Midnight Lightning** (1975), **The Essential Jimi Hendrix** (1978), **The Essential Jimi Hendrix Volume Two** (1979), **Nine To The Universe** (1980), **Kiss The Sky** (1984), **Johnny B Goode** (1985), **Jimi Hendrix Plays Monterey** (1986), **Live At Winterland** (1987), **Radio One** (1988), **Stages** (1991), **The Ultimate Experience** (1993), **Woodstock** (1994), and **Jimi Hendrix: Blues** (1994).*

*Recordings of several important live performances by Hendrix are available on the following various artist compilations – **Woodstock** (1970), **Woodstock Two** (1971), **The First Great Rock Festivals Of The Seventies – The Isle of Wight/Atlanta** (1971), and **Rainbow Bridge** (1971).*

Recording Sessions

*The earliest known Hendrix recording is "My Diary," a single by Rosa Lee Brooks, produced by Arthur Lee in Los Angeles in the early '60s. Hendrix also participated in recording sessions with Little Richard, the Isley Brothers, and Curtis Knight between 1963 and 1965. Late in his career, he appeared on Stephen Stills' **Stephen Stills** (1970) and performed with Love on one track of **False Start** (1970).*

Steve Howe

Considered one of the world's best all-around guitarists, Steve Howe is a versatile player who combines rock, jazz, classical, and country styles. As a member of Yes, he helped develop the progressive rock movement in the early '70s, greatly expanding the boundaries of rock music. Yes' songs, many of which exceeded ten minutes, became showcases for Howe's advanced improvisational skills. Today, Howe continues to expand musical horizons as a solo artist.

The Player

Influences

When Steve was growing up, he enjoyed listening to his parents' records, such as Mantovani, Lawrence Welk, and Les Paul and Mary Ford. The first record he bought was by Bill Haley, which inspired him to learn to play guitar. "I got this strong urge to play the guitar during rock 'n' roll's early days," he recounts. "I was propelled to move to this music. I used to leap around, much to the horror of my parents, occasionally breaking bits of furniture. It brought out a wilder side of myself that I didn't know."

Howe got his first guitar when he was 12, and taught himself to play songs by various early rock 'n' roll guitarists, such as Chuck Berry, Link Wray, Mick Green with Johnny Kidd and the Pirates, James Burton with Ricky Nelson, and Carl Perkins. Santo and Johnny's steel-guitar instrumental "Sleepwalk" inspired him to learn how to play steel guitar later in his career. The Shadows' instrumental "Apache" was one of Howe's favorite songs. He also enjoyed playing blues. "A lot of the music I listened to ranged from Lightnin' Hopkins, Big Bill Broonzy, Muddy Waters,

and early Buddy Guy," he remarks. "I was a bit of a blues player, but I wasn't playing in a blues setting. I don't think of anything I've recorded in the last 25 years as blues."

Country and pop guitarists also had a profound effect. Chet Atkins was a tremendous influence, particularly his *Teensville* album. Howe also enjoyed the playing of Jimmy Bryant, both his duets with pedal-steel guitarist Speedy West, and his recordings with Tennessee Ernie Ford. Howe's other early favorites included Les Paul and Les Spann.

Steve's older brother exposed him to jazz music, and Barney Kessel soon became a favorite. He also enjoyed the playing styles of Kenny Burrell, Django Reinhardt, Tal Farlow, and Charlie Christian, and later he developed a taste for Wes Montgomery's playing. By the time he was 18, Howe had also become interested in classical music, particularly Vivaldi. His favorite classical guitarists include Julian Bream and Carlos Montoya. Steve's more recent influences include Brazilian guitarist Leo Browser, classical guitarist Carlos Barnell, and Celtic guitarist Martin Simpson.

Although most of his guitar influences were excellent technical players, Howe prefers feel and tone over technique. "I relate more to George Harrison than to George

Background

1947 *Steve Howe is born on April 8, in Holloway, North London.*

1959 *He receives his first guitar, an f-hole acoustic, for Christmas.*

1964 *Howe makes his recording debut on the Syndicats single "Maybellene"/"True To Me."*

1966 *He starts playing with the In Crowd.*

1968 *Streve forms Tomorrow with Keith West and scores a hit with "My White Bicycle." He then quits the band and forms Bodast.*

1969 *Steve tours as P.P. Arnold's guitarist, supporting Delaney and Bonnie, who have Eric Clapton on guitar.*

1970 *Howe becomes a member of Yes, joining Jon Anderson, Chris Squire, Bill Bruford, and Tony Kaye.*

1971 *Yes releases* Fragile.

1975 *Howe releases his first solo album,* Beginnings.

1977 *Voted "Best Overall Guitarist" in* Guitar Player's *readers' poll.*

1980 *Yes break up.*

1981 *Howe forms Asia with John Wetton, Geoff Downes, and Carl Palmer. Five consecutive wins in the* Guitar Player *"Best Overall Guitarist" poll make him eligible for inclusion in the magazine's "Gallery of the Greats," at that time an honour shared among only 15 of the world's guitarists.*

1983 *After his fifth consecutive win as "Best Overall Guitarist" in the* Guitar Player *readers' poll, Howe enters the magazine's "Gallery Of The Greats."*

1984 *Howe quits Asia and forms GTR with Steve Hackett, Max Bacon, Phil Spalding, and Jonathan Mover.*

1988 *Anderson, Bruford, Wakeman, and Howe is formed.*

1991 *Anderson, Bruford, Wakeman, and Howe team up with Trevor Rabin, Chris Squire, Tony Kaye, and Alan White, forming a new lineup of Yes. The band releases the album* Union *and goes on tour.*

1992 *Produces an album for British virtuoso jazz guitarist Martin Taylor, and releases his own album,* Turbulence.

Benson," he comments. He has avoided taking any lessons, feeling it is more important for a player to discover his own style by letting his personality emerge through experimentation on the instrument. "I don't read music," he remarks. "I have no education in how to play the guitar other than my own interest."

Approach and Style

Although Howe has no musical training and cannot read music, he has a sophisticated harmonic, rhythmic, and melodic sense. His style is a conglomeration of his diverse influences, and traces of rock, country, jazz, and classical can be heard in the lines he plays.

Howe generally prefers to play barre G and C chord forms, as opposed to the barre E and A forms favored by most rock guitarists. He has also developed many distinctive chord voicings. Like many jazz guitarists, he often uses a chord-soloing approach, sometimes interspersed with single-note lines.

When soloing, Howe tends to avoid the root note, and concentrates on the relative minor or relative minor seventh. His solos are often based on Mixolydian scales, and he likes to play diatonic patterns up and down the guitar's neck. One of his signature licks is a sequenced pattern that cycles through several octaves, producing a call-and-response effect.

Techniques

Because he plays several different styles, Howe uses several techniques on the guitar. He holds his pick with his right-hand thumb and forefinger, and uses the three free fingers to fingerpick the strings. Though he usually flatpicks his chords and lines, he sometimes plays Travis- or Atkins-style, playing an alternating bass pattern with the pick while plucking a melody on the treble strings with his fingertips. An example of this technique can be heard on "The Valley Of Rocks" (*The Grand Scheme Of Things*) and "Clap" (*The Yes Album*).

His right-hand picking technique often makes use of tremolo- and cross-picking. He moves his right hand to various locations along the string for tonal variation. His left-hand technique makes liberal use of pull-offs to open strings and staccato and legato phrasing.

Many of Howe's solos incorporate single-string lines that he plays up and down the neck. He prefers this approach over conventional box patterns across several strings, because he feels that the tone is more consistent. One of his signature licks is an ascending chord scale played in conjunction with several open drone notes, producing a resonant effect similar to 12-string guitar. He also likes the tonal variation produced by using finger slides, slurs, and hammer-on trills, as opposed to picking every note.

The Hardware
Guitars, Strings, and Picks

Howe's first guitar was an f-hole acoustic that his parents gave him as a Christmas present when he was 12. Later, he decided that he really wanted an electric guitar, so he bought a Japanese Guyatone LG50 electric from a friend. This is the guitar that Howe played in the Syndicats. His next guitar was a Burns Jazz electric.

In 1964, Howe bought a brand-new Gibson ES-175D from Selmer music in London. It has remained his main instrument, and has been used on almost every record he has made. "When I went to America for the first time with Yes in 1971, I was still in awe of my 175," he said in *The Steve Howe Collection*. "I carried it as if I was carrying the crown jewels. I'm exactly the same with it now." The guitar is almost stock, except for the volume, tone, and pickup selector knobs and tuning pegs. He also turned the humbucking bridge pickup around to change the tone.

Since then, he has amassed a collection of over 100 guitars, most of which he uses in the studio or on records. It includes several electric archtops (a Gibson Super 400, a Gibson ES-5 Switchmaster, Gretsch 6120, and a Heritage Sweet 16), semi-hollow electrics (a '71 Gibson ES-345TD, '80s Gibson ES Artists, and a Rickenbacker 360), and solidbodies. Howe has owned several Gibson Les Pauls, including a Custom with four pickups, a fancy The Les Paul model, and a couple of Les Paul Juniors. Other favorite solidbodies include a '55 Fender Tele with a humbucking pickup in the neck position, a Fender Broadcaster, and a '67 Fender Stratocaster. The Steinberger GM4T model is one of his current favorite solidbody guitars.

He also owns many double-neck and 12-string electrics, including a Gibson EDS1275 with 6- and 12-string necks, a Danelectro 12-string, a Steinberger 12-string, and a Rickenbacker 12-string. He has often played a Coral electric sitar on record and onstage.

A highly versatile player whose style combines rock, country, classical, and jazz influences, Steve Howe helped define the progressive rock genre in the early '70s as a member of the group Yes.

He started playing an electric lap steel in the early '70s, and it soon became an integral part of his sound. His favorite is a Fender Dual 6 double-neck steel with one neck tuned to *Fm* (*E, B, E, A♭, B, E*), and the other to standard tuning. He also owns a Sho-Bud pedal steel and several Gibson and Fender lap steels.

Acoustic guitars are another important part of Howe's collection. For many years his main steel-string acoustic guitar was a '53 Martin 00-18, which he used to record "Clap," his favorite composition. More recently he favors a custom-made Scharpach SKD acoustic, which is built in Holland. Ever since he borrowed Chris Squire's Guild 12-string to record "And You And I," Howe has been fond of 12-string acoustics. His favorite is a Martin J12-65M, and he also owns a Guild F212CR-NT. Other oft-used acoustic steel strings in

Howe, who had no formal music training, and cannot read music, is nevertheless considered by many to be one of the most outstanding all-round guitar players of his generation.

his collection include a Martin OM-45, and a Gibson Country Western. He also has Gibson L-4C and Gibson L-5 acoustic archtops.

Because of his interest in classical guitar, Howe has acquired a few nylon-string instruments. His main classical guitar is a '73 Kohno No. 10. He also plays a '76 Jose Ramirez 1A flamenco master guitar and an electric Chet Atkins CE, which he uses onstage.

During the '70s, Howe played guitar with a thick plexiglas pick. Nowadays he prefers a conventional heavy-gauge pick. He uses Martin light-gauge strings on his acoustic guitars and Gibson medium-gauge strings on his electrics. The gauges that he uses on his ES-175 are .012, .012, .015, .028, .044, .056.

Amplifiers, Effects, and Devices

Steve's first amp was a small Guyatone model that came with his guitar. Later he switched to a Watkins Dominator, then to a Fender Tremolux, which he used in the Syndicats. He acquired a Vox AC50 in 1966 and started using a solid-state Vox AC100 when he joined Tomorrow, though it caused problems as it was constantly breaking down.

Steve then purchased several Fender Dual Showman amplifier heads and Dual Showman cabinets. He started using a Fender Super Reverb after Yes recorded *Fragile*. By 1978, he was playing through three Fender Twin Reverb tops and six Twin cabinets. He currently uses a combination of Fender Twin Reverbs and Marshall amps onstage.

He often uses the same amps in the studio. He owns several Gibson amps, including a '30s EH-150, and a '70s solid-state Lab Series for recording. He sometimes plays through a Leslie rotating speaker cabinet.

He has always used a wide variety of effects. "I got all the effects virtually the day they came out," he noted in *The Steve Howe Collection*. Some of his favorite effects in the early days of Yes included an Echoplex,

In His Own Words

I never liked the "in-vogue" guitar playing. I've always been a slightly traditional guitarist. Classical and jazz influences me a lot, but my music didn't come out the same, I'm glad to say.
Guitar Player, *April 1973*

I'd be half the guitarist I am if I always went with the same sound. For me, the electric guitar is not so much the notes you play, but what happens when you play. I like the part, I like the melody, but mainly there has to be some texture to the sound, otherwise whatever you play will sound insignificant.
Guitar Player, *October 1993*

A lot of what I do is sheer bluffing. An incredible amount of it is having the gall to do something, even if you don't know what you're going to do. That is creativity.
Excerpt from a previously unpublished interview

What is the Steve Howe sound? It could be the ES-175, but I also play a lot of 12-string acoustic. It's mainly getting a noise out of something that's different.
Excerpt from a previously unpublished interview

What They Say

I remember Steve Howe used to play harmonics when he was with Yes. I was interested by that sound because it was very delicate.
The Edge, Guitar Player, *June 1985*

Stepping into the shoes once filled by Steve Howe can be no easy job. I loved Steve Howe's playing.
Vinny Burns of Asia, The Guitar Magazine, *March 1993*

It was great to hear a guy playing really clean guitar, 'cause when I started playing it was always on the acoustic, so it was refreshing to hear someone avoiding the normal sound around that time, the distorted Les Paul sound.
Steve Stevens, The Guitar Magazine, *June 1993*

Marshall and Maestro fuzz tones, a Cry Baby wah-wah, a Fender volume pedal, and a ring modulator. He also liked to use his amp's reverb and tremolo. More recently, he prefers to use Electro-Harmonix Big Muff distortion pedal, a Roland SDE-3000 digital delay, a Roland SRV-2000 digital reverb, an Eventide Harmonizer, a Yamaha SPX-90 multi-effects unit, and a hand-held E-Bow sustain device.

Howe has experimented with several different guitar synthesizer systems. In 1975 he used Walter Sear's Synthesear. Later he acquired a Roland GR-300 and GR-700, his favorite guitar synthesizer systems. He has also played Stepp and Ibanez guitar synths.

Discography

Howe's recording debut was on "Maybellene"/"True To Me," by the Syndicats, for whom he also appeared on "Howlin' For My Baby"/"What To Do" and "On The Horizon." In 1968, he appeared on Tomorrow's **Tomorrow**, featuring the psychedelic hit "My White Bicycle." Shortly after that he joined Bodast, recording an album with them that, after he had remixed it, was finally released in 1988 as **The Early Years – Steve Howe With Bodast**.

His best work appears on the albums he made with Yes: **The Yes Album**, **Fragile**, **Close To The Edge**, **Yessongs** (live), **Tales From Topographic Oceans**, **Relayer**, **Yesterdays** (a compilation), **Going For The One**, **Tormato**, **Drama**, **Yesshows** (live), **Classic Yes** (a compilation), and **Union**. The 4-CD box set **Yes Years** and the condensed 2-CD package **YesStory** provide a good overview of Howe's playing with Yes.

In the '80s, Howe made the following records with the following groups: With Asia – **Asia**, **Alpha**, **Aqua** (1992); With GTR – **GTR**; With Anderson, Bruford, Wakeman, Howe – **Anderson, Bruford, Wakeman, Howe**.

Steve's solo albums all contain fine examples of his playing. They are: **Beginnings**, **The Steve Howe Album**, **Turbulence**, and **The Grand Scheme Of Things**. He also contributed the track "Sharp On Attack" for the **Guitar Speak** compilation and live performances of "Clap" and "Würm" on **Night Of The Guitar**.

Recording Sessions

In 1967, Howe guested on Keith West's "Excerpt From A Teenage Opera (Grocer Jack)." He also recorded the singles "Sam"/"Thimble Full Of Puzzles" and "On A Saturday"/ "The Kid Was A Killer" with West. In the '70s, he played on Lou Reed's **Lou Reed**, Rick Wakeman's **Six Wives of Henry VIII**, and Alan White's **Ramshackled**. During the '80s he appeared on the Dixie Dregs' **Industry Standard**, Frankie Goes To Hollywood's **Welcome To The Pleasure Dome** and **Liverpool**, Propaganda's **Secret Wish**, Billie Currie's **Transportation**, Paul Sultin's **Seraphim**, Andy Leek's **Say Something**, and Animal Logic's **Animal Logic**. His studio sessions in the '90s include Queen's **Innuendo** and the Bee Gees **Size Isn't Everything**.

Typical Licks

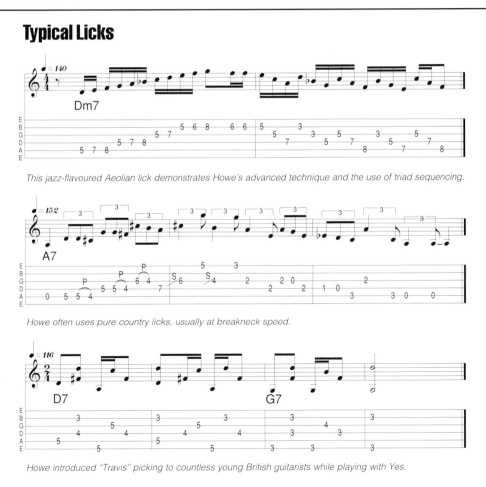

This jazz-flavoured Aeolian lick demonstrates Howe's advanced technique and the use of triad sequencing.

Howe often uses pure country licks, usually at breakneck speed.

Howe introduced "Travis" picking to countless young British guitarists while playing with Yes.

Lonnie Johnson

Lonnie Johnson, one of the best prewar blues guitarists, influenced countless others, including Robert Johnson, T-Bone Walker, B.B. King, Muddy Waters, and John Lee Hooker. He was a diverse player who recorded hundreds of blues, jazz, ballads, and pop songs. With a career that lasted more than 70 years, Johnson had the longest active career of any blues guitarist. His playing in the '20s and '30s paved the way for modern blues and rock guitar styles that did not emerge until nearly 30 years after his recording debut.

The Player

Influences

Because Johnson was rarely interviewed, very little is known about his background and influences. He started learning to play guitar and violin at a very early age, most likely influenced by other musicians in his family. Later he also learned to play mandolin, banjo, kazoo, string bass, and piano. His brother, James "Steady Roll" Johnson, was also a multi-instrumentalist, and the two later worked together as a duet, with Lonnie on guitar and James on piano.

Growing up in New Orleans, Lonnie was exposed to a wide variety of music. He listened to the music of chanters and minstrels, hornpiping sailors, symphonic musicians, brass bands, string bands, barrelhouse and ragtime piano players, pan-Carribbean carnival players, as well as an assortment of singers. By 1910, at the age of 16, he was playing professionally in sporting houses around Storyville, Louisiana.

Approach and Style

Lonnie Johnson was a highly advanced player whose style underwent many changes during his 70-year career. Many of the songs he recorded in the '20s and '30s were complex, innovative compositions performed almost exclusively in the key of *D*. During the '40s, he simplified his style and began playing primarily single-note lines.

Johnson possessed a vast chord vocabulary, and his performances often featured elegant climbing-chord progressions, and distinctive chord voicings. Many of his straightforward blues songs featured diminished-seventh bridges and turnarounds. On his early recordings, he often tuned to dropped-*D* (*D, A, D, G, B, E*, low to high), or dropped the low *E* and *A* or low *E* and *D* strings down a whole step (*D, G, D, G, B, E*, or *D, A, C, G, B, E*, low to high, respectively).

On his early recordings, Johnson simultaneously played a bass line on the lower strings and a melody on the upper strings. Several of his solos and song intros consist of double-stop patterns played on the treble strings. It is not certain whether Johnson played with his fingers or a flatpick on these recordings. Later in his career, he used a flatpick exclusively.

Johnson rarely used set picking patterns, preferring to improvise as he played. His playing displayed excellent phrasing and

Background

1894 *Alonzo Johnson is born on February 8, in New Orleans, Louisiana.*

1902 *Lonnie leaves school to pursue a career as a musician.*

1910 *He frequently plays solo in the New Orleans' red-light district, Storyville.*

1912 *Performs as a violinist in various bands with his brother and father.*

1917 *Johnson acquires his first good guitar and tours the United States and Europe.*

1925 *He lands a long-term recording deal with OKeh Records after winning a blues contest at the Booker Washington Theater in St Louis.*

1927 *Lonnie starts concentrating on guitar after he and his brother, pianist James "Steady Roll" Johnson, part ways.*

1928 *Lonnie pairs with guitarist Eddie Lang and starts recording duets.*

1929 *He tours with Bessie Smith.*

1930 *Johnson gets his own radio show in New York City.*

1939 *Lonnie makes his first recording using an electric guitar for Bluebird sessions. He uses the guitar on only one session.*

1941 *The Lonnie Johnson Trio cuts several live acetates during a gig at Chicago's Boulevard Lounge.*

1947 *Johnson starts using an electric guitar again on Aladdin label recordings.*

1947 *The King label releases "Tomorrow Night," one of Johnson's biggest hits.*

1952 *Johnson's concert tour of England is his last important musical venture of the '50s.*

1960 *He is discovered by jazz DJ Chris Albertson, who convinces him to start recording again.*

1965 *Johnson settles in Toronto and opens the Home Of The Blues Club.*

1970 *Lonnie Johnson dies in Toronto, Canada, on June 16.*

tonality, and he had excellent volume balance between the bass and treble strings.

Techniques

Johnson was as adept at playing with his fingers as he was at playing with a flatpick. Historians are not sure whether he played with his right-hand thumb and index finger, or with his thumb and index and middle fingers on his early recordings. Stefan Grossman, who has carefully studied Johnson's recordings, feels that he probably played primarily with his right-hand thumb and index finger, using the middle finger only occasionally.

Johnson had a well-developed finger vibrato that could approximate the sounds of a zither, mandolin, or bottleneck guitar. When playing solos, he often used a mandolin-like tremolo picking approach. Johnson's pull-offs, triplet patterns, and bent notes were highly influential on jazz, blues, and rock guitarists.

The Hardware

Guitars, Strings, and Picks

Details about Johnson's guitars are very uncertain. A handful of existing photographs provide the only remaining information about what type of guitars he played.

Johnson acquired what he considered his first good guitar in 1917. During the '20s, he primarily played a 12-string guitar, most likely the Grunewald that appears in an early promotional photo. Although no one is certain, many blues historians speculate that Johnson often modified his 12-strings into 9- or 10-string guitars by removing octave strings from the lower courses. His recordings where doubled strings can be heard on the treble notes but not on the bass notes are evidence that this theory may be true.

During the late '30s, Johnson was often photographed performing with a Gibson J-100 acoustic guitar, as well as a large f-hole archtop guitar and a small Martin steel-string acoustic with a 12-fret neck. Sometime during the '40s, he attached a pickup to his J-100, thereby converting it into an electric guitar.

During the '60s, Johnson often performed with a Kay solidbody electric guitar, similar to the one played by Jimmy Reed.

Information about what type of picks or strings Johnson used is unknown.

Amplifiers, Effects, and Devices

Information about Johnson's amplifiers is even harder to come by than information on his guitars. The only amp that can be definitely confirmed as being used by Johnson is a late '30s Supro.

Johnson never used any effects during his career.

Johnson's playing style ranged from complex fingerpicked country blues to straightforward single-note lines. He influenced several eras of blue guitarists, including Robert Johnson, John Lee Hooker, and B.B. King.

Discography

Johnson made his recording debut in 1925 as a session musician and artist on the OKeh label. His first recording, "Won't Do Blues," with Charles Creath's Jazz-O-Maniacs, featured his singing and violin playing. Two days later he recorded "Mr. Johnson's Blues" on guitar under his own name. By the late '20s, OKeh was issuing new Lonnie Johnson records approximately every six weeks.

Some of Johnson's more important early OKeh recordings as a featured artist include: "Falling Rain Blues," a pre-blues parlor duet with his brother called "Nile Of Genago," "Levee Camp Moan Blues," "Section Gang Blues," "Bitin' Flea Blues," "Life Saver Blues," "Blue Ghost Blues," and "St. Louis Cyclone Blues."

Johnson's duets with Eddie Lang in the late '20s feature fine examples of his guitar playing, and he considered these recordings as his greatest musical experience. The two first worked together on "Work Ox Blues," on which they backed Texas Alexander. Some of Lang and Johnson's finest performances include: "Two Tone Stomp," "Have To Change Keys To Play These Blues," "Guitar Blues," "Bull Frog Moan," "A Handful Of Riffs," "Deep Minor Rhythm Stomp," and "Hot Fingers."

In the late '30s, Johnson signed a deal with Decca Records. His Decca debut, "Man Killing Broad," was performed on a 12-string acoustic guitar. Johnson's first session in 1939 for the Bluebird label is notable because it was his first recording with an electric guitar. These are the only electric-guitar performances Johnson recorded until he was signed to the Aladdin label in 1947. In 1948, he recorded one of his biggest hits ever, "Tomorrow Night," for the King label. In the '60s, Johnson released several albums for the Prestige label.

Many of Johnson's recordings have been reissued on CD compilations. The following offer a good overview of various periods of his career: **Lonnie Johnson Complete Recorded Works In Chronological Order** (Document), a seven-CD set of '25 to '32 recordings, **Lonnie Johnson Complete 1937 To June 1947 Recordings In Chronological Order** (RST), **He's A Jelly Roll Baker** (RCA), '39 to '44 recordings, **The Originator Of Modern Blues** (Blues Boy), '41 to '52 recordings, **Me And My Crazy Self** (Charly), '47 to '52 recordings. The following Prestige albums from the '60s have also been reissued on CD: **Losing Game, Blues By Lonnie Johnson, Another Night To Cry, Blues & Ballads, and Idle Hours**.

Jazz Guitar Virtuoso features several fine recordings that Johnson made with Eddie Lang.

Performing almost continuously for more than seven decades, Lonnie Johnson made hundreds of recordings that explored several styles of music, including blues, jazz, ballads, and pop.

In His Own Words

I've been dead four or five times, but I always came back. This time, I knew that some day, somehow, somebody would find me.
On his rediscovery in 1960

I sing city blues. My blues is built on human beings on land – see how they live, see their heartaches, and the shifts they go through with love affairs and things like that. That's what I write about, and that's the way I make my living.
Jazz Monthly, *1963*

You know how the blues will be. You think of some words, and that is how the melody must go. Then you play it a while one way or another to see how you and other people like it. If they ask for it again or if somebody wants to record it, then you've got a blues. I recorded 125 songs against the same chords.
Guitar Player, *November 1981*

What They Say

He was the top. I remember one record of his was strictly jazz, and boy, he was so fast – whoo! With a straight pick. See, he use a straight pick like another man uses three fingers. I've seen guitar players use three fingers wasn't as fast as him.
Johnny Shines, *Guitar Player,* April 1989

Lonnie Johnson has never been recognized as one of the transcendental people who influenced everybody. You can recognize Lonnie Johnson in just about anybody with his voice and elegant style. You can see people copying him right and left. Oh, it's amazing.
Ry Cooder to Jas Obrecht, *1989*

He was a genius. Nobody sound like Lonnie Johnson. You could tell it was Johnson every time he pick up a guitar. Black and white, wherever you are – they loved Lonnie Johnson.
John Lee Hooker to Jas Obrecht, *1992*

Recording Sessions

Johnson had a prolific career as a session musician, starting in 1925 when he was signed to OKeh Records. With his brother, James "Steady Roll" Johnson, he backed singers Cora Perkins, George Hannah, Luella Miller ("Dago Hill Blues"/"Pretty Man Blues"), and Victoria Spivey. In early '27, he teamed with pianist John Erby and backed up Victoria Spivey again ("Blood Thirsty Blues," "Nightmare Blues," and "Dope Head Blues"), Helen Humes, Raymond Boyd, Joe Brown, Irene Scruggs, and Bessie Mae Smith. Later, OKeh sent Johnson to New York to record with Alger "Texas" Alexander ("Levee Camp Moan Blues" and "Section Gang Blues").

In late '27, Johnson joined Louis Armstrong's Hot Five and started recording jazz, including "I'm Not Rough," "Hotter Than That," "Savoy Blues," "I Can't Give You Anything But Love," and "Mahogany Hall Stomp."

In late '28, Johnson joined Duke Ellington's band. He appears on "The Mooche," "Move Over" – credited to Lonnie Johnson's Harlem Footwarmers – and "Hot And Bothered." A few weeks later, Johnson started recording with Victoria Spivey once again, performing on "New Black Snake Blues" and "Toothache Blues." That same week he recorded "Paducah" and "Stardust" with the Chocolate Dandies. Near the end of the year he appeared on another Ellington recording, "Misty Mornin'."

Johnson was only marginally active as a session player during the '30s. In '30 he teamed up with Clara Smith on "You're Getting Old On Your Job"/"What Makes You Act Like That." He also recorded several sides with comedienne Martha Raye. In '37, after a five-year break from recording, he backed up Alice Moore on several recordings on the Decca label, for whom he also recorded with pianist Peetie Wheatstraw and singers Ollie Shepard, Georgia White, and Merline Johnson. In '38 he recorded duets with pianist Roosevelt Sykes, and played on sessions for Red Mike Bailey, Jimmie Gordon, and Johnny Temple.

Johnson signed a deal with Bluebird Records in '39, and appeared on Jimmie Noone And His Orchestra's "New Orleans Hop Scop Blues" and "Keystone Blues," and Johnny Dodd's "Red Onion Blues" and "Gravier Street Blues." One of his last important sessions was with Bob Shoffner And His Harlem Hot Shots on the Mercury 78 "Trouble In Mind"/"Mitzy," recorded near the end of World War II.

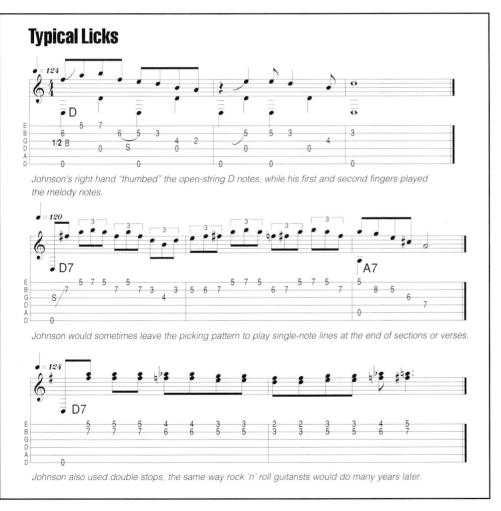

Typical Licks

Johnson's right hand "thumbed" the open-string D notes, while his first and second fingers played the melody notes.

Johnson would sometimes leave the picking pattern to play single-note lines at the end of sections or verses.

Johnson also used double stops, the same way rock 'n' roll guitarists would do many years later.

Albert King

One of the most influential electric blues guitarists, Albert King was highly respected and imitated by many of the world's finest guitarists, including Eric Clapton, Stevie Ray Vaughan, Michael Bloomfield, and Jimi Hendrix. King's music incorporated several different styles, such as rock, R&B, and soul, endearing him to white listeners as well as black audiences. Although he often joked about retiring, King pursued an active playing career up until his death in 1992 at the age of 69.

The Player

Influences

Albert was first exposed to music at an early age by his step-father, Will Nelson, who himself played guitar. Although the young boy showed interest in playing, Albert was not allowed to touch the guitar. A few years later, however, when he was six years old, he started teaching himself to play on a crude guitar that was nothing more than a piece of wire connected to a brick and a wall.

King first heard blues music when he saw a performance by Blind Lemon Jefferson in a park in Forest City, Arkansas, his home town. He also would sneak into clubs to see shows by pianist Memphis Minnie. Later, he started listening to records by blues artists, such as Lightnin' Hopkins, Lonnie Johnson, Elmore James, Howlin' Wolf, and Sonny Boy Williamson. His tastes were diverse, and he appreciated Little Walter's Chicago blues, Son House's Delta blues, and the music of Kansas City blues man Big Joe Turner.

"Stormy Monday" by T-Bone Walker was one of King's biggest influences. He attempted to imitate Walker, but he had so much difficulty that he developed his own style out of frustration. "I couldn't do all those licks and things he was making," he told Dan Forte in *Guitar Player*. "I said, 'I'm going to have to try to do something else with these strings.' So I developed that string squeezing sound."

According to King, he practiced for five years on his own before he joined his first band. In Osceola, Arkansas, he often sat in with a group called Yancey's Band. Later King formed his own three-piece band called the In The Groove Boys and played guitar with them. The band played covers of various blues tunes by Mercy Dee, Howlin' Wolf, T-Bone Walker, and Sonny Boy Williamson. Frustrated with his guitar playing, King hired another guitarist and became the band's drummer before the band decided to continue without him. King left Arkansas and moved to South Bend, Indiana, where he began working with a gospel vocal group called the Harmony Kings.

King enjoyed singing spirituals, but he became frustrated with the other members' lack of professionalism, so he moved to Gary, Indiana, where he got a gig as a drummer with Jimmy Reed. He followed Reed to Chicago where he also played drums for Brook Benton and Jackie Wilson. King often remarked that his ability to play drums had

Background

1923 Albert Nelson is born in Indianola, Mississippi, on April 25.

1939 King begins working in roadhouses as a blues artist.

1941 Albert buys his Guild Acoustic for $1.25.

1953 He moves to Chicago and makes his first recording for the Parrot label.

1956 Changes record labels to St. Louis-based Bobbin Records.

1961 King's first hit, "Don't Throw Your Love On Me So Strong," reaches #14 on R&B charts.

1965 Gets his big break when he is signed to Stax records.

1966 All future releases feature Booker T. and the M.Gs as the session band, greatly improving the quality of King's recording output.

1968 Opening for John Mayall and Jimi Hendrix, King makes his first appearance at San Francisco's Fillmore West.

1969 Performing with the St. Louis Symphony, King becomes the first blues guitarist to record with a symphony orchestra.

1971 John Mayall produces recording sessions for Albert at Wolfman Jack's Studios with an L.A. session band featuring Blue Mitchell, Ernie Watts and Canned Heat bassist Larry Taylor. The record company fails to release the material.

1972 King appears in the Stax feature film Watt Stax '72, staged at the Los Angeles Memorial Coliseum.

1976 Albert headlines the Montreux Jazz Festival's blues show in Switzerland.

1978 Marks the start of a five-year recording exile.

1986 The John Mayall session tapes are rediscovered and released.

1990 King guests on Gary Moore's Still Got The Blues.

1991 Albert is presented with the Pioneer Award from the Rhythm And Blues Foundation.

1992 King dies of a heart attack in Memphis, Tennessee on December 21.

little effect on his guitar playing other than helping him to develop his sense of tempo.

In addition to the blues, King was also a big fan of jazz music, especially big band jazz. Some of King's jazz influences can be detected on his recordings for Bobbin records made during the '50s. Many of the songs that he recorded during this time feature big-band-style orchestration. Part of what gave King's music such a distinctive sound was his willingness to incorporate elements of several different styles in his music, such as R&B, rock 'n' roll, and soul.

King was a self-taught player who learned how to play by ear. When he started making records for Stax in Memphis in the mid '60s, he was taught the different keys by a trumpet player. In the '70s, King took music-theory classes to learn how to voice horn arrangements for his band.

Approach and Style

Albert King developed a distinctive style and vocabulary of signature licks that have been imitated by many guitarists, including Stevie Ray Vaughan, Eric Clapton, Billy Gibbons, and Jimi Hendrix.

King's approach has often been described as "singing." If fact, he would often sing along to himself while he was playing, imagining his licks as vocal lines. He rarely played chords, concentrating instead on single-note lines and lead figures. Many of his songs feature call-and-response interplay between his vocals and guitar playing, where King would follow a sung line with an approximation of that line on the guitar.

String bending was an integral part of King's playing style. He often incorporated semi-tone bends, wide-interval bends, and parallel double-stop bends.

King used pentatonic minor scales almost exclusively, although sometimes his playing veered into Mixolydian scales.

Nonetheless, his playing has a melodic character, resulting mainly from the economy of his style. He rarely played fast lines, preferring instead to emphasize tone and space.

Although King noted that his experience as a drummer had little effect on his guitar playing, he had a well-developed sense of rhythm, and his records often boasted a wide variety of different rhythms. One device that King used often was to have his band emphasize the "one" of the first three bars of the chorus to build a song's intensity. An example of this approach can be heard on "I Believe To My Soul" on his *Blues At Sunrise* album. He also deviated from standard I-IV-V and 8-, 12-, and 16-bar blues progressions. King was very conscientious about keeping his music fresh, so he often incorporated variety into his musical arrangements and playing.

Techniques

The most distinctive element of King's playing was his unorthodox left-handed technique. He kept his guitar strung in the ordinary right-handed manner, but he flipped the guitar over so the high strings were on the top and the low strings were on the bottom. He also used a non-standard, open tuning. According to guitarist Steve Cropper, who recorded with Albert on many of his early Stax sessions, King tuned his guitar to an *Em* chord with a *C* on the lowest string (*C, B, E, G, B, E*, low to high). Other sources, however, claim that his tuning was *E, E, B, E, G♯, C♯*, low to high.

With his left-handed, upside-down technique, King bent notes on the high strings by pulling down on them instead of pushing them up. This accounts for the aggressive sound of his string bends and vibrato, since the hand can exert greater force using the pulling-down method. One technique that King liked to use for solos was to bend a note before striking it, then release the bend after he hit the string. He also liked to bend several strings at once, creating a powerful, screaming sound. He often jokingly attributed

King played left-handed with his guitar "upside down." Because his treble strings are on the top of the neck, his string-bending technique incorporates pulling down on the high strings, accounting for much of his distinctive tone.

this technique to his laziness, claiming that his finger would catch hold of other strings while he was bending notes.

King preferred to play through both pickups on his guitar at once. He left the tone control on full treble and turned the volume for the bridge pickup all the way up, and adjusted the neck pickup volume as he saw fit. King played without a pick, using his bare fingers to pluck the strings and snap them against the fingerboard. He also made liberal use of sustain, and he experimented with feedback.

The Hardware
Guitars, Strings, and Picks

King's first guitars were a variety of primitive, home-made instruments. Indeed, when he started playing it was on a one-string "guitar" that was little more than a piece of wire attached to a wall and a brick. He used a bottle to change pitch on the wire, similar to playing a slide guitar. Later he constructed guitars out of cigar boxes, featuring a neck made from a sapling, and strings that were wires from a whisk broom.

His first real guitar was an old Guild acoustic that he bought for $1.25 from a boy who needed money to take his girlfriend to the movies. "He'd paid $2.00 for it," King told Dan Forte in a 1977 *Guitar Player* interview. "It was getting close to show time, and this girl was getting really upset to get in to see the movie. I offered him my $1.25 for it. She was getting ready to go in with another guy, and he couldn't stand that, so he came over and said, 'Give me the $1.25, man; you can have the guitar.'"

Several years later, King bought an Epiphone electric guitar and an amplifier for $125. He played this guitar throughout the early and mid-'50s until he bought himself a Gibson Flying V in 1958. With its symmetrical shape and uninhibited access to the neck, the Flying V was the ideal guitar for King's unorthodox playing style. This guitar shape remained his favorite for the remainder of his playing career. King named his guitar Lucy, after comedienne Lucille Ball.

In 1974, luthier Dan Erlewine made a custom Flying V for King, who retired his original Gibson shortly thereafter. This Flying V then became King's main instrument. In 1980, Radley Prokopow also made a custom Flying V for King, and ZZ Top guitarist Billy Gibbons gave King a custom-made Flying V for his 65th birthday.

King never used a pick. "I never could hold a pick in my hand," he told *Guitar Player*. "I started out playing with one, but I'd be really gettin' into it, and after a while the pick would sail across the house. I said: 'To hell with this.' So I just play with the meat of the thumb."

Standing 6-foot 4-inches tall and weighing 250 pounds, King had an ominous stage presence that was only outsized by his menacing tone. Here he is seen playing "Lucy," the custom Flying V made by Dan Erlewine.

In His Own Words

I knew I was going to have to create my own style because I couldn't make the changes and the chords the same as a right-handed man could. I always concentrated on my singing guitar sound.
Guitar Player, *September 1977*

When T-Bone Walker came, I couldn't do all those licks and things he was making, so I developed that string-squeezing sound.
Guitar Player, *September 1977*

"Walking From Door To Door" and "Lonesome In My Bed," the first tunes I ever recorded, they sold 350,000 copies... All I got out of it was $14.
Guitar World, *September 1978*

Playing the blues was a life I chose to lead. When I started, there were three things I decided to do: play the blues, play 'em right, and make all the gigs. And I have.
Guitar World, *July 1991*

What They Say

He was the only bluesman I know of who had a completely comfortable synthesis with modern black music – R&B, so to speak – and sold copiously to a black audience as well as the white audience.
Mike Bloomfield, Guitar Player, *September 1977*

Albert... had a wonderful stage presence, he was very congenial and warm, he was relaxed onstage, and related to the public. He just went onstage and said, "Let's play."
Bill Graham, Guitar Player, *September 1977*

Albert King can blow Eddie [Van Halen] off the stage with his amp on standby.
Joe Walsh, Guitar World, *September 1988*

I remember seeing him and B. B. King jam at the Fillmore, and Albert cut B. B. to death, man. He had that big Acoustic amp, and it sounded like bombs exploding.
Mike Bloomfield, Guitar Player, *April 1993*

In a 1972 interview, King mentioned that he preferred Black Diamond strings. He used light-gauge strings with a wound *G* on the first three strings and medium-gauge strings on the lower three.

Amplifiers, Effects, and Devices

King never provided any details about what type of amplifiers he used in the early days. In the '60s, he played through Acoustic amps before switching to a Roland JC-120 Jazz Chorus solid-state amp in the late '70s. King used only a few effects, including the chorus effect on the Roland amp and an MXR Phase 90 phase shifter.

Discography

King made his recording debut on the single "Bad Luck Blues"/"Be On Your Merry Way" that he recorded in the early '50s for Chicago's Parrot label, for whom he also recorded "Walking From Door To Door" and "Lonesome In My Bed." Several of his early recordings for the Parrot label can be heard on **Door To Door***, issued by Chess Records.*

A few years later, King began recording for Bobbin Records and King Records. He recorded for these labels until 1963, including the album **The Big Blues***. Many of these recordings are featured on Modern Blues'* **Let's Have A Natural Ball***, and Bellaphon's* **Travelin' To California***.*

King's big breakthrough came in 1965, when he was signed to Stax Records. His Stax debut, **Born Under A Bad Sign***, was a huge success and helped Albert reach a white audience. King's other Stax recordings include* **Live Wire/Blues Power***,* **I'll Play The Blues For You***,* **Lovejoy***,* **The Lost Session***,* **Wednesday Night In San Francisco***,* **Thursday Night In San Francisco***,* **The Pinch***,* **Years Gone By***,* **King Does The King's Thing** *(later reissued as* **Blues For Elvis***),* **I Wanna Get Funky***,* **Blues At Sunrise***,* **Chronicle** *(featuring one side by Albert King and the other by Little Milton),* **Montreux Festival***, and* **Jammed Together***, featuring guests Steve Cropper and Pops Staples. Many of King's most popular Stax performances are included on* **The Best Of Albert King – Vol. 1** *(Stax),* **King Of The Blues Guitar** *(Atlantic France),* **Laundromat Blues** *(Edsel), and* **Masterworks** *(Atlantic).*

After King stopped recording for Stax, his records were issued by several different labels. These records include **Albert Live** *(Utopia),* **New Orleans Heat** *and* **Truckload Of Lovin'** *(both on Charly),* **Albert** *and* **King Albert** *(both on Tomato),* **San Francisco '83** *and* **I'm In A Phone Booth Baby** *(both on Fantasy).*

Recording Sessions

Albert rarely appeared on other artists' records, though notable guest performances include Toru Oki's **Toru Oki Blues Band** *(Japanese import) and Albert Brooks' comedy album* **A Star Is Bought***. King's last recording was "Oh, Pretty Woman," on Gary Moore's* **Still Got The Blues***.*

Typical Licks

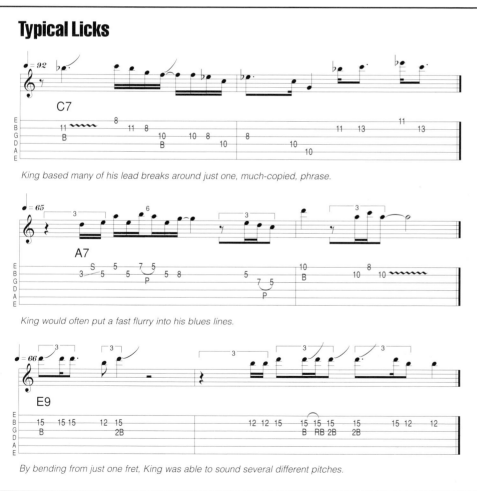

King based many of his lead breaks around just one, much-copied, phrase.

King would often put a fast flurry into his blues lines.

By bending from just one fret, King was able to sound several different pitches.

B.B. King

Known as the "King Of The Blues," B.B. King is the most popular and famous artist of the blues genre. Dubbing himself the "Blues Boy from Beale Street," which was shortened to the nickname "Blues Boy," then finally "B.B.," King has had a prolific recording and performing career since making his debut on KWEM in the late '40s. To this day, he performs as many as 300 shows a year, and he has issued more than 70 albums. His 1965 record, Live At The Regal, *is considered one of the finest blues-guitar albums ever made.*

The Player

Influences

In his youth, B. B. King was exposed primarily to gospel music. Both of his parents were part-time gospel singers, and King himself started his musical career by singing spirituals with the Elkhorn Jubilee Singers.

At eight years old, King was first exposed to guitar when his uncle's brother-in-law, a sanctified preacher named Archie Fair, came to visit. Fair eventually taught the young King how to play C, F, and G chords, and how to put them together into a I-IV-V progression. In his early teens, King purchased his first guitar with wages he earned as a plantation worker. He started trying to play jazz, blues, gospel, and country-and-western songs that he heard on the radio.

Some of the first blues music King ever heard was on 78s owned by his aunt, including Blind Lemon Jefferson, Lonnie Johnson, Robert Johnson, Bumble Bee Slim, and Charley Patton. A few years later, during World War II, he started playing on street corners. When he noticed that customers gave him more money to play blues songs, King decided to become a blues artist. Some of his favorite blues guitarists include T-Bone Walker ("Stormy Monday" was particularly influential), Lonnie Johnson, Blind Lemon Jefferson, Elmore James, Clarence "Gatemouth" Brown, Lightnin' Hopkins, Lowell Fulson, and Big Joe Williams with Sonny Boy Williamson.

King also enjoyed the slide playing of guitarists such as Earl Hooker, Robert Nighthawk, and his cousin Bukka White, but he never could figure out how to play slide. "I feel that I've got stupid fingers because I could never do it," King told Jas Obrecht in a 1991 *Guitar Player* interview. King attributes the development of his distinctive vibrato technique to his attempts to imitate the sound of a slide guitar.

King developed a fondness for jazz music, and he particularly enjoyed the playing of Charlie Christian, Django Reinhardt, Barney Kessel, and Kenny Burrell. He especially liked the phrasing of these guitarists. King also enjoyed the playing of jump-blues and pop guitarists, such as Bill Jennings with Louis Jordan's Tympany Five, and Johnny Moore of Johnny Moore And The Three Blazers. King claims that Moore's playing exposed him to 9th and 13th chords.

Background

1925 *Riley B. King is born on September 16, near Itta Bena, Mississippi.*

1946 *B. B. quits sharecropping and moves to Memphis, where he makes his living "busking," and shares a room for almost a year with his second cousin, Bukka White.*

1948 *He finally manages to pay off his debts to his former plantation boss. Sonny Boy Williamson invites King to play on his radio show broadcast on KWEM.*

1949 *B. B. nearly loses his life rescuing his Gibson acoustic from a fire started by two men fighting over a girl called Lucille. Starts to record for the Bullet label.*

1950 *King starts recording for Modern Records.*

1951 *His cover of Lowell Fulson's "Three O'Clock Blues" hits #1 on the U. S. R&B charts.*

1952 *His first marriage ends in divorce.*

1962 *B. B. signs to ABC Records.*

1965 *He releases* Live At The Regal.

1969 *King's single "The Thrill Is Gone," which features an impressive string arrangement, gains massive crossover appeal and reaches #15 on the U. S. pop charts. This occasions King's first tour of Europe.*

1971 *B. B. is voted third in the U.K.'s New Musical Express' guitarist poll behind Eric Clapton and Jimi Hendrix.*

1972 *King founds FAIRR (Foundation for the Advancement of Inmate Rehabilitation and Recreation) with F. Lee Bailey.*

1975 *B. B. becomes the first guitarist to enter Guitar Player magazine's Gallery Of The Greats in recognition of his five consecutive wins in the Electric Blues category in the magazine's readers' poll.*

1987 *King is awarded a Lifetime Achievement Grammy.*

1990 *B. B. appears at a tribute festival to John Lennon in Liverpool.*

When King moved to Memphis, Tennessee, in the late '40s, he found jobs in nightclubs playing music by Louis Jordan, Dinah Washington, and Roy Brown. Soon he got work singing commercials on WDIA, the first all-black-operated radio station. During this period, King studied briefly with Robert Lockwood, Jr.

Although B.B. King is best-known as a guitarist, he also plays several other instruments, including piano, bass, drums, harmonica, violin, and clarinet. He notes that his proficiency on other instruments has influenced his guitar playing. "It affects my phrasing, and it makes me a little more fluent," he explains. He is also inspired by the playing of several horn players, such as Cootie Williams, Johnny Hodges, Bobby Hackett, Cleanhead Vinson, and Louis Jordan.

B.B. is a self-taught musician, but he learned to read music later in his career. "Reading music is what I call spellin'," he told Tom Wheeler in a 1980 *Guitar Player* interview. "I spell; I read slowly. If the metronome is not goin' too fast, I can do it pretty good." King is an avid music fan who owns tens of thousands of records. Even today he still listens to a wide range of music and is inspired by many newcomers as well as his old favorites.

Approach and Style

Because King never learned how to play while he is singing, he has never developed much of a rhythm style. Instead, he concentrates on playing fills and solos. He often uses a call-and-response approach, where he will play a short phrase on the guitar after he has sung a line, like a dialog between the guitar and the vocals.

Most of King's lines are based around pentatonic minor scales. However, he will sometimes use additional notes to

complement the key of the song that he is playing. For example, he will often add a major third in order to outline a dominant seventh tonality. He is also fond of playing chromatic figures, which give his music a sophisticated, jazzy feel. His phrasing is economical, consisting primarily of sparse, melodic, single-note lines and sustained notes. He can play quite quickly, but he prefers to emphasize soulful emotions over technical displays of speed.

Several characteristics of King's soloing style include grace notes, blue notes, and T-Bone Walker-style duplicate notes, where the same pitch is played on adjacent strings. He also incorporates wide-interval jumps, either by skipping strings or by sliding up or down a string as much as an octave.

B. B. King launched his career in the late '40s as a DJ at Memphis radio station WDIA, where he performed commercials for Pepticon. At this time he was playing an inexpensive Gibson archtop electric and a Gibson amp.

Although King primarily plays single-note lines, he occasionally intersperses chords into his solos and fills. He particularly likes to play 9th chords, an approach he picked up while attempting to play like T-Bone Walker. King admits that he knows only a few chords, and that he never learned too many because he does not play rhythm.

Techniques

Perhaps the most distinctive element of King's playing is his fast, powerful, and dramatic vibrato technique, which he developed by trying to imitate the sound of a slide guitar. To create this effect, he usually holds the note with his left-hand forefinger, removes his thumb off of the neck, and pivots his wrist back and forth very quickly. Many guitarists have tried to duplicate King's vibrato, but none have been able to match his distinctive touch.

His string-bending technique is equally idiosyncratic. He bends strings mostly with his third finger, but he can bend strings with any one of his left-hand fingers including his forefinger and pinky. King usually uses just one finger to perform the bend, and only occasionally uses the other free fingers to support the bend. Sometimes he will hit a note one fret lower than the intended pitch and then bend the note up to pitch.

Playing exclusively with a flat pick, he generally uses downstrokes to pluck the strings. Sometimes he will rake the strings, dragging the pick across muted strings before he hits the desired note.

King prefers to play through both pickups at once. He adjusts the tone and volume controls often to create different tones and textures. He also likes to experiment with controlled feedback to generate sustain.

The Hardware

Guitars, Strings, and Picks

King's first instrument was a piece of wire strung in between two nails in a wall and tightened with a brick. When he was 14, he bought a Stella acoustic guitar with wages that he earned working on a plantation. After hearing T-Bone Walker's "Stormy Monday," King decided that he wanted to play electric guitar, so he acquired an inexpensive black Gibson f-hole archtop that he fitted with a DeArmond pickup. This was the guitar that King played when he got his job playing on radio station WDIA.

During the '50s, King played a widely varying selection of guitars, including a Gibson ES-5, a Fender Broadcaster, a Gibson Byrdland, and various Gretsches, Epiphones, and Silvertones.

In 1958, he purchased a Gibson ES-335

With his idiosyncratic vibrato technique and singing lead-guitar style, King is one of the most influential blues guitarists ever. Here he is seen playing "Lucille," one of his trademark Gibson ES-355 thinline electric guitars.

semi-hollow thinline electric. A year later he bought a Gibson ES-355, which has remained his favorite type of guitar ever since. In 1980, Gibson started making the B.B. King Custom model, which is similar to an ES-355, except it has no f-holes. This model, which became known as the B.B. King Lucille model in 1988, is King's current favorite and he owns several of them.

King also owns a couple of acoustic guitars, but he does not play them onstage. They include a National resonator guitar, a Gibson L-00 Blues King, and a custom-made Gibson J-200 with fancy abalone inlays and a built-in transducer pickup.

King uses a stiff medium pick and strings his guitars with sets of Ernie Ball light top/heavy bottom strings, gauged .010, .013, .017, .030, .045, .054.

Amplifiers, Effects, and Devices

King's first amplifier was a Gibson from the mid-'40s that he used with his DeArmond pickup-equipped Gibson archtop. During the '50s, he used whatever amps were available to him, and he was often photographed playing through tweed-covered Fender amps during this era.

King started using Fender Twin Reverb amps in the mid-'60s, and he recorded many of his critically acclaimed ABC releases using these amps. At this time he did not carry his own amps on the road with him, and instead he had the promoter provide a suitable amp for him. By the early '70s he switched to solid-state Gibson SG amps because Fender had changed the design of the Twin Reverb, and he did not like the sound as much as the old ones. In the late '70s, King became fond of Gibson Lab Series amps, and he used these throughout the early '90s. Currently, King prefers Fender's '65 Twin Reverb reissue.

King does not use any effects.

In His Own Words

I feel that I'm still singing when I play. That's why I don't play a lot of notes maybe like some people. When I'm playing a solo, I hear me singing through the guitar.
Guitar Player, *September 1980*

I've always been conscious of being put down as a blues player. So I've had one thing that I always tried to keep in mind: It's always better to know and not need, than to need and not know. I practice hard trying to be able to do things that nobody would expect me to do.
Guitar Player, *July 1991*

I'm like a test pilot for the airplane – he don't know much about it, he just flies it. An amp and a guitar, I don't know much about 'em. I just play – or at least try.
Guitar Player, *June 1992*

What They Say

Usually in a good concert you'll hear people say "ooh" or "aah" at various times, but when B. B. plays they all go "ooh" at the same time and "aah" at the same time. He doesn't just play his guitar; he plays his audience.
David Bromberg, Guitar Player, *September 1980*

He's the father of the squeezing of the string of the electric guitar. The original "Sweet Little Angel" made me cry when I first heard it, when I heard his voice. He'd sing in a long-meter way and, man, that guy can go so high with his voice.
Buddy Guy, The Guitar Magazine, *September 1991*

There's only one B. B. There's a lot of imitations, lot of people pick up the guitar and follow this man – many, many of 'em. Used to be everybody that pick up a guitar try to sound like B. B. King. But you can tell when the main person, the main man, hit it.
John Lee Hooker, Guitar Player, *September 1993*

Discography

King made his first recordings in 1949 for Nashville's Bullet label. He recorded four songs for Bullet, including "Miss Martha Take A Swing With Me," "How Do You Feel When Your Baby's Packed Up To Go," and "I've Got The Blues."

In 1950, King caught the attention of Ike Turner, who helped him to land a deal with Modern Records. King went on to record for this label and its subsidiaries RPM, Kent, and Crown throughout the '50s. Many of King's early recordings have been reissued by the Ace label on compilations that include: **Singin' The Blues/The Blues**, **The Best Of B.B. King** volumes 1 and 2, **The Fabulous B.B. King**, **The Memphis Masters**,

Across The Tracks, **One Nighter Blues**, **Lucille Had A Baby**, and **Do The Boogie**. United Records has also reissued many of King's '50s recordings on the following albums: **B.B. King, 1949-1950**, **Singing The Blues**, **The Blues**, **The Great B.B. King**, and **I Love You So**.

King signed to ABC records in 1962 and issued his ABC debut, **Mr. Blues**, that year. In 1965, ABC released King's classic **Live At The Regal**, considered by many critics to be his finest record, if not one of the best blues records ever. Since then King has issued dozens of records for various labels, including Bluesway and MCA, his current label.

The following B.B. King albums are available on MCA: **Live At The Regal**, **Blues Is King**, **Live And Well**, **Completely Well**, **Live In Cook County Jail**, **Now Appearing At Ole Miss**, **Midnight Believer**, **Take It Home**, **There Must Be A Better World Somewhere**, **Love Me Tender**, **Blues 'N' Jazz**, **Six Silver Strings**, **King Of The Blues**, and **Blues Summit**.

The following B.B. King albums were reissued by United Records: **My Kind Of Blues**, **The Soul Of B.B. King**, and **King Of The Blues**.

In 1992, MCA released the **King Of The Blues** box set, a retrospective of King's career from 1949 through to 1991. This is highly recommended for anyone who wants an overview of King's recording career.

Recording Sessions

In the '70s, King collaborated with vocalist Bobby "Blue" Bland on several albums. The most notable of these include **Together For The First Time... Live**, and **I Like To Live The Love**.

King has guested on a handful of albums in his career, including recording sessions with Miles Davis and Ray Charles. In the late '80s, he recorded "When Love Comes To Town" with U2, included on their **Rattle And Hum** album.

Typical Licks

This lick from a blues in C minor shows B.B. setting up the IV chord with a two-part lick.

B.B. slides up from a blues-scale position one into position two and includes the sixth.

This is an example of the classic call-and-response phrasing used by the "King of the Blues."

Freddie King

Although Freddie King is often described as a Texas bluesman, he blended several different styles of music and forged his own distinctive sound. He was one of the first blues guitarists to break through to a pop audience, and his instrumental hits exposed many young white listeners to the blues. With a fast, flamboyant style, King influenced many rock and blues guitarists, such as Michael Bloomfield and Jerry Garcia. His songs have been covered by Jeff Beck, Eric Clapton, Dave Edmunds, Peter Green, Mick Taylor, and ZZ Top.

The Player

Influences

Freddie's mother Ella and his uncle Leon both played guitar, and they taught him how to play when he was six. King's earliest musical influences were blues and gospel music. He enjoyed listening to records by several blues artists, including T-Bone Walker, Robert Johnson, Lightnin' Hopkins, Sonny Boy Williamson, and John Lee Hooker. His idol at this time was Louis Jordan, and King later remarked that he tried to make his guitar sound like Jordan's alto saxophone.

When his family moved to Chicago when he was a young teenager, King started going out to blues clubs and watching performances by Muddy Waters, Howlin' Wolf, and Little Walter. While hanging around in these clubs, he often had the opportunity to sit in with the bands. He made friends with Jimmy Rogers, who played guitar with Muddy Waters. Rogers and Eddie Taylor, who was Jimmy Reed's lead guitarist, taught King how to play with a fingerpick and a thumbpick.

King eventually worked with Waters, Wolf, and Little Walter, and he became friends with Otis Rush, Magic Sam Maghett, and Jody Williams. During this time, King also experienced the music of B. B. King and Robert Lockwood, Jr., who influenced Freddie. "I picked up the style between Lightnin' Hopkins and Muddy Waters and B. B. King and T-Bone Walker," he said in an interview published by *Living Blues*. "That's in-between style, that's the way I play. I play country and city."

One day, Freddie and Magic Sam overheard Hound Dog Taylor working on "Taylor's Boogie." King and Magic reworked Taylor's song and wrote "Hideaway," which later became King's first hit. Throughout his career, Freddie often covered songs by his favorite musicians such as T-Bone Walker, B. B. King, and Albert King.

Freddie's mixture of Delta-, Texas-, and Chicago-blues styles resulted in a distinctive form of music that defied categorization. Many of his early instrumental hits appealed to pop audiences who were also buying records by the Ventures and Duane Eddy. King incorporated several other styles of music into his playing, including country and western swing. His western swing influences are most evident in the instrumental "Remington Ride." Later in his career, he covered funk tunes, such as Bill Withers'

Background

1934 *Freddie Christian is born on September 3, in Gilmer, Texas.*

1940 *At the early age of six, Freddie has already learned how to play the guitar.*

1949 *Looking to meet prominent blues recording artists like Muddy Waters, T-Bone Walker and John Lee Hooker, he travels to Chicago.*

1950 *King moves to Chicago with his family.*

1952 *He forms the Every Hour Blues Boys, with Jimmy Lee Robinson.*

1953 *King participates on his first recording sessions for Parrot records with Little Sonny Cooper's band, Earlee Payton's Blues Cats, and Smokey Smothers.*

1954 *Freddie moves permanently to Chicago with his family.*

1956 *Freddie makes his recording debut as an artist for Chicago's El-Bee label.*

1960 *Freddie is signed to the King label by talent scout Alphonse "Sonny" Thompson and records six titles under his own name for Sydney Nathan's King/Federal label. He starts touring.*

1961 *The single "Hideaway" reaches #5 on the R&B charts and #29 on the pop charts. King releases his first album.*

1966 *Freddie leaves the King/Federal label.*

1968 *He is signed to Atlantic's Cotillion subsidiary by saxophonist King Curtis.*

1969 *King participates in his first tour of Europe.*

1970 *He is signed to Leon Russell's Shelter label.*

1973 *Freddie co-produces on Jimmy Rogers' comeback LP, Gold Tailed Bird.*

1974 *Freddie records and tours with Eric Clapton.*

1976 *Freddie King dies of pancreatitis on December 18, in Dallas, Texas, at the age of 42.*

"Ain't No Sunshine" and Dave Mason's "Feelin' All Right." King admitted that he was also influenced by many other guitarists, including Steve Cropper, Kenny Burrell, and Chet Atkins.

Approach and Style

The most identifiable attribute of King's playing style was his aggressive, percussive attack and his piercing, slightly distorted tone. His early vocal recordings featured sparse, straight-ahead blues guitar accompaniment based around pentatonic minor scales. He stretched out more on his instrumentals, which, although they too were primarily centered around pentatonic minor scales, broke away from the blues and

incorporated elements of pop, country, and rock music. King often added 2nd and 6th intervals to the pentatonic scale, which gave his licks a jazzy feel.

King's playing was primarily centered around box patterns in the root position, but he used the full range of the patterns, and he was very resourceful at coming up with inventive melodies within these limitations. To add variety to his instrumentals, he often interspersed muted bass-note runs with melodic single-note lines played in the middle or upper registers. Sometimes he even quoted other songs, such as the "Peter Gunn Theme" interlude in the middle of "Hideaway."

King rarely played straight rhythm guitar,

although some of his songs are predominantly rhythm-guitar figures punctuated with lead lines every other measure. He favored major, minor, and ninth chords. He also frequently played harmonized double-stop figures or simple double-stop lines, such as the Elmore James lick he plays at the beginning of "Takin' Care Of Business."

Like many of the other great blues guitarists, Freddie possessed a distinctive vibrato and note-bending style. His vibrato was fast and wide, most closely resembling B. B. King's style. Freddie made frequent use of bent notes, generally bending in half- or whole-step intervals.

King's lead lines display a sophisticated sense of rhythm. Some of his distinctive touches included syncopated phrasing, triplet pull-offs, and cross-picked patterns.

Techniques

King's technique is distinguished by his use of both a thumbpick and a fingerpick that he wore on his first finger. He used the thumbpick for downstrokes and the fingerpick for upstrokes. He would pick entire lines with either the thumbpick or fingerpick. He often used both picks for fast tremolo picking on a single string and to play cross-picked figures on adjacent strings. A good example of the latter technique can be heard on the melody line of "Side Tracked."

King frequently incorporated hammer-ons and fast trills in his lead lines, such as the open-string hammer-ons heard on "Hideaway." He also utilized pull-offs, such as the triplet pattern he played on "Driving Sideways." Occasionally, King would quickly drag the picks across the strings while holding a chord, a technique known as

One of the three Kings of the blues, Freddie King recorded several instrumentals in the early '60s that crossed over to pop audiences and exposed many white listeners to blues music. Here he is seen playing a Gibson ES-355.

"raking". "Sen-Sa-Shun" contains a good example of this raking technique.

King usually picked between the pickups, with his right hand positioned just below the neck pickup. He draped his left-hand thumb over the top edge of the neck, occasionally using his thumb to fret notes while playing chords. Most of his string bends were executed with the third finger of his left hand, using his first and second fingers for support. He also used his third finger for vibrato.

Keeping all of the guitar's tone and volume guitars about halfway up, King almost always played through both pickups at once. He would adjust the controls to make slight adjustments to the tone.

Although King enjoyed the playing of bottleneck guitarists, he never learned to play slide. However, he often used slurs and finger slides to imitate the licks played by bottleneck guitarists. "My fingers are too heavy," he told Dan Forte. "I play too hard.

Eric Clapton (seen here behind King) was heavily influenced by Freddie's music in the early '60s. He returned the favor in the mid '70s by bringing King on tour with him and releasing one of his records.

I wish I could play slide, but I can't. I do some of the same licks, though, as Elmore James, Earl Hooker, and guys like that."

The Hardware

Guitars, Strings, and Picks

King's first guitar was a Silvertone Roy Rogers acoustic that he got when he was six years old. Details about what kind of guitars he used during the '50s are unknown, but by the time he started recording for the King label, Freddie was playing a gold-top 1954 Les Paul solidbody electric with two single-coil P-90 pickups. He recorded most of his early instrumental hits with this guitar.

In the mid-'60s he switched to a stereo Gibson ES-355 semi-hollow thinline electric, which was his main guitar up until his death. He owned several ES-355s, as well as a few other Gibsons, including an ES-335, an ES-345, a Les Paul, and two Firebirds. "I used to use Fenders, but not anymore," he told Dan Forte in an interview for *Guitar Player*. "Fender is a good sounding guitar, but for the way I play I think Gibson is the best."

King never played guitar with a flatpick. Instead, he preferred to wear a steel finger-pick on his right-hand forefinger and a plastic thumbpick on his thumb. He liked to use light-gauge Ernie Ball strings on the top three strings (.010, .011, and .012) and Gibson medium-gauge on the bottom three.

Amplifiers, Effects, and Devices

Details about King's early amplifers are also unknown. In the late '60s and early '70s, he played through a Fender Twin Reverb. Towards the end of his career, he used a 1972 Fender Quad combo amplifier with four 12-inch speakers.

King plugged directly into the amplifier and did not use any effects.

In His Own Words

I play my guitar like Louis Jordan used to play his horn. That's the same sound I get.
Guitar Player, *January 1977*

The young whites started people looking at me, B.B. King, and all the rest of us. If it wasn't for them, I think the blues would still be in the same old black market. But now it's a bigger market. Johnny Winter, John Hammond, Paul Butterfield, Mike Bloomfield – he hung around us as a kid in Chicago – they're really blues cats. It went okay for me.
Guitar Player, *January 1977*

I have never used one [flatpick]. I use a steel finger pick on the index and a plastic thumbpick. Jimmy Rogers and Eddie Taylor taught me how to play like that. Robert Junior Lockwood can play with all three fingers.
Guitar Player, *January 1977*

What They Say

I think of all the people I've ever played with, the most stimulating in an onstage situation was Freddie King. Freddie could be pretty mean, but subtle with it. He'd make you feel at home and then tear you to pieces.
Eric Clapton, Guitar Player.

He was one of the best guys to work with. The only thing, he didn't like competition. But he didn't worry about me. Different style. We got along together fine. He was a likable guy.
Lowell Fulson.

Freddie King, who is my man at the moment, does a bend and he's pulling it a good inch to get that sound, he works for it. If you are going to hit a note you've got to work for it.
Pete Townshend, Guitar Player, *June 1972*

Discography

King made his debut as a solo artist in 1956 on the single "Country Boy"/"That's What You Think," which he recorded for Chicago's El-Bee label. The single was not a hit and he did not make any recordings until nearly four years later.

*King signed to the King/Federal label in 1960 and started recording several singles featuring a vocal on the A-side and an instrumental on the B-side for them. The B-side of his first single for the label, "I Love The Woman"/ "Hideaway," became a success on both rock 'n' roll and R&B radio stations. In 1961, the label issued King's first album, **Freddie King Sings**, which they later followed up with the instrumental collection **Let's Hide Away And Dance Away**. This was more successful, leading the label*

*to issue several more instrumental collections, including **Freddy King Gives You A Bonanza Of Instrumentals** and **Freddy King Goes Surfin'**, which was the same record as **Let's Hide Away And Dance Away**, only with added canned applause. The King label also released the albums **Girl-Boy-Girl**, featuring vocal duets with Lulu Reed, in 1962 and **17 Original Greatest Hits**. King's early recordings have been reissued by Rhino (**Hideaway: The Best Of Freddie King**), Ace (**Freddie King/Blues Guitar Hero** and **Blues Guitar Hero – The Influential Early Sessions**), Charly (**Takin' Care Of Business**), and Modern Blues (**Freddie King Sings/The Original Hits** and **Just Pickin'**).*

*In the late '60s, King signed a deal with Cotillion Records, which released **Freddie King Is A Blues Master** (1969) and **My Feeling For The Blues** (1970), both produced by Texas saxophone legend King Curtis and later reissued by WEA. King then inked a deal with Leon Russell's Shelter label and recorded the soul-influenced **Gettin' Ready** (1971), **Texas Cannonball** (1972), and **Woman Across The Water** (1973). In 1974 he signed to the Polydor label and recorded the album **Burglar**, which featured a guest appearance by Eric Clapton. The following year, King moved to Clapton's label, RSO, and released **Larger Than Life**, his final studio recording.*

*Several of King's live performances were recorded and released: **Live In Antibes, 1974** (French Concerts), **Rocking The Blues Live** (Crosscut), and **Live At The Texas Opry House, April 20, 1976** (P-Vine).*

*Vestapol Productions has discovered rare video footage of King's concerts and television performances and issued them on the following video tapes: **Freddie King In Concert**, **Freddie King The!!!!Beat 1966**, and **Freddie King Dallas, Texas, January 20, 1973**.*

Recording Sessions

*The very first recordings featuring King's playing were made in 1953 during sessions with Little Sonny Cooper for the Parrot label. In the late '50s, King appeared on Howlin' Wolf's recordings of "Wang-Dang Doodle" and "Back Door Man." King participated in few other recording sessions, with the exception of Jimmy Rogers' **Gold Tailed Bird** (Shelter), which he also produced.*

Typical Licks

Freddie often started off his blues solos with this type of opening phrase.

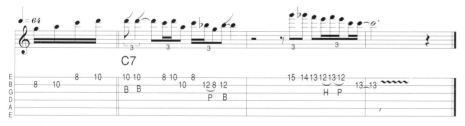

This much-copied lick demonstrates King's smooth playing over triplets.

Freddie liked to repeat his bends over and over, across one or two bars.

Mark Knopfler

Mark Knopfler burst onto the scene in the late '70s with his dynamic, yet understated, fingerstyle playing on Dire Straits' "Sultans Of Swing." His melodic, lyrical playing has graced several film soundtracks, and he has recently branched out into several projects, including collaborations with his hero Chet Atkins, and all-acoustic ventures with The Notting Hillbillies. An idiosyncratic stylist, Knopfler remains an original and independent voice in the often-imitative and trend-following world of rock music.

The Player

Influences

Knopfler spent his early years in Scotland, where he was exposed to Celtic music. When he was about nine years old, he was introduced to rock 'n' roll when he heard his uncle Kingsley playing boogie-woogie piano. Mark started listening to the radio and began buying records. Lonnie Donegan was an early favorite of his, and he encouraged his mother to buy skiffle records for him.

Mark started playing guitar by the time he was 15. His favorite music during this period was rock 'n' roll, and he enjoyed listening to the Beatles, the Rolling Stones, the Kinks, and Hank Marvin And The Shadows. He also enjoyed rockabilly and rock 'n' roll from the '50s, including music by Elvis Presley (with Scotty Moore on guitar), Ricky Nelson (with James Burton on guitar), Duane Eddy, the Fireballs, Jerry Lee Lewis, and the Everly Brothers (with Chet Atkins on guitar).

It was around this time that Knopfler was introduced to the music of Bob Dylan. "I was hugely influenced by him about the age of 14 or 15, going 'round to girls' houses, drinking 75 cups of coffee, smoking 90 cigarettes, and listening to *Blonde On Blonde* 120 times," Knopfler told Dan Forte in a *Guitar Player* interview. "I heard Bob Dylan from the very beginning, the 'Hard Rain' days, and went with him all the way up, and I'm still with him. I still think he's great." A few years after Dire Straits' debut, Mark was given the opportunity to play on a Bob Dylan album (*Slow Train Coming*), and he has worked with Dylan several times since then.

When Mark was 16, he started listening to American blues artists. He was particularly interested in early blues guitarists, such as Blind Willie McTell, Blind Blake, and Lonnie Johnson. Eventually he began listening to Chicago blues, and he particularly enjoyed Howlin' Wolf and B. B. King's playing, crediting King's *Live At The Regal* as one of his favorite blues albums.

Knopfler played rock 'n' roll in his early bands, and later he started playing acoustic guitar in folk clubs, using a guitar he had borrowed from a friend. During this time he learned how to fingerpick, and eventually he began mimicking the clawhammer and frailing styles of many folk and Celtic guitarists.

During the late '60s, Knopfler greatly expanded his musical interests. His favorite rock bands at this time were the Doors, and

Background

1949 *Mark Knopfler is born in Glasgow, Scotland, on August 12.*

1955 *Mark moves with his parents from Glasgow to Newcastle, England.*

1964 *Mark gets his first guitar, and teaches himself to play by playing along with records and the radio.*

1977 *Knopfler forms Dire Straits with brother David Knopfler (rhythm guitar), John Illsley (bass), and Pick Withers (drums).*

1978 *Dire Straits' debut album,* Dire Straits, *is released. The single "Sultans Of Swing" becomes a Top Ten hit on pop charts in the U.S. and U.K.*

1979 *Knopfler guests on Bob Dylan's* Slow Train Coming. *Dire Straits have the biggest selling debut album in the U.S.*

1980 *Mark's brother and founder member, David Knopfler, quits the band.*

1982 *Knopfler scores his first soundtrack, for the movie* Local Hero.

1984 *He produces Bob Dylan's* Infidels.

1985 *Dire Straits release their most successful album to date,* Brothers In Arms. *Mark guests on Chet Atkins' album* Stay Tuned.

1986 *Dire Straits play a benefit concert for Prince Charles' charity, Prince's Trust, at Wembley Arena, London.*

1988 *Dire Straits headlines at Nelson Mandela tribute concert at Wembley Stadium, London.*

1989 *Following a gig in 1986, Mark rejoins the line-up of Brendan Croker and Steve Phillips to form a country-blues band called The Notting Hillbillies.*

1990 *Mark collaborates with his long-time hero Chet Atkins to make the album* Neck And Neck, *for which he initially refuses to accept any payment.*

Head, Hands & Feet, featuring Albert Lee. He also started listening to western swing, ragtime, slide guitar, country blues, and jug-band music, and he wrote several waltzes and rags. He started teaching children basic guitar and singing, and joined a rockabilly/R&B band called the Cafe Racers, with whom he began to develop his fingerstyle technique. "I was playing a rhythm/lead thing with a plectrum, sort of like Mick Green," he told Joel Siegel in a 1979 *Guitar Player* interview. "Then, a sort of synthesis happened between fingerpicking and getting plectrum-type effects by just using my fingers."

Knopfler's biggest guitar influence during this period was J. J. Cale. "I listened to a lot of J. J. Cale around the time my style was developing," Knopfler told Dan Forte. "He's very, very special to me." Much of Cale's influence can be detected in Knopfler's tone and chord structures.

Knopfler's film soundtracks, which he recorded during the '80s, reveal several other important influences, including Italian film music composer Ennio Morricone and traditional Irish music.

Knopfler is an inventive guitarist with a melodic style that meshes elements of country, rockabilly, blues, and Celtic music. His primary guitar is a Stratocaster, and he coaxes a variety of tones out of it playing only with his fingers.

Approach and Style

Mark's style is characterized by liberal use of triads, arpeggios, and diminished runs. His use of triads is largely due to his reliance on using his thumb and two fingers to play and his preference of plucking chords instead of strumming them. He uses arpeggios to create lines that fit nicely over chord changes. He also frequently plays chromatic runs.

His left hand delivers fast, narrow, stinging vibrato reminiscent of, but more subtle than, B. B. King. He also frequently uses half-step slides for chords and single notes. Another favorite device of his is a descending figure where he will play a pattern of notes, then repeat it on several lower fretboard positions.

F, *Dm*, and *Bm* are some of his favorite keys for composition. "It's that slightly comic, melodramatic thing," he told Dan Forte. "I call it 'spaghetti music.' They're almost tongue-in-cheek – deliberately exaggerated."

Although he performs most of his songs in standard tuning, Mark occasionally uses open tunings, especially for slide. He tuned a National resonator guitar to open *G* (*D*, *G*, *D*, *G*, *B*, *D*, low to high) for "Water Of Love" and he tuned to *B♭* (*F*, *B♭*, *F*, *B♭*, *D*, *F*, low to high) for "Telegraph Road." He used a capo placed at the third fret on the latter.

Knopfler often mixes styles within a song. He frequently plays country-style pedal-steel licks that are followed by Celtic-inspired pull-off patterns. Some of his rhythms are reminiscent of reggae, while others recall rockabilly. But even though he borrows heavily from several styles, he puts them together in a distinctive, simple, and direct manner that retains and embellishes his own personality.

Techniques

Mark plays almost exclusively with his thumb and first two fingers. "Playing with your fingers has something to do with immediacy and soul," he told *Guitar Player*. "You're absolutely in touch with what's going on." He anchors his third and fourth fingers on the top of the guitar just below the high-*E* string, and rests the heel of his right hand against the bridge. He picks mostly with the flesh of his thumb and fingers, but occasionally uses his nails to snap the strings. This gives him considerable control over dynamics, and his lines often vary from subtle, warm textures to aggressive, percussive tones.

Knopfler generally plays chords by grabbing several strings and plucking them all at once, giving his chords a pianistic attack. He also utilizes claw-hammer and frailing techniques, where he percussively hammers downstrokes with his thumb, followed by upstrokes that he plucks with his fingers. He uses these techniques for chords as well as single-note lines. To play fast lines, he makes liberal use of hammer-ons and pull-offs. A particularly good example of this can be heard on his last solo on "Sultans Of Swing."

Although he plays primarily with his fingers, Knopfler occasionally uses a flatpick to strum rhythms, especially on acoustic guitars. The title cut to *On Every Street* is one example where Knopfler plays guitar with a pick. He is also an adept slide player. He wears his slide on his little finger, although he started out wearing it on his third finger. "It just felt more comfortable," he explained to Andy Ellis in *Guitar Player*. "When I realized I needed more fingers to do other things, the slide went on the little finger."

Another important aspect of Knopfler's technique is his control of attack. His finger-style technique generates a percussive attack, but sometimes he uses a volume pedal to swell softly into a note. "It gives you more of a speaking voice, something that approximates a steel guitar," he told Ellis.

Knopfler prefers the "in-between" settings on a Strat – the bridge/middle or the neck/middle pickup combinations.

The Hardware

Guitars, Strings, and Picks

Mark acquired his first guitar when he was 15, a red, Strat-shaped Hofner V-2, which he played for several years. He also played a borrowed acoustic in folk clubs, but did not own an acoustic guitar until many years later.

In the late '60s, Mark purchased his first National metal-body resonator guitar, a 1928 tricone, from Steve Phillips, a guitar builder who later collaborated with Mark on the Notting Hillbillies project. Knopfler also bought an early '60s Les Paul Special around this time, which was his main guitar until the mid-'70s when he switched to a Fender Stratocaster. Since then, Strats and Strat-style guitars have been his main electrics.

Knopfler's current main electric guitar is a late-'80s Pensa-Suhr, featuring active EMG pickups (a humbucker in the bridge position and single-coils in the middle and neck positions), and a Floyd Rose tremolo unit. He owns several other Pensa-Suhr guitars, including a prototype Rudi Pensa Strat. In the early '80s his main guitar was a red Schecter Strat. Knopfler stills plays this guitar often, and he also owns a red Schecter Telecaster copy with Seymour Duncan vintage pickups. Other solidbody electrics in his collection include several maple- and rosewood-neck '60s Fender Stratocasters, a Fender Telecaster Custom with a rosewood neck, and a 12-string Burns Baldwin. On *Brothers In Arms*, he started using a Les Paul Custom that is wired with a phase switch.

Knopfler recently acquired a 1953 Gibson Super 400 archtop electric with original Alnico pickups. He used this guitar on several tracks for *On Every Street*. Other non-solid-body electrics that he has played include the Gibson ES-335 semi-hollow thinline that he used on Bob Dylan's *Slow Train Coming*.

Although he is best-known for his clean Stratocaster tones, Mark Knopfler also uses various other guitars, both in the studio and on stage. Here he is playing one of his favorites, a 1953 Gibson Super 400.

Knopfler also owns several National resonator guitars. His main National is a 1936 Style O with 14 frets clear from the body and an L.R. Baggs bridge transducer. He also owns a '30s Duolian. He plays many different acoustic guitars, including a pair of custom Ovation Adamas 12- and 6-strings, an Ovation Legend, a Gibson J-45, a Taylor, a 1925 Gibson L-3 archtop with a round soundhole, and a few acoustics custom-made by Steve Phillips. He also sometimes plays nylon-string guitar, including a Gibson Chet Atkins electric classical guitar and a Ramirez classical.

Knopfler strings his guitars with D'Addario XL-120 strings (.009-.042). He uses D'Addario XL-115W strings (.011 and a wound third string) on his Super 400.

Amplifiers, Effects, and Devices

When he was playing with the Cafe Racers, Knopfler used a 30-watt Selmer Thunderbird amplifier. In the early days of Dire Straits, he switched to Music Man combos that featured two 12-inch speakers. In the early '80s, he preferred Mesa Boogie amplifier heads, which he played through standard Marshall cabinets. At this time he also used a Fender Vibrolux for the amp's tremolo effect.

More recently, Knopfler's setup consists of Soldano 100-watt heads that have been modified by Pete Cornish to segregate the preamp from the power sections. The amps are connected to 4x12 Marshall cabinets loaded with Electro-Voice 12-inch speakers.

Knopfler uses very few effects, preferring the sound of a guitar connected to an amp. His effects rig includes a t.c. electronics 2290 delay unit, an Alesis Quadraverb, a Boss CS-300 Super Chorus, a Zoom 9010 multi-effects unit, and a rack-mounted Dunlop Cry Baby wah-wah unit. He uses an Ernie Ball volume pedal to control volume swelling effects. In the early days of Dire Straits, Knopfler's effects setup consisted of a Morley volume pedal and an MXR analog delay. His wireless unit is made by Sony.

Discography

Knopfler made his recording debut as a member of Dire Straits, and the bulk of his recorded output appears on the records he has made with that group. These records include: **Dire Straits**, **Communique**, **Making Movies**, **Love Over Gold**, **Twisting By The Pool**, the live album **Alchemy**, **Brothers In Arms**, and **On Every Street**. The greatest hits compilation, **Money For Nothing**, contains several of Dire Straits' biggest hits prior to **On Every Street**. The **Hope And Anchor Front Row Festival** compilation contains a fine early live performance by the band on the cut "Eastbound Train."

Knopfler has also composed the soundtracks to several films, including **Local Hero**, **Cal**, and **The Princess Bride**.

In the late '80s, Knopfler recorded with a group he assembled called the Notting Hillbillies. The group released one album, **Missing... Presumed Having A Good Time**.

Recording Sessions

Shortly after his debut with Dire Straits in the late '70s, Knopfler was asked to guest on several albums. His most important early guest appearances include Steely Dan's **Gaucho**, Van Morrison's **Beautiful Vision**, and Bob Dylan's **Slow Train Coming**.

In the mid-'80s, Knopfler produced and played on Dylan's **Infidels**. He also guested on albums by Bryan Ferry, Phil Everly, Phillip Lynott (**Solo In Soho** and **The Phillip Lynott Album**), and Kate and Anna McGarrigle's **Love Over And Over**. He joined his brother and ex-Dire Straits member David Knopfler on **Release** and played on Dire Strait's bassist John Illsley's **Never Told A Soul**.

Towards the end of the '80s, Knopfler began working with one of his guitar heroes, Chet Atkins. He first appeared on Atkin's **Stay Tuned**, then later collaborated with him on **Neck & Neck**, which is credited to Chet Atkins and Mark Knopfler. He also guested on Atkins and Jerry Reed's 1992 collaboration **Sneakin' Around** and Atkins' **Read My Licks**.

Typical Licks

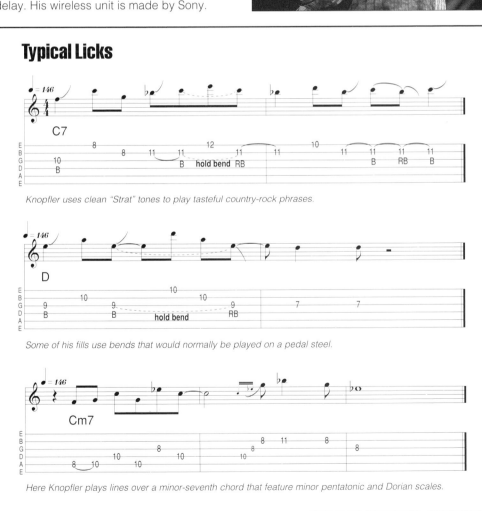

Knopfler uses clean "Strat" tones to play tasteful country-rock phrases.

Some of his fills use bends that would normally be played on a pedal steel.

Here Knopfler plays lines over a minor-seventh chord that feature minor pentatonic and Dorian scales.

Johnny Marr

In the mid-'80s, Johnny Marr emerged as the "guitar anti-hero." As a member of the Smiths, he emphasized rhythms and textures. His paucity of solos and lead-guitar lines contrasted starkly to the flamboyant styles of popular hard-rock and heavy-metal guitarists at that time. Able to create many different tones, Marr is not as immediately identifiable as most guitar stylists, but his playing blends perfectly and supports the song. Currently a member of The The, Marr continues to defy the guitarist's traditional roles.

The Player

Influences

Marr grew up in a household where music was always around. His parents enjoyed listening to country music, and Johnny was often given instruments as gifts when he was a child. One of his first instruments was a toy harmonica, and later his parents gave him a plastic guitar. His father, who played accordion, taught him how to play the harmonica, and his uncle first taught him how to play guitar. Marr never had any formal musical training, however, and he learned to play music either by playing along with records, or in bands. "It sounds corny, but there was never really a time when I didn't have a guitar," he told Scott Isler in a *Musician* magazine interview.

In the mid-'70s Marr became fond of glam or "glitter rock" bands, such as T. Rex, Sweet, Gary Glitter, Roxy Music, and David Bowie. He cites T. Rex's Marc Bolan as his first real influence. Marr saved his money to buy singles every week, and he played along with, and learned parts from, these records. During this period, he also became interested in Motown music. He attributes his

fascination with Motown music as being the primary influence for his chordal approach.

When his family moved to Wythenshaw, in the north of England, Marr met many other musicians, and he had started playing in groups by the time he was 12. It was also around this time that he decided that he wanted to become a professional musician. Billy Duffy, who later became The Cult's guitarist, became friends with Marr and taught him a few chords. Marr's main influences at this time included Keith Richards, George Harrison, and John Lennon, whom he preferred for their rhythmic playing styles. Andy Rourke, who later became the Smiths' bassist, was a big fan of Neil Young, and he exposed Marr to West Coast American music. Another friend exposed him to Pentangle, featuring Bert Jansch, and Fairport Convention, featuring Richard Thompson.

"I started to get into guitar players as such," he told Joe Gore in a *Guitar Player* interview. "When I got into Nils Lofgren, there was no turning back. He had a lot of cool and a lot of flash, but he had respect for the song and the melody." Marr mentions that it was his desire to emulate Lofgren that influenced him to play guitar with a thumbpick.

Marr was also heavily influenced by

Background

1963 *John Maher is born on October 31 in Manchester, England.*

1976 *Marr starts playing guitar.*

1982 *He teams up with Stephen Morrissey, and the duo starts writing songs.*

1983 *The Smiths issue their first single on the Rough Trade label after turning down an offer from Factory Records. They play their debut gig at London's Rock Garden.*

1984 *The Smiths first album,* The Smiths, *is released and reaches #2 in the British album charts.*

1985 *The album* Meat is Murder *goes straight in at #1 in the U.K.*

1986 *The Smiths cancel an appearance at the Artists Against Apartheid benefit gig at London's Royal Albert Hall after Marr is injured in a car accident.*

1987 *Increasingly in demand as a session player, Marr guests with Brian Ferry and Billy Bragg, fueling speculation that the Marr/Morrissey team is disintegrating. Shortly afterwards, Marr quits the Smiths.*

1988 *He goes on tour with the Pretenders and performs with Midge Ure at Nelson Mandela's 70th Birthday Tribute at Wembley Stadium, England.*

1989 *Marr begins working with Matt Johnson and becomes a member of The The.*

1990 *Marr works with three-piece band Stex.*

1991 *He collaborates with New Order's Bernard Sumner on* Electronic.

1993 *The The releases* Dusk.

American punk and new-wave music in the late '70s. Some of his favorite albums from this period include Patti Smith's *Horses*, the Talking Heads' *Talking Heads '77*, and Television's *Marquee Moon*. He also mentions that James Honeyman-Scott of the Pretenders was a big influence on him. "After Patti Smith, I thought, 'Great, I can play big loud chords on a Les Paul through a Fender Twin Reverb, instead of sitting around with an acoustic guitar,'" Marr told Gore. "I could pick like Bert Jansch, but I wanted to look like Ivan Kraal from the Patti Smith Group. From then on, I didn't look back."

One of the most original guitarists to emerge from England's post-punk scene in the mid-'80s, Johnny Marr defies the traditional notion of a guitar hero by emphasizing tones and rhythms over flashy lead playing.

After he left the Smiths, Marr became interested in the music of early '70s funk groups, such as the Ohio Players, the Fatback Band, and the Isley Brothers. These influences are evident in Marr's recent work with The The.

Approach and Style
Favoring textures and tones, Marr is more of a rhythm player than a lead guitarist. His playing is characterized by odd chord sequences that sometimes use clashing major and minor tonalities. With the Smiths he often mixed elements of African highlife with '60s pop-influenced progressions, resulting in a highly melodic mixture.

Marr's playing is primarily based around chords rather than scales. Many of his parts consist of double-stops or triads, and even his single-note lines are usually arpeggios. Marr favors major 7th and 6th chords, though he frequently uses standard major and minor chords as well. His African highlife-influenced lines rely heavily on thirds. He also has a tendency to emphasize the interval between the third and the fifth or the minor third within a major chord, and he often plays chromatic lines or semitones.

In the studio, Marr builds sophisticated tracks by overdubbing several guitar parts. Sometimes he simply builds layers by repeating the same notes on each track, but more often he works out harmonies and counterpoints. He also records a wide variety of tones on the tracks, including acoustic, electric, clean, and distorted sounds.

To expand the guitar's tonality, Marr often experiments with open tunings. He likes the sound of ringing open strings, and open tunings give him more possibilities to use open strings in various keys. With the Smiths, he often tuned his guitar up a whole step to F♯ (F♯, B, E, A, C♯, F♯, low to high). Some of his favorite open tunings include open

G (D, G, D, G, B, D, low to high), open D (D, A, D, F♯, A, D, low to high), and open A (C, F, C, F, A, C, low to high). He uses a capo to match the key of the song that he is performing. He also likes to play "Nashville-strung" guitars, where the guitar is tuned to standard tuning, but the bottom four strings are replaced with a lighter gauge and tuned up an octave or two higher than normal.

Techniques
Marr plays with a thumb pick and his fingers. In general, he uses the pick for downstrokes and uses his fingers for upstrokes. To play fast lines, he grasps the thumb pick between his forefinger and thumb and uses alternate picking, or else he will alternate between picking with the thumb pick and with his fingers. Sometimes he is very aggressive with the latter technique, and he snaps strings against the fretboard, producing an effect similar to slap-bass technique.

Marr often plays octave harmonics by fretting notes with his left hand while lightly touching the string an octave higher than the fretted note with his forefinger and picking behind his forefinger with the thumb pick. He adopted this technique from watching Nils Lofgren play.

Simultaneously striking notes with his fingers and the thumb pick, Marr sometimes adopts a pianistic approach, where he grabs a chord instead of strumming it. He will also play arpeggios with the thumb pick and his fingers in a "rolling" motion, similar to the technique used by banjo players. His right-hand technique accounts for much of his distinctive sound.

Marr has occasionally experimented with unorthodox techniques. For "Stop Me If You Think You've Heard This One Before," and "This Charming Man," both by the Smiths, he tuned his guitar to an open chord and dropped a metal-handled knife on the strings at random. He has also used a slide for sound effects, rather than playing conventional slide guitar lines. He likes to create sounds with a slow attack by hitting a note with the guitar's volume control turned all the way down and slowly swelling the volume up. He also frequently experiments with feedback and the guitar's vibrato bar.

The Hardware

Guitars, Strings, Picks

Marr's first guitar was a ¾-size Strat-shaped Vox electric solidbody that he bought with money he earned delivering newspapers. As he became more involved with music, Marr generally favored Strat-style guitars. He owns several Stratocasters, including a Fender '57 reissue Strat, a couple of '63 Strats that he bought from John Entwistle, a '69 Strat that he bought from Jeff Beck, and a 12-string Strat. Marr also occasionally plays Telecasters, including a recent-make Fender Tele, a Tele-style guitar custom-made by Roger Giffin, and a custom-made Tele-style guitar with a green-finished, quilted-maple top.

Another one of Marr's favorite guitars is his 1959 Gibson Les Paul that he acquired while he was with the Smiths. Other Gibsons in his guitar arsenal include a '59 ES-355 and a 12-string ES-335-12. He also owns several Epiphone electrics, including a Casino hollowbody and a Coronet solidbody.

Marr frequently played Rickenbackers when he was with the Smiths, but he rarely plays them now. Some of the Rickenbackers in his collection include a '66 330 and a model 1993 12-string electric hollowbody that once belonged to Pete Townshend.

Marr has dabbled with guitar synthesizers, and he occasionally plays a Roland GR-50 unit or a Casio MIDI guitar that he uses to

Although he was only a member of the Smiths for about four years, Marr recorded much of his most memorable and popular work with the band, which included bassist Andy Rourke, drummer Mike Joyce, and singer Morrissey.

control various synthesizers. In the studio, he often uses acoustic guitars for overdubs and rhythm tracks. His favorite acoustics are Martins, particularly D-28s, though he also enjoys playing Gibson J-200s.

Inspired by Nils Lofgren, Marr started playing with a thumbpick and his fingers in the late '70s. He wears an Ernie Ball thumbpick on his right hand and strings his guitars with Ernie Ball Regular Slinkies, gauged .010 to .046.

Amplifiers, Effects, and Devices

In the recording studio, Marr favors clean-sounding amplifiers. With the Smiths he used

In His Own Words

I'm not into that self-important, egotistical showing off. I'm too into songs, lyrics, and singers to do it. The whole thing to me smacks of spandex trousers and blond perms.
Musician, *September 1989*

I really like the idea of not knowing what I'm doing. Ultimately, I end up with something more original, a little more from the heart than from the head.
Guitar Player, *January 1990*

I've always believed that any instrumentalist is basically just an accompanist to the singer and the words. That's born out of being a fan of records before I was a fan of guitar players.
Guitar Player, *January 1990*

Rock music from the '50s was built on the guitar, but if you look at the late '70s and the advent of the "SSL" [mixing desk], and at least 14 tracks of drums and drum reverbs, then you've got 12 years of music being built on drums and production. If I was 14 now, the first thing I'd have would be a computer, some reverb, and a sampler.
The Guitar Magazine, *June 1991*

What They Say

Johnny Marr was my guitar hero 'cause to me he had everything – he played so simply compared to these other supposed heroes, yet he was really flash, and when I first saw him with his shades, his mop top and his Rickenbacker, I thought he was just so cool.
Bernard Butler of Suede, The Guitar Magazine, *November 1992*

Johnny Marr is the master of combining guitar sounds. On the track "How Soon Is Now" what he's playing is so layered, it doesn't even sound like guitar.
Johnny Hickman of Cracker, The Guitar Magazine, *July 1994*

Roland JC-120 solid-state amps, Fender Twin Reverbs, Fender Showmans, and Fender Bassmans. On stage he uses a more sophisticated rig, consisting of a Mesa Boogie Quad preamp, a Mesa Boogie 295 tube power amp, and a speaker cabinet loaded with two Electro-Voice 10-inch speakers.

Marr has a small rack of effects that houses a t.c. electronics 2290 multi-effects unit, an Eventide H3000S Ultra-Harmonizer, a Yamaha GEP50 guitar effects processor, and a Roland GP-8 guitar effects processor. He also uses the circuitry from a Dunlop Cry Baby wah-wah pedal that is placed inside an Ernie Ball volume pedal.

Discography

In the late '70s, Marr participated in his first recording session at Nick Lowe's studio. This performance has never been released.

Marr made his recording debut with the Smiths in the early '80s. All of the Smiths albums feature fine, prominent examples of Marr's playing. Studio albums include: **The Smiths**, **Hatful Of Hollow**, **Meat Is Murder**, **The Queen Is Dead**, **The World Won't Listen**, **Louder Than Bombs**, and **Strangeways, Here We Come**. The Smiths recorded one live album, **Rank**, and an EP, **The Peel Sessions**, which was recorded live in BBC studios.

Since he became a full-time member of The The, Marr has recorded several albums with the band, including **Mind Bomb**, **Dusk**, and **Hanky Panky**. His playing can also be heard on the following The The EPs: **Shades Of Blue** and **Dis-infected**. Marr's playing can be heard on six of the nine tracks on **Solitude**, a collection of several The The songs from the band's entire career.

In 1991 Marr was also briefly a member of Electronic, a collaborative project between him and New Order's Bernard Sumner. The band released one record, eponymously titled **Electronic**.

Recording Sessions

After Marr left the Smiths, he became involved in several recording projects. As a guest musician, he appears on Bryan Ferry's **Bête Noir**, the Talking Heads' **Naked**, the Pretenders' single "Windows Of The World"/"1969," Kirsty MacColl's **Kite** and **Electric Landlady**, Sandie Shaw's **Hello Angel**, and Paul McCartney's **Choba B CCCP – The Russian Album**.

Typical Licks

Play this intro with a '60s fuzz box to hear one aspect of Johnny Marr's style.

Marr often plays a clean, bright melodic figure over gentle, 8th-note rhythm guitars.

The rhythm guitar plays the chords while Johnny uses a bright, jangly tone for a bass figure.

Scotty Moore

In Memphis' Sun Studios in 1954, Scotty Moore, Bill Black, and Elvis Presley combined elements of Nashville country music and Mississippi blues to create rock 'n' roll. Moore's Travis-picked rhythms, bluesy leads, and boogie runs influenced many of the early rock guitarists who followed in his footsteps, including Jeff Beck and Jimmy Page. Moore's playing shared the spotlight with the vocalist, making the electric guitar the definitive rock 'n' roll instrument as well as a symbol of youth and rebellion.

The Player

Influences

Scotty Moore grew up in a musical family. His father and three older brothers played country songs on guitar as well as banjo, fiddle, and mandolin. When he was eight years old, Scotty started learning to play guitar. One of his brothers taught him how to play a few chords, but Scotty essentially learned how to play on his own by listening to music on the radio and records.

By the time Scotty was 15, he decided that he wanted to become a professional musician. In 1948, while serving in the armed forces, he formed his first band, and in 1952 in Memphis, Tennessee, he became a member of Doug Poindexter's Starlite Wranglers. With these bands, Moore played country, blues, and pop music in honky tonks. He attributes his experience in honky tonks as the basis for the formative rock 'n' roll sounds he developed a couple of years later with Elvis Presley. "Elvis, Bill Black, and myself somehow or another knocked down some doors to release what I've always called honky tonk music," Moore said in his December '92 *Guitar Player* interview. "All of

us were playing basically the same kind of stuff in clubs, though not exactly the way we did it with 'That's All Right Mama' and that stuff. You played whatever was popular, the number one pop song, whatever. If you had a country band you'd play a pop song with country instruments, and vice versa. Everyone just wanted to dance. As long as you made music everyone could dance to, they didn't care."

Moore's primary influences were country/ pop guitarists Chet Atkins and Merle Travis. "They were my idols," Moore told *Guitar Player*. "But I couldn't play with my thumb and fingers or duplicate note-for-note what they were doing. I would take a little phrase – blues, country, whatever – and turn it around to make it fit something I was trying to do." When recording with Presley, Moore generally used his own version of Atkins- or Travis-style picking, using a thumbpick and his fingers. Ironically, Atkins eventually played rhythm behind Moore's lead guitar on several early Presley recording sessions for RCA.

Moore was also influenced by blues guitarists, and cites B. B. King as an early favorite. "I've always said if you can't play a little blues in any kind of song it ain't worth the paper it's written on," says Moore. "I loved

Background

1931 *Winfield Scott Moore is born on December 27, in Gasden, Tennessee.*

1939 *Scotty starts playing guitar.*

1952 *He leaves the armed services and moves to Memphis to work with his brother at a cleaning plant. He meets Sam Phillips of Sun Records and begins working as a session musician.*

1954 *Moore and bassist Bill Black make their first recordings with Elvis Presley at Memphis, Tennessee's, Sun Studios.*

1958 *Elvis Presley joins the army and Scotty starts his own small record company.*

1965 *Moore records his first solo album, The Guitar That Changed The World.*

1968 *Scotty plays on Elvis' Comeback television special. Shortly afterwards he retires from his career as a musician.*

1976 *Moore comes out of retirement to record with Billy Swan.*

1991 *Scotty performs at the 15th Anniversary Elvis Tribute in Memphis.*

1992 *He releases an album with Carl Perkins and tours Europe for the first time. He also releases a cassette with Carl Perkins, 706 Re-Union, as a limited edition.*

Muddy Waters, Lightnin' Hopkins – you name 'em. I didn't even know their names back then." Traces of Moore's blues influences can be heard on his fills and lead breaks, such as on "Mean Woman Blues."

Jazz is another favorite of Moore's, but he admits that he cannot play it. He is particularly fond of Barney Kessel, Tal Farlow, and Johnny Smith's playing.

In general, Moore enjoys any style of music that features guitar. "I was just into everybody," he admits. "As long as he played guitar he was fine with me. I heard something on the radio, and if there was a guitar player on it, I loved it. Even now, whenever I hear guitar I turn it up. And boy, there's some good ones out there these days."

Approach and Style

Moore's playing approach can best be described as a hybrid of several different styles, primarily country, blues, and pop. He developed his style as a result of playing various types of music in honky tonks and having to duplicate other instruments' parts due to a shortage of musicians in the band. "I've always said I was forced into my way of playing," he told *Guitar Player*. "That was the best thing I could find to make it sound like there was more of us than there was. You do the best you can with what you've got to do at the time."

While playing with the Starlite Wranglers, Moore often imitated steel-guitar and horn parts he heard on popular records. His horn-influenced lines later became a considerable element of his playing with Elvis Presley. He would pluck two-, three-, or four-note chord fragments to make his guitar sound like horn-section harmonies. When he was playing with Presley's stripped-down, three-piece band, Moore used a lot of open chords and open strings to fill in the spaces.

Moore favored basic major, minor, 7th,

and 6th chords, though he occasionally played 13th and 9th chords as well. Instead of playing full barre chords, he usually played fragments that imply a full chord.

Despite the apparent simplicity of Moore's style, he is actually a complex player who mixes approaches at will. On many Elvis singles, he uses Atkins-style fingerpicking for the rhythm, then immediately switches to single-note lines for fills and leads.

Most of Moore's leads are centered around major or pentatonic minor scales, but he sometimes plays chromatic lines and arpeggios. His Atkins-style leads are especially impressive, with alternating bass lines and melodic structures that make them sound like songs within the song.

Techniques

Because of the sparse, three-piece instrumentation on Presley's early recordings, Moore developed a hybrid lead/rhythm playing technique that was loosely based on Atkins- and Travis-picking. Moore uses a thumbpick and three of his fingers, playing alternating bass lines on the lower strings

More than 40 years after he first began to make records with Elvis, Moore is still an active guitarist who often tours and records. Here he is seen with his legendary Gibson Super 400.

with the thumbpick and plucking melody lines or chords on the treble strings with his fingers. "I tried to keep a rhythm going and nose on in with stabs here and there," he says. "I just dialed in and was reaching for it."

By playing staccato chords and using slap-back echo, Moore turned simple rhythms into complex-sounding patterns. A prime example of this technique can be heard on "Mystery Train," where he simply alternates an open E and an open A chord plucked with his fingers between a steady, lower, open E-string pattern that he strikes with the thumbpick.

Sometimes, Moore played with a flatpick instead of a thumbpick and fingers. On a few of the earliest Presley songs, such as "Blue Moon Of Kentucky" and "Harbor Lights," Moore is probably playing with a flatpick. He may have also grabbed the thumbpick between his thumb and forefinger, clutching it like a flatpick.

For his lead breaks, Moore often used a few fancy left-hand techniques. For example, he plays a stunning succession of double-stop triplet pull-offs on the first lead break on "Shake, Rattle, And Roll." He also frequently used slides and slurs for leads and rhythms. Because of the heavy gauge strings that he used on his guitars, Moore did not bend strings very often.

The Hardware

Guitars, Strings, and Picks

Moore's first guitar was a Kalamazoo flat-top acoustic that was probably a hand-me-down from one of his brothers. He traded this for a Sears Silvertone Gene Autry guitar that his brother owned while the same brother was serving in the Navy in World War II. When he was 15, Moore saved the money that he made growing cotton to buy himself a Gibson flat-top acoustic.

Moore recalls playing a variety of inexpensive Japanese electric guitars during the early '50s. By the time he became a member of Doug Poindexter's Starlite Wranglers in 1952, he was playing a Fender Esquire. He says that he did not like the small body, however, and he soon abandoned the Esquire in favor of the guitar that he later used on the earliest Elvis Presley recording sessions, a gold-finished Gibson ES-295 archtop hollowbody electric.

About a year after making his first recording with Presley, Moore acquired a Gibson L-5 archtop hollowbody electric. He used this for several years until he got himself a Gibson Super 400, which, like the previous two guitars, is also a hollowbody archtop electric. Moore still owns and plays the blonde Super 400 that he acquired in the '50s while playing with Elvis. In the early '60s, he bought a sunburst Super 400 with a sharp "Florentine"

Mixing elements of country music and the blues, Scotty Moore was one of the earliest rock 'n' roll guitarists. He made his first records with Elvis Presley in 1954 and inspired countless rockabilly and rock guitarists.

cutaway. This is the guitar that he used for the Elvis "Comeback" television special.

One of Moore's most recent guitar acquisitions is a Gibson Country Gentleman that was given to him by Chet Atkins. "Chet called and asked if I needed a guitar," recalls Moore. "I said 'No, I'm not playing. I don't really need one.' He said 'Well I'm going to give you one.' A few months went by and he showed up at my office and brought this guitar in. Chet's a jewel."

Moore plays with a thumbpick. From the '50s through the '70s, he strung his guitars with Gretsch Chet Atkins heavy-gauge strings.

Amplifiers, Effects, and Devices

During the early '50s, while he was playing with Doug Poindexter and the Starlite Wranglers, Moore used a tweed-covered, "TV-front" Fender Bassman amplifier. He probably used this same amp on his first recordings with Elvis Presley.

To duplicate the slapback tape-echo effects that were created in the studio, Moore purchased an Echo-Sonic amplifier with a built-in echo unit for use onstage. The amp was made by Ray Butts of Cairo,

In His Own Words

I'm coming out the chute after 20 years. It's kind of like getting on a bucking horse. The old fingers have been going through misery, let me tell you.
On his emergence from retirement in 1992, Guitar Player, December 1992

Most of the things we recorded, if you listen close you can hear that we were having a good time. And Elvis always had a good time on stage. That was really his forte.
Guitar Player, December 1992

Elvis is a symbol of an era. I don't think it's the man as much as it is his music. Elvis, Bill Black, and myself somehow or another knocked some doors down to release what I've always called honky tonk music. It's a time people wouldn't mind going back to.
Guitar Player, December 1992

What They Say

When I was ten or eleven, I started listening to rock 'n' roll. The first things that really got me off were the early Sun records with Scotty Moore.
Robert Fripp, Guitar Player, May 1974

The record that made me want to play guitar was "Baby, Let's Play House" by Elvis Presley. I just sort of heard two guitars and bass and thought, "Yeah, I want to be part of this." There was just so much vitality and energy coming out of it.
Jimmy Page, Guitar Player, July 1977

If you want to get into it, I would say buy any Sun record that you can get your hands on. When I first heard Scotty Moore play on Elvis' Sun sessions, it blew me away.
Brian Setzer of Stray Cats, Guitar Player, September 1983

Illinois. Butts' amps were also used by Chet Atkins, Roy Orbison, and Carl Perkins. "I heard Chet using it on a couple of records and started investigating how he got that sound," recalls Moore. "When I found out it was Ray's amp, I drove up to Cairo, Illinois, to get him to build me one. Ray built only about five or six of those amps." Moore first used the Echo-Sonic on "Mystery Train," recorded on July 11, 1955.

Besides the built-in echo in the Echo-Sonic amp, the only other effect that Moore used on his guitar was tape echo that was created in the studio with a pair of tape recorders.

Discography

Moore's first recording was with Doug Poindexter and his Starlite Wranglers on the single "My Kind Of Carryin' On"/"No She Cares No More For Me," released in May, 1954 (Sun). Shortly afterwards, Moore, Elvis Presley, and Bill Black recorded "That's All Right"/"Blue Moon Of Kentucky" at Sun Studios. He played on every Elvis session in the '50s, including the following albums: **Elvis Presley**, **Elvis**, **Loving You**, **Elvis' Christmas Album**, **Elvis' Golden Records**, **King Creole**, **For LP Fans Only**, **A Date With Elvis**, and **Elvis' Gold Records Vol. 2**. The box set, **Elvis – The King Of Rock 'n' Roll: The Complete 50's Masters** contains all of his studio sessions with Elvis and rare live recordings. **The Complete Sun Sessions** album is a good, though less detailed, overview of Moore's finest moments with Elvis. Moore played on many of Elvis' albums in the '60s, including **Elvis Is Back**, **G.I. Blues**, and **NBC TV Special**, the soundtrack to Elvis' "Comeback" special.

Moore also made a few solo records. In the late '50s he recorded "Have Guitar Will Travel," (Fernwood). In the mid-'60s he recorded **The Guitar That Changed The World**, and in 1970 he released **What's Left**, with Elvis' drummer D.J. Fontana. In 1992, he released **Moore Feel Good Music** and **706 Re-Union – A Sentimental Journey** with Carl Perkins, on his own Belle Meade label.

Recording Sessions

Besides his work with Presley, Moore did not do any session work until the '60s, when he played on several Chess/Checker releases, including Dale Hawkins' "Class Cutter" and recordings with Harvey And The Moonglows, and Eddie Hill and Texas Bill Strength. In the '60s, he was a producer for Sun Records, and played on a few of these sessions, including Danny Stewart's "I'll Change My Ways" and a six-string bass part on Jerry Lee Lewis' "When I Get Paid." In the '70s, he played on "EP Express" with Carl Perkins, Billy Swan's **Billy Swan** and **You're O.K., I'm O.K.**, Ral Donner's **1935-1977 "I've Been Away For A While Now…"** and Phil Sweet's **Memphis Blue Streak**. He did not appear on any records in the '80s, but in the '90s he played on Chip Young's **Having Thumb Fun With My Friends** and "Little Buster" and "Shame, Shame, Shame" on **Lee Rocker's Big Blue**.

Typical Licks

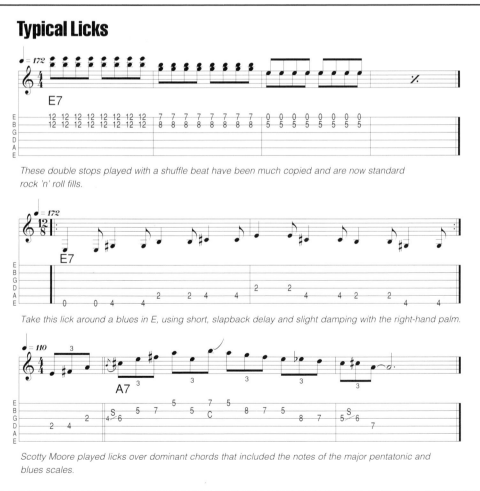

These double stops played with a shuffle beat have been much copied and are now standard rock 'n' roll fills.

Take this lick around a blues in E, using short, slapback delay and slight damping with the right-hand palm.

Scotty Moore played licks over dominant chords that included the notes of the major pentatonic and blues scales.

Muddy Waters

Nicknamed "The Father Of Chicago Blues" and "The Father Of Electric Blues," Muddy Waters possessed a strong understanding of the power of simplicity and emotion. An impressive slide and acoustic guitarist, his influence extended from Chicago to London, where his music was embraced by many young rock guitarists in the early '60s. Mixing urban blues with rural Delta blues styles played through an electric guitar, Waters developed a raw, stripped-down band sound that became the blueprint for modern blues and rock 'n' roll.

The Player

Influences

Waters' father played blues guitar, but Muddy was sent to live with his grandmother when he was three years old, so it is unlikely that his father had a lasting influence on him. While growing up on Stovall's Plantation in Clarksdale, Mississippi, Waters enjoyed making music by banging on a kerosene can and singing. Later he tried to learn to play accordion and the Jew's harp.

When Waters was 13, he started playing the harmonica, and he learned to play the guitar when he was 17. He taught himself to play chords and picked up a few lead patterns by watching his friend Scott Bohannon play the guitar. Eventually he had become proficient enough to join a band and play in juke joints. For a brief period, he played harmonica in a band with guitarist Robert McCollum, who later became known as the blues artist Robert Nighthawk. Around this time, Waters also sang in gospel groups.

With money that he had saved while working on the plantation, Waters bought 78s by Blind Blake, Blind Lemon Jefferson, Blind Boy Fuller, and Charlie Patton. At a local juke joint he was exposed to the playing of Son House, who became one of his biggest influences. It was House who taught Waters how to play slide guitar. Around this time, Muddy also became heavily influenced by the Delta-blues style of guitarist/singer Robert Johnson. Waters' Delta-blues influences are evident on his first recordings, which were captured by Alan Lomax in 1941 and 1942 for the United States Library Of Congress.

Waters learned to play a variety of different musical styles in juke joints and at country balls. To please the clientele, he needed to know how to play country blues, pop songs, and country-and-western standards. When he moved to Chicago in 1943, he became exposed to big-band music, ballad singers, and the urban-blues stylings of Lonnie Johnson, Tampa Red, and Big Bill Broonzy. Although Waters' style remained deeply rooted in Delta blues, he quickly developed his own sound, playing electric slide guitar by mixing elements of urban and Delta blues.

By the mid-'40s, Waters was working with Claude "Blue Smitty" Smith, playing covers of Robert Johnson and Leroy Carr songs that he learned from 78s. They also performed a

Background

1915 *McKinley Morganfield is born on April 4, in Rolling Fork, Mississippi.*

1918 *Moves to Clarksdale, the center of the famed Delta, home of the blues.*

1930 *Muddy forms his first quartet and plays pop, hillbilly, and blues.*

1932 *Buys his first guitar, a second-hand Stella.*

1935 *Muddy starts to play guitar and sing.*

1941 *Waters makes his first recordings for the Library of Congress.*

1943 *Muddy moves to Chicago, where he meets and befriends blues legend Big Bill Broonzy.*

1944 *He receives his first electric guitar from his uncle.*

1946 *His second commercial session is organized by Lester Melrose for Columbia Records.*

1947 *Waters starts recording for Chess Records.*

1948 *"I Can't Be Satisfied" becomes a hit in Chicago and the South.*

1953 *"Hoochie Coochie Man" becomes Waters biggest seller and spends many weeks in the R&B Top Ten.*

1955 *Chuck Berry asks for advice from Muddy, who tells him to go to Chess Records with his audition tape.*

1958 *Waters makes his first trip to England during the height of the folk revival.*

1959 *He plays Carnegie Recital Hall, along with James Cotton and Memphis Slim.*

1960 *Waters headlines the Newport Jazz Festival.*

1968 *Takes part in sessions with Paul Butterfield and Mike Bloomfield for the album Fathers And Sons.*

1969 *His right hand is paralyzed in an automobile accident. He recovers a year later.*

1972 *Muddy works with Rory Gallagher, Steve Winwood and Mitch Mitchell on The London Sessions.*

1976 *Appears at The Band's farewell gig.*

1977 *He performs for President Jimmy Carter at White House staff picnic. He wins a Grammy for Hard Again.*

1983 *Muddy Waters dies on April 30, in Chicago, Illinois.*

few original compositions. Smitty showed Waters how to play using his fingers and a slide at the same time, helping Waters to shape the style that became his trademark during the late '40s and early '50s, when he made his early recordings for Chess.

Approach and Style

When he was approached by Alan Lomax at Stovall's Plantation, Waters style was very similar to the fingerpicked Delta-blues style favored by Son House and Robert Johnson. Using a bottleneck slide, Muddy played either picked chordal rhythms or simple, single-note bass lines. All of the notes were either open strings or produced by touching the slide to the strings.

Waters started using metal fingerpicks while he was playing in clubs in Chicago as a backup musician for Sonny Boy Williamson. This was an attempt to generate more volume out of his acoustic guitar. When he later got an electric guitar, he stopped using the fingerpicks. Waters' style became more sophisticated after Claude "Blue Smitty" Smith showed him how to play by fretting notes with his index, middle, and ring fingers while wearing the slide on his little finger. From then on, he played by alternating fretted notes with slide patterns.

Waters used a variety of open tunings during his career. In the early days, he generally preferred open D (D, A, D, F#, A, D, low to high) and open A (E, A, E, A, C#, E, low to high). In the '50s, he started using open G (D, G, D, G, B, D, low to high) more frequently, and later he preferred open E (E, B, E, G#, B, E, low to high). Towards the latter part of his life, Waters kept his guitar in standard tuning because he did not want to mess with changing tunings or guitars while performing live.

His use of open tunings allowed him to use open strings quite liberally. If a song was in a different key than the guitar was tuned to, he placed a capo on the neck according to the appropriate key. Waters generally played chords on the upper three strings, with the slide placed straight above the fret, and he played single-note bass lines with the slide on the lower strings.

Waters' early songs seldom broke away from standard 12-bar blues structures, but in the early '50s he began to experiment with groove-oriented arrangements that became his signature style on songs such as "Hoochie Coochie Man" and "I Just Want To Make Love To You." Waters often doubled his vocal melodies with slide guitar lines. "Me and my guitar, we have a conversation and talk together," he once commented.

Techniques

Although Waters' slide playing was sparse and economical, it was by no means simple. He had an acute sense of tone, and his playing frequently made effective use of

Armed with a Les Paul and a huge, powerful voice, Muddy Waters recorded many blues classics for Chess Records in Chicago during the '50s and early '60s.

microtones (notes in between the standard 12 notes in a scale), which gave his lines a distinctive, inimitable sound.

Waters started playing slide by wearing it on his left-hand middle finger, but when he started fretting notes as well as playing with the slide, he began to wear it on his little finger. He eventually became adept at playing chords while fretting notes simultaneously with his fingers and the slide.

Waters played with a thumbpick and his fingers. He often damped the treble strings with his right-hand fingers, and he picked notes with the thumbpick. He liked to pat his right-hand palm rhythmically against the strings, creating a clicking sound by touching the strings against the pickup.

For most of his rhythm work, Waters preferred to play through the neck pickup or both pickups at once, but for leads he often switched to the treble pickup because he liked the clarity and the bite.

The Hardware

Guitars, Strings, and Picks

Waters first guitar was a second-hand Stella acoustic that he bought from Ed Moore for $2.50 in 1932. He often bragged that he made 50 cents playing the guitar on the first day that he owned it. Later he saved up 11 dollars to buy himself a Sears Silvertone acoustic. Waters did not have a guitar when Alan Lomax located him to make the Library Of Congress recordings in 1941, so Waters borrowed Lomax's Martin flat-top acoustic.

When he arrived in Chicago, Waters was still playing acoustic guitars. After about a year of struggling to be heard over the chatter of people in nightclubs, he acquired his first electric guitar from his uncle. He could not remember what type of guitar it was, but he mentioned that it was a cheap, off-brand electric. By the time he made his first recordings for the Chess label, Waters owned a hollowbody Gretsch archtop electric fitted with a single DeArmond pickup. Soon after that he acquired an early '50s Gibson Les Paul gold-top solidbody, with two single-coil P-90 pickups. He used this guitar until 1957, when he purchased his trademark Fender Telecaster. The Tele underwent several modifications over the years. It was painted red, the knobs were replaced with ones from a '60s Fender amplifier, the nut was raised, and a thicker neck was placed on the guitar. "I think the big neck has a lot to do with the big sound," Waters told Tom Wheeler in *Guitar Player* in 1983. Waters set up his Tele with heavy strings (the *E* string was a .012), and a high action.

Waters used a sawed-off bottleneck for a slide in the early days, but later started using a short chrome Craftsman socket. When he

Known as the "Father Of Electric Blues," Muddy Waters created a raw, stripped-down style of music that influenced several generations of Chicago blues artists, as well as many rock guitarists.

first arrived in Chicago, he played with a metal thumbpick, but soon switched to a plastic version. "No way could I use a regular flatpick," he recalled.

Amplifiers, Effects, and Devices

Like most early electric blues guitarists, Waters used whatever amplification was readily available. While playing in Chicago clubs, he most likely used a variety of different Fender and Gibson amps, but this has not been documented in any detail. Later in his career, he expressed a preference for his Fender Super Reverb combo with four 10-inch speakers. "I don't like the Twin – different sound," he commented. Waters also liked to play through Johnny Winter's Music Man amplifiers.

Except for the misguided *Electric Mud* album, which featured liberal amounts of wah-wah and fuzztone guitar, Waters never used any effects. "If you've got to have big amplifiers and wah-wahs and equipment to make your guitar say different things, well, hell, you can't play no blues," he remarked in reference to *Electric Mud*.

In His Own Words

I had a part of my own, part of Son House, and a little part of Robert Johnson. Really, though, it was Son House who influenced me to play. I was really behind Son House all the way.
Downbeat, *1969*

No matter what you do, some things come out all different, just your own. It's like singing. Your face, and what you're doing on your face, will change the tone of your voice. That's where my tone is.
Guitar Player, *August 1983*

I can't make the guitar say as much as my voice, but I try to get it as close as I can. I'm no hell of a guitar player, not the best guitar walkin' around the streets. But the feeling that I put into my guitar – a lot of players can't put it there.
Guitar Player, *August 1983*

What They Say

The first guitarist I was aware of was Muddy Waters. I heard one of his records when I was a little boy, and it scared me to death.
Jimi Hendrix, Rolling Stone

Muddy was real modest about his own guitar playing. He didn't feel like he was that great. I remember him saying, "Well, even an old man probably can outplay me, but I got something now that works."
Johnny Winter, Guitar Player, *August 1983*

Muddy's music turned me on when I was about 13 years old, you know, because it's so simple. It's so natural. I fall back on these players that hit all the right notes.
Slash, Guitar Player, *May 1993*

Muddy Waters is one of the great performers of all time. He's won more awards than I could name. His music is well known around the world, comes from a good part of the country, and represents accurately the background and history of the American people.
U. S. President Jimmy Carter, August 1977

Discography

Waters' first recordings were for the U.S. Library Of Congress in 1941 and 1942, and are available on MCA's **Muddy Waters – The Complete Plantation Recordings**.

Waters made his first recordings in Chicago in 1946. "Mean Red Spider" features him on lead vocals and guitar. He also recorded "Jitterbug Blues," "Hard Day Blues," and "Burying Ground Blues," which weren't released until the '70s. His '40s Chicago recordings are featured on **Chicago Blues: The Beginning** and **OKeh Chicago Blues**.

Waters began recording for Chess Records in 1947. He fronted Guitar Slim's band on "Gypsy Woman" and "Little Annie Mae." In 1948 he recorded "I Can't Be Satisfied"/"Feel Like Going Home," his first big hit.

Chess has released several albums featuring Waters' music: **The Best Of Muddy Waters, Muddy Waters Sings Big Bill Broonzy, Muddy Waters At Newport, 1960, Folk Singer, The Real Folk Blues, Muddy, Brass & Blues, More Real Folk Blues, Electric Mud** (originally released on Cadet), **After The Rain, Fathers And Sons, Sail On, They Call Me Muddy Waters, McKinley Morganfield A.K.A. Muddy Waters, Live (At Mister Kelly's), The London Muddy Waters Sessions, Can't Get No Grindin', London Revisited With Howlin' Wolf, "Unk" In Funk, The Muddy Waters Woodstock Album, Rolling Stone, Rare And Unissued,** and **Trouble No More/Singles (1955-1959)**. Chess' **Muddy Waters – The Chess Box** is an excellent overview of Waters' Chess recordings.

Muddy Waters albums released on other labels include: **Muddy Waters, 1958** (recorded live in England), **Mud In Your Ear, Muddy Waters Live, 1965-'68, Live In Paris, 1968,** and **Live In Antibes, 1974**.

In the '70s Johnny Winter helped Waters to sign with Columbia. The albums **Hard Again, I'm Ready, Muddy "Mississippi" Waters Live,** and **King Bee** all contain fine examples of Waters' latter-day music.

Waters also recorded several movie soundtracks, including **Mandingo, The Last Waltz, Dynamite Chicken,** and **Street Girls**.

Recording Sessions

Waters appeared on records by many other Chicago blues artists. These albums include the Baby Face Leroy Trio's **Chicago Blues: The Early 1950s**, Otis Spann's **The Blues Never Die!, Half Ain't Been Told, The Blues Is Where It's At, Take Me Back Home, Heart Loaded With Trouble, Bottom Of The Blues, Nobody Knows Chicago Like I Do,** and **Rarest Recordings**, Little Walter's **The Best Of Little Walter, The Best Of Little Walter, Vol. 2, Boss Blues Harmonica,** and **Little Walter**, Jimmy Rogers' **Chicago Bound** and **Jimmy Rogers**, Sonny Boy Williamson's **One Way Out** and **Down And Out Blues**, Junior Wells' **Blues Hit Big Town**, Luther Johnson's **Chicken Shack**, Johnny Winter's **Nothin' But The Blues**, Willie Dixon's **The Chess Box**, and John Lee Hooker's **Live At Cafe Au-Go-Go**.

Typical Licks

Muddy often used to end a blues chorus with a turnaround similar to this.

Some of Muddy's tunes use a strong riff as the backbone of the tune (let the bend release into a pull-off).

Muddy embellishes the melody by playing bottleneck licks in between his vocal lines.

Jimmy Page

With Led Zeppelin, Jimmy Page shattered conventional notions of rock-guitar playing. His orchestrated, multi-tracked guitar parts brought rock music to a new level of sophistication, and his playing encompassed several diverse influences, including the blues, classical, Celtic, Indian, and Arabic music. On Led Zeppelin's early albums, Page set the foundation for many heavy-metal groups that followed and influenced many of today's current crop of rock guitarists.

The Player

Influences

Jimmy Page was heavily inspired by early rock 'n' roll music. He remarks that Elvis Presley's "Baby Let's Play House," with Scotty Moore on guitar, made him interested in playing. He also liked the music of Ricky Nelson (with James Burton on guitar), Gene Vincent, and Buddy Holly. One of the first things he learned to play on the guitar was the chord solo to Buddy Holly's "Peggy Sue." He was particularly fond of Burton's string-bending style, and later learned how to play the solo to Ricky Nelson's "My Babe" from Jeff Beck.

Although Page owned the popular instruction book *Play In A Day* by Burt Weedon and took a few guitar lessons, he primarily taught himself to play by ear and he did not learn to read music until several years later.

Page later became interested in the playing style and studio approach of Les Paul. "That's where I heard feedback from first," Page told Steve Rosen in *Guitar Player*. "Also vibrato and things." Many of Page's overdubbed guitar parts and studio experiments with Led Zeppelin were influenced by Les Paul's records made during the '50s.

Like many other young British rock guitarists in the early '60s, Page became fascinated with the blues. He comments that he was introduced to the blues through Chess Records' rock 'n' roll artists, such as Chuck Berry and Bo Diddley. Hubert Sumlin, who played guitar with Howlin' Wolf, was a huge influence on Page, and many Led Zeppelin songs were based around Howlin' Wolf songs. Page's other blues-guitar influences include Elmore James, B. B. King, Freddie King, Albert King, Otis Rush, and Matt "Guitar" Murphy, whom Page saw onstage with Muddy Waters in the early '60s. He also enjoys the Delta-blues styles of artists such as Robert Johnson, whose "Travelling Riverside Blues" was covered by Led Zeppelin.

Page adopted several influences beyond rock and blues music, which accounts for the distinctive sound of his playing. Celtic music influences show up in much of his acoustic guitar playing. He cites Bert Jansch, John Renbourn, and Davey Graham as particularly important figures in the development of his fingerpicking style as well as the composition of his solo acoustic guitar pieces "Black Mountain Side" and "Bron-Yr-Aur." He also enjoys Spanish flamenco and classical guitar.

In the mid-'60s, Page became fascinated

Background

1944 *James Patrick Page is born on January 9, in Heston, Middlesex, England.*

1959 *Jimmy starts playing guitar, partly by watching his friends and guitarists at music stores.*

1960 *He joins his first band, Neil Christian's Crusaders.*

1966 *He joins the Yardbirds as bass guitarist.*

1967 *Jimmy plays on Jeff Beck's album,* Truth.

1968 *The Yardbirds break up and Page forms the New Yardbirds, which eventually becomes Led Zeppelin.*

1969 *Led Zeppelin's first album hits gold in the U.S. They play at the 16th Annual Newport Jazz Festival, which features heavy-rock acts for the first time in its history.*

1970 *Led Zeppelin play gigs in Copenhagen under the name The Nobs, after Eva Von Zeppelin objects to the group using her family name.*

1974 *The group launch their own record label, Swansong.*

1975 *Jimmy breaks a finger during rehearsals for the Madison Square Gardens concerts in New York.*

1977 *With Page ill, and the death of Robert Plant's 5-year-old son, Led Zeppelin's tour of the U.S. collapses.*

1979 *Zeppelin play at the Knebworth Festival in England, their first gig in two years.*

1980 *Led Zeppelin disbands after the death of drummer John Bonham.*

1982 *Page records the* Death Wish II *soundtrack.*

1985 *The remaining members of Led Zeppelin reunite for the Live Aid concert at Wembley Stadium, London.*

1987 *Zeppelin settle out of court with R&B artist Willie Dixon, who claims that "Whole Lotta Love" is based on his song "You Need Love."*

1988 *Page releases his first solo album,* Outrider. *Led Zeppelin reforms for the Atlantic Records 40th-Anniversary celebration.*

1993 *Page and ex-Whitesnake vocalist David Coverdale release the album* Coverdale Page.

1994 *Page and Robert Plant reunite for MTV's* Un-Led-ded *television special.*

with Indian music. He attended concerts by sitar maestro Ravi Shankar, and discovered Indian classical music during several trips to India. He later developed a liking for Arabic music and, prompted by William S. Burroughs, went to Marrakesh to learn about Moroccan music. His Arabic influences are especially prevalent on Led Zeppelin's "Kashmir."

Jazz and country are the only styles of music that Page does not say were influential. Although he has played pedal steel on several songs and plays guitars equipped with a Parsons-White *B*-string bender, he says that Chuck Berry's "Blue Feeling" and the Byrds' live version of "Eight Miles High" inspired him to dabble with those instruments.

Approach and Style

Page's style is characterized by his unique amalgamation of different musical influences. His playing borrows liberally from rock, blues, classical, Celtic, Indian, and Arabic music.

Although Page played on hundreds of sessions and with the Yardbirds during the '60s, he recorded his most lasting and influential work with Led Zeppelin during the late '60s and '70s.

Many of his single-note lines are centered around standard minor pentatonic blues scales, but he often ventures into exotic-sounding, non-Western modal scales. A few of his songs employ odd meters, which he says are influenced by Indian music and some of Howlin' Wolf's blues songs.

He frequently tunes his guitars to open or alternate tunings to take advantage of ringing open strings and unisons that create a full, lush rhythm sound. His favorite tunings (all low to high) include *D, A, D, G, A, D*, used on "Kashmir" and "Black Mountain Side," *E, A, D, A, D, E* ("The Rain Song"), *C, A, C, G, C, E* ("Friends," "Bron-Yr-Aur," and "Poor Tom"), and open *A* (*E, A, E, A, C♯, E*, low to high), used on "Celebration Day." He also uses open *C* (*C, G, C, E, G, C*, low to high), open *G* (*D, G, D, G, B, D*), and open *E* modal (*E, B, E, A, B, E*).

Page often plays the same chord shapes up and down the neck in conjunction with open strings. He also likes to use classical-influenced contrapuntal and contrary lines, a good example of which is the introduction to "Stairway To Heaven." He often assumed the role of orchestrator as well as player in the studio, and his studio performances feature multi-tracked guitar parts and complex harmonies.

Techniques

Page's right-hand technique centers around a hybrid picking style. "It's a cross between fingerstyle and flatpicking," he told Steve Rosen in *Guitar Player*. "My fingerpicking is a cross between Pete Seeger, Earl Scruggs, and total incompetence." For fast rhythms and single-note lines, Jimmy mainly relies on the flatpick.

His left-hand technique comprises liberal use of the usual rock guitarist's arsenal of vibrato, hammer-ons, and pull-offs. Many of his leads feature quick triplet pull-off patterns played on one or two strings. He often uses open strings as pedal tones in pull-off patterns.

Page usually bends strings with his left-hand ring finger, supporting the bend with the index and middle fingers. His bending technique is aggressive, and he often plays over-extended bends that reach as high as two whole-steps. Sometimes he bends open strings by pressing down on them behind the nut, as on his solo break on "Heartbreaker."

Always open to exploring new sounds, Page adopted a few "non-conventional" playing techniques, such as using feedback and electronic effects. While he was a studio guitarist, he started experimenting with playing the guitar with a violin bow, using it to strike chords percussively or draw sustaining lines from the strings. His solo on "Dazed And Confused" features a good example of this.

The Hardware

Guitars, Strings, and Picks

Page's first guitar was a Spanish-style acoustic with steel strings, given to him by his parents, on which he taught himself to play. He later bought a Hofner Senator, on which he installed a pickup to make it an electric. His first true electric guitar was a Grazioso. By the time he joined Neil Christian's Crusaders, Page was playing a hollowbody Gretsch 6120 Chet Atkins electric. Next, he acquired a stereo Gibson ES-355 that he later traded for a black, three-pickup Gibson Les Paul Custom. He used the Custom on most of his mid-'60s studio sessions; it was stolen or lost during his first trip to the U.S. with the Yardbirds.

While in the Yardbirds, Page started playing a white '66 Fender Telecaster with a maple neck given to him by Jeff Beck. Shortly afterwards, he also acquired a '58 Gibson Les Paul Standard. Since then, the Telecaster and Les Paul have remained Page's main electric guitars. He currently owns several Telecasters equipped with Parsons-White *B*-string benders.

He also has a '59 Les Paul Standard he acquired from Joe Walsh while touring the U.S. with Led Zeppelin, a mid-'70s Les Paul with a Parsons-White device, and an early-'90s Les Paul fitted with a TransPerformance Digital Tuning System, a computer-controlled bridge device that automatically changes tunings.

Page used several different 12-string electric guitars in the studio, including a Vox 12-string and a Fender Electric XII. Onstage he uses a Gibson EDS-1275 double-neck electric with separate 12- and 6-string necks. The doubleneck was custom built at the Gibson factory in the early '70s.

Page owns over 100 guitars. Other notable electrics that he uses often include an early-'60s Lake Placid Blue Fender Stratocaster, an early-'60s Danelectro that he assembled from the parts of two guitars, and a Gibson ES-5 Switchmaster that he used on the *Death Wish II* soundtrack.

Some of Page's favorite acoustic guitars include Martin D-18, D-28, and D-45 flat-tops, a Gibson Everly Brothers model given to him by Ronnie Wood, and a Gibson-made Cromwell from the '20s. He borrowed a Gibson J-200 for *Led Zeppelin I*, and recorded many of his acoustic guitar parts on Led Zeppelin records playing an inexpensive Harmony.

Page is often described as a heavy-metal or hard-rock guitarist, but his playing was heavily influenced by a diverse mixture of styles, including blues, classical, Celtic, Indian, and Arabic.

Page plays with heavy Herco Flex 75 picks. His slide is a piece of chrome tubing. All of his guitars are strung with Ernie Ball strings – light-gauge Super Slinkies on his electrics, and Earthwood phosphor-bronze strings on his acoustics.

Amplifiers, Effects, and Devices

Page used a variety of different amps during his early studio session days, including a Burns and a Fender Super Reverb. One of his favorite amps was a small Supro combo with a single 12-inch speaker. He used this amp on many Led Zeppelin albums as well.

With the Yardbirds, Page played through Vox AC30 amps. With Led Zeppelin, he switched to 100-watt Marshalls, customized to 200-watts of output for onstage use. During Led Zeppelin's first U.S. tour, he played through solid-state Rickenbacker Transonic amps. In the studio, he sometimes plugged his guitar into a Leslie. His solo on "Good Times Bad Times" from *Led Zeppelin I* is one example of this.

Page owns a large collection of amplifiers, including several Marshalls, Voxes, Hiwatts, and Fenders. The Fender Vibro-King and Tonemaster are among his new favorites.

Page uses only a limited amount of effects. He used a Roger Mayer Tonebender fuzztone with the Yardbirds and on recording sessions in the '60s. Onstage with Led Zeppelin he used a Vox Cry Baby wah-wah pedal, an Eventide Harmonizer, and an Echoplex. On Led Zeppelin's *In Through The Out Door* he used a Gizmotron sustain device on "In The Evening" and an MXR Blue Box for his solo on "Fool In The Rain." He frequently employs several outboard effects in the studio, including digital delays and digital reverb, compressors and limiters.

In the '80s Page experimented with guitar synthesizers and played a Roland GR-700 unit on the *Death Wish II* soundtrack.

In His Own Words

My vocation is more in composition really than in anything else – building up harmonies using the guitar, orchestrating the guitar like an army, a guitar army.
Guitar Player, *July 1977*

I've got two different approaches, like a schizophrenic guitarist, really. Onstage is totally different than the way that I approach it in the studio.
Guitar Player, *July 1977*

I was always a sloppy guitarist. I never had the technique of a John McLaughlin. I suppose you make up with originality what you don't have in technique.
Musician, *November 1990*

What They Say

Jimmy Page is very critical of his playing, but if he plays something good, he knows it's there.
Ron Wood, Guitar Player, *December 1975*

He's a genius. He's a great player, a songwriter, a producer. Put it this way, he might not be the greatest executor of whatever, but when you hear a Page solo, he speaks.
Eddie Van Halen, Guitar World, *July 1990*

Jimmy Page's solos are fantastic, but it's his sense of composition that has everybody down. He carries a total sense of vision. To me, he's the one who took over what Jimi Hendrix was doing.
Carlos Santana, Guitar Player, *January 1991*

Page had the ability not only to think up a good riff but also write a great song round it and get the right guitar sound. On "Whole Lotta Love" you can hear the riff driving things along without ever obscuring Plant. He was a great arranger – the band always came first for him.
Joe Satriani, The Guitar Magazine, *February 1992*

Discography

Page's recording debut was with Neil Christian's Crusaders on the single "The Road To Love"/"Big Beat Drum" in 1962. He also played on their follow-up single, "A Little Bit Of Someone Else"/"Get A Load Of This." He then joined Carter-Lewis And The Southerners, playing on the singles "Sweet And Tender Romance"/"Who Told You," "Your Momma's Out Of Town"/"Somebody Told My Girl," and "Skinnie Minnie"/"Easy To Cry." In early '64, he joined Mickey Finn And The Blue Men and recorded the singles "Pills"/"Hush Your Mouth" and "Sporting Life"/"Night Comes Down."

He made his first solo recording, "She Just Satisfies"/"Keep Moving," in 1965. His other solo singles, "Skin Deep"/"Zoom, Widge And Wag" and "Teensville"/ "Grotty Drums," did not credit him on the label. In 1966, he worked with Eric Clapton on several blues recordings for **Blues Anytime** (Immediate).

In the summer of '66, Page joined the Yardbirds. He and Jeff Beck share guitar duties on the single "Happenings Ten Years Time Ago"/"Psycho Daisies" and the song "Stroll On," which appeared on the **Blow Up** soundtrack. All of Page's Yardbirds studio recordings after Beck quit the group in 1966, including previously unreleased rarities, appears on EMI's **The Yardbirds – Little Games Sessions & More**. A live album, **Live Yardbirds Featuring Jimmy Page**, was released in 1971, but was quickly withdrawn.

The best examples of Page's guitar playing are his work with Led Zeppelin. The band released eight studio albums – **Led Zeppelin I**, **Led Zeppelin II**, **Led Zeppelin III**, an untitled fourth album known as "Led Zeppelin IV," **Houses Of The Holy**, **Physical Graffiti**, **Presence**, and **In Through The Out Door**. **The Song Remains The Same** soundtrack is the only legitimate Led Zeppelin live recording. An album of left-over studio tracks, **Coda**, was released in 1982. Atlantic's four-CD **Led Zeppelin** box set provides an excellent overview of the band's music, plus the previously unreleased "White Summer/Black Mountain Side" and "Travelling Riverside Blues." Atlantic's **Led Zeppelin – Boxed Set 2** contains the remaining Led Zeppelin material.

In 1982 Page recorded the soundtrack to the film **Death Wish II**. He recorded two albums with the Firm in the mid-'80s, **The Firm** and **Mean Business**. He released his first solo album, **Outrider**, in 1988. In 1993 he made **Coverdale Page** with ex-Whitesnake vocalist David Coverdale. In 1994 he recorded **No Quarter** with Robert Plant.

Typical Licks

Jimmy Page was one of the first guitarists to play fast blues licks over high-energy rock rhythms.

This lick shows Page playing a line from the D major pentatonic scale, giving his licks a country-rock flavour.

Jimmy had great "chops" for his era. Here he sequences a D minor pentatonic scale over a dominant chord.

Recording Sessions

Page had a prolific career as a studio guitarist in the '60s, and he played on hundreds of sessions for artists, ranging from the Who, the Kinks, and Them to Burt Bacharach, Paul Anka, and Petula Clark. One of his first sessions was for the song "Diamonds" by Jet Harris and Tony Meehan. Some of his better-known sessions include "Baby Please Don't Go"/ "Gloria" with Them, "You Really Got Me" and "All Day And All Of The Night" with the Kinks, the Who's "I Can't Explain"/ "Bald Headed Woman," and Donovan's "Sunshine Superman." He also played on the debut albums by these three groups, and co-wrote the song "Revenge" on the Kinks first album. The CDs **Session Man Vol. 1** and **Session Man Vol. 2** contain a good sampling of Page's mid-'60s session work.

After joining the Yardbirds, Page's only major session was for Jeff Beck's "Beck's Bolero," which he co-wrote. After the Yardbirds broke up, his one notable session was for P.J. Proby's **Three Week Hero**, featuring Led Zeppelin's lineup.

Page guested on a few records during Led Zeppelin's early years, including Screaming Lord Sutch's **Lord Sutch And Heavy Friends** and Joe Cocker's **With A Little Help From My Friends**. After Led Zeppelin broke up, he appeared on John Paul Jones' soundtrack to **Scream For Help**, "One Hit To The Body" on the Rolling Stones' **Dirty Work**, "Heaven Knows" and "Tall Cool One" on Robert Plant's **Now And Zen**, and "Sea Of Love" on Plant's **The Honeydrippers Vol. 1**.

Keith Richards

With a playing style that is recognizable from when he strikes his first chord, Keith Richards is one of rock 'n' roll's most original rhythm-guitar stylists. Using a 5-string guitar usually tuned to open G, he has developed a distinctive chordal vocabulary and syncopated rhythmic style few guitarists can duplicate. As a member of the Rolling Stones he has explored several musical genres, including rock 'n' roll, blues, country, reggae, and funk. He remains a powerful and influential force in rock 'n' roll after more than 30 years in the limelight.

The Player

Influences

Keith was first exposed to music at an early age by his grandfather, who was a guitarist, fiddler, and saxophonist. Apparently inspired by the movies he saw on weekends as a child, a five-year-old Richards told his playmate Mick Jagger that he wanted to be like Roy Rogers and play guitar.

Keith received his first guitar when he was 13, and this was also the time when he first heard rock 'n' roll music. Elvis Presley's "That's All Right" was the first song he learned. Richards never learned to read music. He taught himself to play by listening to records by Cliff Richard, Ricky Nelson, Buddy Holly, and Chuck Berry, who became one of his biggest influences. "Chuck was my man," Richards told Tom Wheeler in *Guitar Player*. "He was the one that made me say as a teenager, 'I want to play guitar.' I spent so long learning from him and his records that there's got to be so much influence in there."

In 1959, Richards started attending Sidcup Art College, where he was exposed to a wide range of music, including jazz, blues, and American folk. At school he picked up playing tips by watching and listening to other guitarists. He learned to play songs by folk artists Ramblin' Jack Elliot and Woodie Guthrie, and he started playing in bands. Richards notes that Don Everly's rhythm playing with the Everly Brothers heavily influenced his own rhythm style.

Blues music had a profound effect on Richards, and he started listening to records by John Lee Hooker, Jimmy Reed, Willie Dixon, Fred McDowell, Blind Willie McTell, Elmore James, Slim Harpo, Robert Johnson, and Big Bill Broonzy. Muddy Waters was one of Keith's favorite blues artists. The Rolling Stones adopted their name from Waters' "Rollin' Stone," and the band later backed up Waters on several occasions. "If we could turn people on to Muddy, Jimmy Reed, Howlin' Wolf, and John Lee Hooker, then our job was done," Richards remarked to Jas Obrecht In *Guitar Player*.

Richards was also heavily influenced by country music. He learned several country-and-western songs when he first started playing guitar, but it wasn't until 1968, when he met Gram Parsons of the Byrds and the Flying Burrito Brothers, that his interest in country music was renewed. Parsons acquainted Richards with the various styles of

Background

1943 Keith Richards is born in Dartford, Kent, on December 18.

1956 Keith receives his first guitar.

1962 Richards forms the Rolling Stones with Mick Jagger and Brian Jones.

1963 The Rolling Stones are signed to Decca.

1965 The single "Satisfaction" goes to number 1 on U.S. and U.K. pop charts.

1967 Richards and Mick Jagger are arrested on drug offences. Found guilty, they are initially jailed, then released on bail. On appeal, the sentences are quashed.

1968 He is introduced to Gram Parsons, who piques his interest in country music.

1971 Keith and the other Rolling Stones emigrate to France for tax purposes.

1972 The Rolling Stones release Exile On Main Street, considered by many critics to be their finest album.

1977 Keith is arrested in Toronto and charged with possession of heroin and intent to traffic. Faced with the very real possibility of a 30-year jail sentence, he was admitted into a New York clinic for addiction therapy.

1978 In court in Toronto, he pleads guilty to possession of heroin. Impressed by his efforts to come off heroin, the judge imposes a suspended sentence, on condition that Richards continue the therapy regime and plays a benefit concert for the Canadian Institute for the Blind.

1985 Richards, Ron Wood, and Bob Dylan make the closing appearance at the Live Aid concert in Philadelphia.

1986 The Stones win a Lifetime Achievement Grammy.

1987 Keith produces and appears in movie Hail! Hail! Rock 'n' Roll, a celebration of Chuck Berry's contribution to rock 'n' roll.

1988 Richards releases his first solo album, Talk Is Cheap, and goes on tour in the U.S. backed by the X-Pensive Winos, featuring Bobby Keyes on saxophone.

1989 The Rolling Stones are inducted into the Rock And Roll Hall Of Fame.

1992 Richards releases Main Offender.

country music and introduced him to open tunings and the "Nashville stringing" technique that Keith later used on "Wild Horses" (*Sticky Fingers*). "He taught me the mechanics of country music, the different styles," Richards told Joseph Bosso in *Guitar World*. "He filled me in on the inside details, the Nashville style as opposed to the Bakersfield style."

Over the years with the Rolling Stones, Richards has explored several other styles of music, including R&B, funk, reggae, English ballads, soukous, flamenco, and East Indian.

Approach and Style

Richards is best known for his idiosyncratic rhythm playing. His signature is a I-IV progression played on a 5-string guitar in open *G* tuning (*G, D, G, B, D*, low to high). He plays the I by barring straight across a fret, and voices the IV by fingering a 4th and a 6th on the second (first fret) and fourth (second fret) strings respectively (a Cadd9 chord). His chords are usually single- or double-note embellishments of barre chords. Richards favors suspended chords, including sus2, sus4, and sus2/sus4 chords.

Playing a 5-string Telecaster tuned to open G, Richards has created some of rock 'n' roll's most memorable riffs on songs such as "Brown Sugar," "Honky Tonk Women," and "Start Me Up."

Richards primarily plays in open *G* or standard tuning, but he also uses open *D* (*A, D, F♯, A, D*, low to high, starting on the fifth string) for "Street Fighting Man" and "Jumping Jack Flash," and open *E* (*B, E, G♯, B, E*, low to high, starting on the fifth string).

Although Richards' chordal vocabulary may be simple, his detailed rhythmic approach gives his playing a great amount of variety. He often employs swing shuffle rhythms and eighth-note syncopations. "There's a tension between the 4/4 beat and the eighths going on with the guitar," he explained to Tom Wheeler in *Guitar Player*. Many of his phrases begin on the pick-up to beat one, anticipating the rhythm, then hanging over into the bar line. Richards gives his rhythms personality by using slides, bends, hammer-ons, and pull-offs to execute chord changes. For added variety, he interjects arpeggios, double-stops, triads, and single-note punctuations.

Richards' lead playing, with its heavy reliance on double-stop licks, betrays his Chuck Berry influences. His leads are often extensions of his rhythms, although he has occasionally been known to unleash bluesy minor- and major-pentatonic single-note licks.

Techniques

Richards' playing technique is fairly straightforward. When using open tunings, he barres major chords with his left-hand forefinger. He uses the barre as a foundation for chordal variations that he frets with his left-hand middle and ring fingers. He often drapes his thumb over the neck to fret bass notes, but he frets notes with his little finger only occasionally. Sometimes he also uses a capo, which is most frequently placed at the second or fourth fret.

Richards is especially fond of using double-stop and triple-stop bends, and he adds a country flavor to many of his lines with pedal-steel bends, where he bends the third string up a whole step while holding a double-stop on the first and second strings. The intro to "Honky Tonk Women" contains a good example of this technique.

Richards generally strums downstrokes with a flatpick, but he also sometimes plucks chords by grabbing strings with his free fingers to produce a percussive tone. He is adept at Travis-picking and clawhammer techniques, but he rarely plays in this manner any more.

In the late '70s, he started playing staccato, "clicking" rhythms, muting the strings by resting his right-hand palm against the bridge. An analog delay adjusted to a slap-back echo setting gave these rhythms a double-time feel. The song "She's So Cold" is a good example of this technique.

The Hardware

Guitars, Strings, and Picks

Keith's mother helped him to buy his first guitar, a Rosetti Spanish acoustic with gut strings. When he went to art school, he bought himself an old f-hole Hofner archtop acoustic and put a Japanese pickup on it to make it an electric.

In the early days of the Rolling Stones, Richards played a variety of different electric guitars, including Epiphones, Gretsches, and Gibsons. For many years his favorite guitar was a Gibson Les Paul, but in the late '60s he began to favor Fender Telecasters. The Telecaster remains the guitar that he uses most frequently today. His main Telecaster is a black '72 Tele Custom with a humbucking pickup in the neck position and a single-coil pickup at the bridge. Richards also plays several early '50s blonde Teles that are set up as 5-string guitars with the low-*E* string removed. Most of these Teles have been modified with Gibson PAF humbucking pickups installed in the neck position. Other Teles in his collection include a sunburst '67 and a rosewood Tele. Richards also likes to play a blonde '57 Fender Stratocaster that he bought from Ron Wood.

One of Richards' favorite new electrics is the Ernie Ball Music Man Silhouette. He owns several of these, including one with a *B*-string bender. His Silhouettes are early versions from the late '80s, featuring Schaller pickups.

Richards plays several Gibson guitars. He owns several Les Paul Juniors, including a double cutaway '58 TV model, and a single cutaway '57 with a sunburst finish. Other Gibsons in his collection include a black L-5S with a single humbucking pickup, and an L-6S.

Although Richards owns several custom-made guitars, he generally keeps them at home. He owns guitars made by Tony Zemaitis, Ted Newman Jones, Doug Young, and Joseph Jesselli. Most of these luthiers have made him special 5-string guitars. Other interesting electrics in Richards' collection include several aluminum-neck Travis Beans, a Guild Bluesbird, and a Supro Resolectric.

Richards also plays a variety of different acoustic guitars. In the mid-'60s, he often played Harmony and Guild 12-strings. He also owns several Martins, including a D-45, 000-28 herringbone, 0-18, 0-21, and D-18. Richards' Gibson acoustics include a J-200, which he often sets up with "Nashville stringing," a Hummingbird, and a late-'80s L-1 reissue.

On rare occasions he plays a wood-body Dobro resonator guitar. He also likes classical guitars, including a Velasquez classical that he plays in the studio and a solid-body Sadowsky gut-string electric that he uses onstage.

Keith uses Ernie Ball medium-gauge picks and Ernie Ball strings (.010-.046). The gauges on his 5-string guitars are .011, .015, .018, .023, .042.

Onstage and in public, Keith has always projected a "bad boy" image. His numerous drug busts during the '60s and '70s helped establish this persona, which still lingers, even though he is now an avowed family man.

Amplifiers, Effects, and Devices

Richards cannot remember any particular details about his first amp, other than it looked like a radio. In the early days of the Rolling Stones, Keith played through Harmony amps for a short period before getting Vox amps. During the early '70s, he used Ampeg V-4 amplifiers, and started using a combination of Fender and Mesa Boogie amps run into an Ampeg SVT in the late '70s. The Fender and Mesa Boogie combination remains his favorite to this day. Onstage, Keith plays through a Mesa Boogie Mark III Simul-Class, a 1957 Fender Twin, 50-watt Marshall Super Leads, and a 1956 Fender 4x10 Bassman.

In the studio, Keith prefers to play through small amps, such as a Fender Champ or inexpensive Kay and Silvertone amps. He also likes blackface Fender Deluxe Reverbs and Fender Bandmasters, and has experimented with playing through a Leslie in the studio.

In His Own Words

I'll never be a George Benson or a John McLaughlin. I've never tried to be. I've been more interested in creating sounds, and something that has a real atmosphere and feel to it.
Guitar Player, *November 1977*

Most people don't know what a band is. The musicians are there to contribute to the band sound. The band isn't there for showing off solos or egos.
Guitar Player, *April 1983*

If I'm a guitar hero, I never really entered the competition – I forgot to fill in the application form.
Guitar World, *March 1986*

I'm interested in what I can do with somebody else – how we can interact and play things back and forth and pick up a dropped beat and fling things against the ceiling to see if they stick.
Guitar Player, *December 1992*

What They Say

There's no man on earth who knows more about or cares more about rock 'n' roll.
Chet Flippo, It's Only Rock And Roll

He likes to think of himself as the resident tyrant, but really he's just a pussycat, to be perfectly honest. He just does what he is told.
Mick Jagger, The Rolling Stones (Best Of Guitar Player *special issue*)

I don't need to hear the rest of the band if Keith is there. The thing with me and Keith is we just have a go at things. We just enjoy playing it, and I just follow what he's doing.
Charlie Watts, The Rolling Stones (Best Of Guitar Player *special issue*)

To me, Keith Richards is the all time genius of coming up with guitar hooks that songs are built around, a lick that's the immediate hook.
Walter Trout, The Guitar Magazine, *January 1993*

Richards uses only a few effects, either onstage or for recording purposes. In 1965, he used a Maestro fuzztone to play the hook on "Satisfaction," but he has rarely used a fuzztone or distortion box since then. In the '70s, he occasionally used an MXR Phase 100, most notably on "Shattered," from the album *Some Girls*, and he plugged into an MXR Graphic EQ onstage. His current effects setup consists of a Cry Baby wah wah, an MXR analog delay, and a t.c. electronics 2290 multi-effects processor. In the studio, he sometimes uses a Palmer amp simulator. His wireless unit is made by Sony.

Discography

Almost all of Richards' recorded performances were made with the Rolling Stones. He made his recording debut on the Rolling Stones' single "Come On," a cover of a Chuck Berry tune. The Rolling Stones have made the following studio albums: **Rolling Stones**, **12 x 5**, **December's Children (And Everybody's)**, **Out Of Our Heads**, **Rolling Stones Now**, **Aftermath**, **Between The Buttons**, **Their Satanic Majesties' Request**, **Beggar's Banquet**, **Let It Bleed**, **Sticky Fingers**, **Exile On Main Street**, **Goats Head Soup**, **It's Only Rock And Roll**, **Black & Blue**, **Some Girls**, **Emotional Rescue**, **Tattoo You**, **Undercover**, **Dirty Work**, **Steel Wheels**, *and* **Voodoo Lounge**.

The Rolling Stones have also made the following live records: **Got Live If You Want It**, **Get Yer Ya-Ya's Out**, **Love You Live**, *and* **Flashpoint**.

Several greatest-hits compilations provide good overviews of the band's recordings from the '60s and '70s, but there has yet to be a greatest-hits record compiling their work from the '80s and '90s. Recommended compilations include: **Big Hits, Vol. 1 (High Tide And Green Grass)**, **Big Hits, Vol. 2 (Through The Past Darkly)**, **Hot Rocks (1964-1971)**, **More Hot Rocks (Big Hits And Fazed Cookies)**, **Still Life**, **Flowers**, **Metamorphosis**, **Sucking In The Seventies**, *and* **Made In The Shade**.

Richards made his first solo album, **Talk Is Cheap**, *in 1988 and released a second,* **Main Offender**, *in 1992. In 1991, Virgin released* **Live At The Hollywood Palladium, December 12, 1988**, *a live album recorded during Keith's 1988 U.S. tour with the X-Pensive Winos.*

Recording Sessions

Richards has guested on only a handful of records. During the '70s, he appeared on several of Ronnie Wood's solo albums, including **I've Got My Own Album To Do**, **Gimme Some Neck**, *and* **Now Look**. *In the '80s, he recorded a new version of "Jumpin' Jack Flash" with Aretha Franklin, and backed up Chuck Berry in a live performance that was recorded for the soundtrack to the film* **Hail! Hail! Rock 'n' Roll**.

Typical Licks

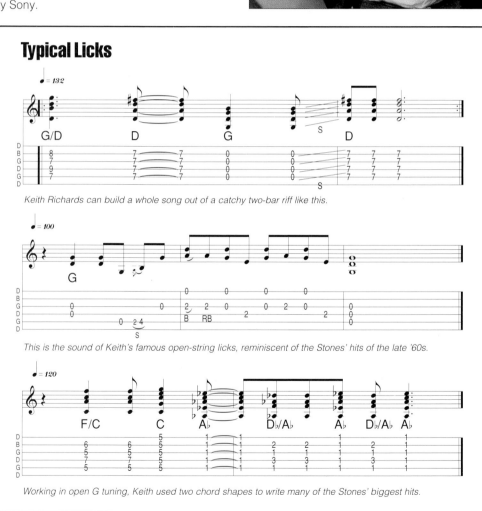

Keith Richards can build a whole song out of a catchy two-bar riff like this.

This is the sound of Keith's famous open-string licks, reminiscent of the Stones' hits of the late '60s.

Working in open G tuning, Keith used two chord shapes to write many of the Stones' biggest hits.

Carlos Santana

Carlos Santana is one of the most original guitarists to emerge from San Francisco's blues/rock/psychedelia scene in the late '60s. Combining blues, rock, jazz, and Latin music, he developed a highly melodic, emotional style that earned him a reputation as one of the world's leading electric guitarists. A deeply spiritual person, Carlos is an advocate of the healing properties of music. Ever since his legendary appearance at the 1969 Woodstock festival, Carlos has touched the lives of countless music fans with his stirring music and positive message.

The Player

Influences

Carlos Santana grew up around music. His father was a violinist in mariachi bands, and he later compelled Carlos to play guitar. Carlos' involvement with music began when he started playing violin at the age of five. He learned to play several classical music pieces, including compositions by Beethoven, and Von Suppe's *Poet And Peasant Overture*. "I hated the violin," he told Dan Forte in *Guitar Player*. "Anything I played on the violin sounded like Jack Benny when he was fooling around."

His father had a nylon-string acoustic, and Carlos' interest soon shifted to this instrument. He learned how to play a few basic chords and Mexican folk songs from his father, and later his brother Jorge also taught him chords. Although he doesn't read music, Carlos has studied several music theory books, including *The Thesaurus Of Scales And Melodic Patterns*.

When he was 11, Carlos was exposed to blues and rock 'n' roll when he saw a band in Tijuana that played songs by Bobby Bland, Ray Charles, B. B. King, and Little Richard.

"When I heard them playing I said, 'Oh man! This is the stuff I want to get into,'" he told Forte. He became friends with Javier Batiz, the band's guitar player, who showed him how to play blues. Soon afterwards, Carlos was playing Top 40 and R&B songs in Tijuana clubs and bars.

He moved to San Francisco in the early '60s, and a few years later he was listening to music by white blues artists, such as Paul Butterfield and Cream, whose *Fresh Cream* was highly influential on him. He became familiar with the music of several traditional blues guitarists, including Muddy Waters, Little Milton, Otis Rush, and Jimmy Reed, and also enjoyed the music of harmonica players James Cotton, Little Walter, and Junior Wells. Stevie Ray Vaughan is one of Carlos' more recent blues influences.

By the late '60s, Santana had become fascinated with jazz. He enjoyed the music of several jazz instrumentalists, including John Coltrane, Charles Lloyd, McCoy Tyner, Thelonius Monk, Miles Davis, John Handy, and the groups Weather Report and the Jazz Crusaders. He also appreciated jazz guitarists Charlie Christian, Django Reinhardt, and Wes Montgomery, whom he often saw playing in clubs. He also witnessed several

Background

1947 Carlos Santana is born on July 20, in Autlán de Navarro, Mexico.

1953 His father teaches him how to play the violin.

1961 Carlos starts playing guitar.

1962 He moves to San Francisco.

1966 Carlos meets keyboardist Gregg Rolie at a jam session and starts his first band, The Carlos Santana Blues Band.

1968 Santana makes his recording debut on the album The Live Adventures Of Mike Bloomfield And Al Kooper.

1969 The group Santana releases its debut album, Santana, and appears at the Woodstock Festival. Carlos later admits to being high on LSD while appearing on stage.

1971 Santana's South American tour ends in disaster when the Peruvian authorities confiscate $400,000 worth of equipment.

1972 Santana are featured in a movie about the famous Fillmore East.

1973 Carlos commits his spiritual life to following the guru Sri Chinmoy. He collaborates with John McLaughlin on Love, Devotion, Surrender.

1975 Santana perform at a benefit for S.N.A.C.K. [Students Need Athletics, Culture, and Kicks] in San Francisco.

1978 The Soviet authorities cancel a planned concert and movie by Santana and the Beach Boys.

1986 He produces the soundtrack to the movie La Bamba.

1988 Columbia Records releases Viva Santana!, a three-record retrospective of Santana's career.

1989 Santana guests on John Lee Hooker's The Healer.

1992 Santana is signed to Polydor Records and starts his own Guts & Grace label.

shows by jazz-rock fusion pioneer Harvey Mandel. In the late '70s, he cited John McLaughlin, George Benson, and Pat Martino as some of his favorite guitarists.

Carlos developed a keen sense of melody by listening to vocalists. He used to practice by playing along with records by Johnny Mathis, Aretha Franklin, Dionne Warwick, and Marvin Gaye, duplicating the feel of the vocal melody. Although he cites few rock artists as influences, Carlos enjoyed the music of the Beatles, Yardbirds, and Eric Clapton. Jimi Hendrix is one of his favorite rock guitarists.

Despite the Latin and Afro-Cuban rhythms often heard in his music, Santana remarks that he was not very heavily influenced by Latin or Mexican music. However, he has cited several Latin and Spanish guitarists as influences, including Gabor Szabo, Brazilian guitarist Bola Sete, and flamenco guitarist Paco de Lucia. He also enjoys reggae music, especially that of Bob Marley.

Approach and Style

Santana is a melodic player who mainly plays single-note lines. "The point of music is to tell stories with a melody," he said to Dan Forte in a *Guitar Player* interview. "I sing through the guitar. The main theme is always haunting melodies."

His playing is centered around pentatonic minor and major scales, blues scales, and diatonic modes, particularly the Dorian mode. However, he often plays intervals outside of the pentatonic scales, giving the music refreshing melodic twists. His occasional use of the harmonic minor scale and arpeggiated major triads reveals his jazz-saxophone influences.

Rhythm is an especially important element of Carlos' style. Sometimes he plays simple two- or three-note patterns, but he changes the rhythm of the patterns for variety. His playing is characterized by syncopated rhythm motifs and rhythms that accelerate ahead or drop behind the beat. He uses rests and mixed rhythmic groupings to create a sense of tension and drama. He often employs sustained notes, sometimes holding a single note for as long as a minute.

Many of Carlos' lines consist of call-and-response phrases played in the upper and middle registers of a scale. Other stylistic devices that he often employs include chromatically descending 4ths, minor 3rd intervals that descend by whole steps, and ascending bends. He also likes to bend a note up to pitch and hold it for several beats.

Although he is primarily a soloist, Carlos has an identifiable rhythm style that is characterized by two-chord vamps and scalar chord progressions. One of his signature vamps is a Im-IV pattern, such as that heard on "Evil Ways."

Ever since making his debut at San Francisco's Fillmore Theater, Santana has favored the thick tone and sustain characteristics of dual-humbucker solidbody electrics. His current favorite is a Paul Reed Smith.

Techniques

Santana's most noteworthy technique is his ability to control feedback to sustain desired notes. "First of all, you find a spot between you and the amplifier where you both feel that umbilical cord," he explained to Jas Obrecht. "When you hit the note, you immediately feel a laser between you and the speakers. You can hear it catch, like two trains coupling together."

The key to his playing lies in his right-hand technique. He holds his pick between his thumb and forefinger, and possesses excellent command of rhythm. Using alternate picking techniques, he executes quick tremolo-picked glissandos and skips back and forth across adjacent strings with ease.

Santana makes liberal use of left-hand pull-offs and hammer-ons to increase his playing speed. Sometimes, he trills between two notes with hammer-ons or pull-offs without picking notes with his right hand. He prefers to keep his left-hand fingers in a tight, four-note range on the fingerboard, instead of attempting wide interval stretches.

Carlos' frequent use of bent notes reveals his jazz and blues influences. He bends notes with his ring finger, using the forefinger and middle finger to support the bend. He generally bends notes up a whole step, although sometimes he may push a note even higher. He also employs unison bends, where he bends a note up a whole step on the third string, while simultaneously striking the second string two frets lower. Sometimes he slides up or down a half-step into the desired note, evoking the jazz-influenced phrasing of George Benson and Wes Montgomery.

To generate vibrato, Carlos uses either his first or third finger. "I call these the emotion expression fingers," he told Obrecht. "You can tickle it with the index finger, and you can get total emotion with the ring finger." Lately he has started using a vibrato bar as well. "It's not something I go wild with. I try to fingerpaint with the notes. It's easier to use the whammy when you're playing up tempo, because then you're like a surfer making your own waves."

The Hardware

Guitars, Strings, and Picks

When Carlos started playing guitar, he used a nylon-string acoustic that his father kept around the house. His father gave him his first guitar in the late '50s, which Carlos recalls was an old hollow-body Gibson. He has never provided details about what kind of guitar he used in his early days in San Francisco.

Carlos generally favors solid-body electrics with two humbucking pickups. In the late '60s, when he formed the Santana Blues Band, he played a '63 Gibson SG. Later, he acquired a '68 Gibson Les Paul, and he played a late '60s SG at the Woodstock festival in 1969. He has owned several Les Pauls and SGs, including a three-pickup SG Custom, since. In the early '70s, he started playing a Gibson L-6S, which features a 6-position rotary switch for tonal variations. A few years later he started endorsing Yamaha guitars. During this period he played a Yamaha SG-2000, a double-cutaway solidbody with two humbuckers and intricate custom inlays on the body. In the early '80s, he discovered Paul Reed Smith electrics, which are currently his main guitars. His favorite Paul Reed Smiths were built between 1979 and 1981, and are equipped with Gibson PAF humbucking pickups.

He has used various other electrics from time to time, including a Fender Stratocaster that he played on "She's Not There," a hollowbody archtop Gibson Byrdland that he used for *Amigos*, and a custom guitar built by luthier Linda Manzer.

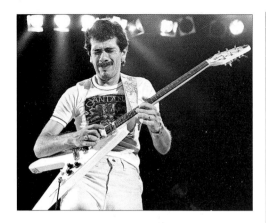

Carlos Santana's playing is characterized by his stirring, emotional lines and an innate sense of melody. Inspired by blues, jazz, and Latin music, he has developed a truly unique style.

Carlos plays acoustic guitar only occasionally. In the late '70s, he expressed a fondness for his Yamaha nylon-string Yamaha classical.

Santana plays with large, triangular heavy-gauge nylon picks. "I just got in the habit of playing with big ones like that when I was in Tijuana," he told Jas Obrecht. "I can turn them any way I want to, and even if I make a mistake, it just keeps rotating. If the pick is weird, I've still got two other edges." In the late '70s, he used strings gauged .008, .011, .014, .024, .032, .042, but now he uses Ernie Ball or D'Addario strings gauged .009-.042.

Amplifiers, Effects, and Devices

Carlos has provided few details about his early amplifiers. On the first Santana records, he played through Fender Twin Reverbs.

In the mid-'70s, he started using Mesa Boogie amplifiers. "My brother Jorge turned me on to them," he told Dan Forte. "He came over and said, 'You got to try this amp.' Man, it sustained like crazy and was pure. So I never gave it back to Jorge." Carlos has owned several Boogie amps through the years, including an early Mark I combo and a Mark IV head, which he currently favors for live performance. He also uses an early-'70s 100-watt Marshall onstage for distorted rhythms. The amp heads are connected to small open-back cabinets loaded with a single 12-inch Altec speaker.

Santana has never been a big fan of effects. "Gadgets sound too generic," he explained to Jas Obrecht. "The emotion creates all the things you are supposed to create, not the gadgets." The only effects that he likes to use are a wah-wah and chorus pedals, his current favorites being Ibanez or Boss chorus pedals and Morley wahs. He has also used DOD and Ibanez octave dividers and a Cry Baby wah.

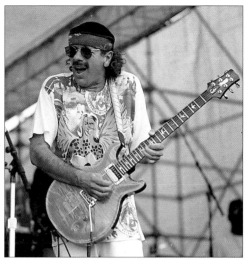

Discography

The bulk of Carlos Santana's recorded output appears on albums by his band Santana. With the group, he has made the following albums: **Santana** *(1969),* **Abraxas** *(1970),* **Santana III** *(1972),* **Caravanserai** *(1972),* **Welcome** *(1973),* **Borboletta** *(1975), the three-record live album* **Lotus** *(1975),* **Amigos** *(1976),* **Festival** *(1976), the double live album* **Moonflower** *(1977),* **Inner Secrets** *(1978),* **Marathon** *(1979),* **Zebop!** *(1981),* **Shangó** *(1982),* **Beyond Appearances** *(1985),* **Havana Moon** *(1985),* **Freedom** *(1987),* **Blues For Salvador** *(1987),* **Persuasion** *(1989),* **Spirits Dancing In The Flesh** *(1990), and* **Milagro** *(1991).*

Viva Santana!, a three-record package, provides an excellent overview of Santana's career prior to 1988 and features several outtakes and live performances, as well as studio versions of his best work.

Carlos recorded three solo albums in the late '70s and early '80s: **Oneness** *(1979),* **Silver Dreams – Golden Reality** *(1979), and the double album* **The Swing Of Delight** *(1980).*

He has also collaborated on projects with several musicians. He recorded **Carlos Santana & Buddy Miles! Live!** *with drummer Buddy Miles in 1972,* **Illuminations** *with Turiya Alice Coltrane in 1973, and* **Love, Devotion, Surrender** *with guitarist John McLaughlin in 1973. In 1994, he released the album* **Santana Brothers**, *featuring his brother Jorge and nephew Carlos Hernandez on guitar.*

Recording Sessions

Carlos made his first recorded appearance on **The Live Adventures Of Mike Bloomfield And Al Kooper** *in 1968, where he appeared on the track "Sonny Boy Williamson." Since then, he has guested on several records, including Luis Gasca's* **Luis Gasca** *(1971), Papa John Creach's* **Papa John Creach** *(1971), Narada Michael Walden's* **Garden Of Love Light** *(1977) and* **Awakening** *(1979), Herbie Hancock's* **Monster** *(1980), Boz Scaggs'* **Middleman** *(1980), and John Lee Hooker's* **The Healer** *(1989).*

Typical Licks

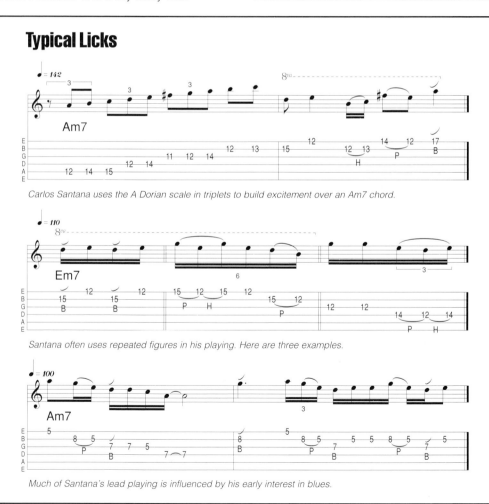

Carlos Santana uses the A Dorian scale in triplets to build excitement over an Am7 chord.

Santana often uses repeated figures in his playing. Here are three examples.

Much of Santana's lead playing is influenced by his early interest in blues.

Joe Satriani

One of the most successful rock instrumentalists, Joe Satriani made guitar virtuosity palatable to the masses. Possessing an astonishing command of the instrument, he has established a reputation as a master, based not only on his own success, but also on the talents of his students, who include Steve Vai, Metallica's Kirk Hammett, and Primus' Larry Lalonde. Although his music is technically sophisticated, he has written many attractive melodies, such as the ballad "Always With Me, Always With You."

The Player

Influences

Joe Satriani came from a musical family. His mother and sisters played piano, and his sister Marion played folk songs on guitar. Joe experimented with piano, but he never received any formal instruction on it.

In 1964 Joe saw the Beatles on *The Ed Sullivan Show*, and decided that he wanted to play drums. Shortly thereafter he received his first set of drums and started learning to play. He enjoyed the music of many '60s rock bands, such as the Beatles and the Rolling Stones, but it was the music of Jimi Hendrix that had the most profound effect on the youngster. When he heard of Hendrix' death on September 18, 1970, Joe decided to abandon the drums and start playing guitar.

During his teens, Satriani listened mainly to rock guitarists. Some of his favorite players were Led Zeppelin's Jimmy Page, Tony Iommi of Black Sabbath, Eric Clapton with Cream, Johnny Winter, Jeff Beck, and Joe Walsh.

In high school, Joe took music classes from instructor Bill Wescott, who taught him about music theory, modes and scales, and how to read music. Wescott exposed Satriani

to the music of various composers, including Eric Satie, Bartók, Chopin, Handel, and Harry Partch, and Joe became interested in more adventurous styles of music, such as the works of Frank Zappa. Joe started practicing 13 hours a day, a routine that he maintained until he was 20.

Satriani says that Wes Montgomery was the only true jazz guitarist who influenced him. "Wes Montgomery, to me, was perfect," he told Jas Obrecht in *Guitar Player*. "Before that there were all these smoking jazz guys, but very few of them touched me." Joe also enjoyed the playing of fusion guitarists, such as Al Di Meola, Allan Holdsworth, and John McLaughlin. He learned the enigmatic scale from a songbook for McLaughlin's *Birds Of Fire* and later used this scale as the basis for the song "The Enigmatic" on his debut album, *Not Of This Earth*. Joe also studied bebop for a short period, but he says he could not improve on the explorations of Charlie Parker, Bud Powell, and Dizzy Gillespie in that genre. For a short period in 1975, Joe studied with jazz pianist Lennie Tristano.

Several other styles of music have been highly influential on Satriani. He particularly enjoys funk music, ranging from the '70s works of James Brown and Sly Stone to the

Background

more modern sounds of Prince and De La Soul. He also likes the blues, and cites John Lee Hooker as one of his favorite blues artists. Arabian, Japanese, and Chinese music are a few of his non-Western influences.

Some of Satriani's more recent favorites include ZZ Top and various late '70s and '80s new wave and post-punk bands, such as Gang Of Four. In a 1994 interview, he listed albums by Nirvana, Nicky Skopelitis, and Urge Overkill as some of his current favorites.

Approach and Style

With an advanced understanding of music theory and extremely well-developed technique, Satriani is a true virtuoso. His songs make effective use of several scales and modes. Although Joe often uses standard pentatonic minor and blues scales, he throws in additional notes that give the phrases a distinct personality. He frequently solos in the Dorian mode, but he is also well-versed in the Aeolian, Lydian, Mixolydian, and Phrygian dominant modes. Some of his slower, melodic ballads are based around major or minor scales. He occasionally plays

Emerging in the late '80s, Satriani has maintained a highly successful career as a rock guitar instrumentalist. All of his records since 1988's Surfing With The Alien *have been certified gold, and he plays to large audiences worldwide.*

in unorthodox scales and modes, such as the enigmatic mode (root, flatted second, major third, raised fourth, raised fifth, raised sixth, and major seventh), which was the basis of his song "The Enigmatic."

Satriani has strong compositional skills, and his songs rarely revert to traditional rock clichés. They are highly melodic and lyrical, with unusual melodic structures often based around riffs, arpeggios, and rhythms, instead of standard chord progressions. "In my mind I see the melodies, solos, and rhythms as being the chords," Satriani told Jas Obrecht in *Guitar Player*. For solo sections, he often changes keys to add drama and contrast. He also uses a wide variety of non-conventional chords, intricate, complex arpeggios, and innovative chord progressions.

He generally plays in standard tuning, occasionally tuning the entire guitar down a half-step. "Flying In A Blue Dream" features an acoustic guitar tuned to open *F* (*C, F, C, F, A, C*, low to high), and he sometimes uses a "Nashville-strung" acoustic for rhythm-guitar parts. He has also recorded with guitars set up in *D* diminished tuning.

Techniques

Satriani is a fluent technician who makes use of the guitar's entire fretboard. He has a wide reach that enables him to execute arpeggios that span from the fifth to the twelfth fret. Using his wide reach, along with left-hand hammer-ons and pull-offs, Satriani has developed a versatile legato phasing technique that gives his playing a fluid tone. Instead of relying on box patterns like most rock guitarists, he uses finger slides, position shifts, and lateral motion to take advantage of the full range of the fretboard.

Sometimes he uses his left hand exclusively to sound notes. He might play a succession of hammer-ons and pull-offs on a single string while moving his left hand up and

down the neck. Sometimes he will hammer a single note on each string to execute extremely fast arpeggios, often simultaneously reaching behind his left hand with his right to damp the strings.

Joe has developed several unorthodox techniques that allow him to create interesting sound effects. He created a train sound on "The Snake" (*Surfing With The Alien*) by pulling the *G* string over the *B* and *E* strings and rubbing it against the frets. To end his first solo to "The Enigmatic" (*Not Of This Earth*), he pulled the *B* string off the fingerboard.

Joe holds his pick between his thumb and forefinger and usually keeps the edge of his right-hand palm on the vibrato arm, which he uses frequently, both to raise and lower pitch. A favorite vibrato-bar technique of his involves lowering the bar, striking a harmonic, and slowly raising the pitch, sometimes as much as an octave. To create a growling sound, he picks a fretted note and slides his left hand up the neck while depressing the bar and keeping the pitch the same. Sometimes he taps or scrapes the strings with the vibrato arm.

Joe's thick, high-gain distortion tone enables him to create a wide variety of interesting harmonic effects. He uses several different techniques to generate harmonics, including striking the string with the pick and the edge of his thumb, reaching above the pick with his forefinger, and placing his left hand at various nodes along the string.

Satriani also uses a variety of different tapping techniques. Depending on the tone he wants, he taps the strings with either his fingertips, the edge of his pick, or by clenching his right-hand thumb and forefinger together. On the songs "Midnight" (*Surfing With The Alien*) and "New Blues" (*The Extremist*) he uses his right and left hands to tap interweaving parts on separate parts of the neck.

The Hardware

Guitars, Strings, and Picks

One of Joe's first guitars was a Hagstrom III with a tremolo tailpiece. His next guitar was a '54 Fender Stratocaster, and he later moved on to a succession of electrics, including various Gibson Les Pauls and Fender Telecasters.

In the '80s, when he was signed to Relativity Records, Satriani accepted an endorsement deal with Ibanez guitars. Since then, various Ibanez solidbodies have been his main guitars. In the late '80s he played Ibanez 540 Radius guitars, equipped with a Floyd Rose-style vibrato tailpiece and DiMarzio Pro 151 and Al Di Meola model humbucking pickups. Joe bends the bars on his vibrato units so the arm rests parallel with the guitar body, and he installs only two vibrato springs in the body. For the Mick Jagger tour, Joe played a custom-built Ibanez Stratocaster replica with three single-coil pickups.

In 1990, Ibanez introduced the JS-6 Joe Satriani guitar, developed according to Joe's specifications. It features a basswood body, Ibanez Edge vibrato tailpiece, and DiMarzio PAF Pro and Fred model humbucking pickups. In '91, Ibanez introduced a mahogany body version of the JS-6, with a standard tailpiece. In 1993, Joe helped Ibanez develop a new guitar based on a Fender Telecaster. Introduced in 1995, this model features four single-coil pickups placed in groups of two in the traditional Tele pickup configuration.

Joe uses several other electric guitars in the studio, including a '58 Fender Esquire and a Rickenbacker 12-string.

After releasing *Surfing With The Alien*, Joe began using acoustic guitars on his records. His acoustic instruments include a Yamaha APX steel-string, an Ibanez N800TB acoustic/electric steel-string, a Gibson Chet

Satriani has an incredible comprehension of music theory, great technique, and an innate sense of melody. Several of his students, including Steve Vai and Kirk Hammett, are some of the most acclaimed guitarists in rock music.

Atkins CE electric classical guitar, several Dobro resonator guitars, and a Deering 6-string banjo that he tunes to *F♯, B, E, A, C♯, E* (low to high).

Joe uses heavy-gauge picks and sometimes plays with a glass slide. He uses D'Addario XL-120+ strings, gauged .0095-.044.

Amplifiers, Effects, and Devices

Satriani's main amplifiers are Marshalls. He has used several different Marshalls, including a 1968 100-watt Super Bass head modified by Todd Langer, a 1969 100-watt Super Lead head, a 1979 100-watt Mark II head, an '80s Jubilee Series model, and a 1992 6100BK 30th Anniversary 100-watt head. The amps are connected to Marshall 4x12 cabinets that are loaded with 25-watt Celestion 12-inch speakers. On stage, Joe boosts the signal from his Marshalls with a Mesa Boogie Strategy 500 power amp.

Joe also experiments with various amps in the recording studio. He has recorded with a Fender Princeton Reverb, various Soldano amp heads, a Mesa Boogie Dual Rectifier, a

In His Own Words

Whatever is considered standard operating procedure, I generally try to go the other way, just to see what happens – usually with good results. I take chances a lot.
Guitar Player, *February 1988*

There will always be a return to roots going on, because the sound that a beginner makes has a lot of validity. There will always be room for a very simple approach to songs.
Guitar Player, *January 1989*

I'd rather someone said, "Man, that's a great solo! I'll never forget it," than, "Man that was a great solo; that guy's got some technique." That's the accolade I don't care for.
Guitar Player, *November 1989*

When I try to move forward with techniques, there's a discipline sitting back there. That's important, because I think you have to know how to practice. You have to know how to work so you don't get discouraged.
Guitar Player, *January 1994*

What They Say

As long as he's making music, I'll always find an inspiration to play. I see what he does as pure integrity in music. Integrity with his own intuition. That all shows in his playing.
Steve Vai, Guitar World, *April 1990*

Joe was by far my most thorough teacher. He knew what it meant to teach. He taught all the fundamentals, but he also set a great example. For instance, he would never tell me to practice and not practice himself. He would never tell me to memorize something that he hadn't memorized. He was, by far, my biggest influence.
Steve Vai, Guitar World, *April 1990*

I think you're born with a feel for certain things – like the way Joe Satriani phrases notes just has a certain beauty; it's something he was born with.
Rowan Robertson, Guitarist, *August 1990*

Peavey 5150, a Roland JC-120 combo, and a 17-watt amp head built by Matt Wells. He also uses a variety of preamps and direct recording devices, including a Mesa Boogie Quad Preamp, a Chandler Tube Driver, and a Scholz Rockman.

His current effects setup consists of an Eventide DSP-4000, a DigiTech Smart Shift pitch transposer, a Cry Baby wah-wah pedal, and Boss DS-1 distortion, CE-2 chorus, and OC-2 octave pedals. Other effects that he has used live or in the studio include an Eventide H3000 Ultra Harmonizer, a t.c. electronics 2290, a Dyno-My-Piano TriStereo Chorus, an Echoplex, and various digital delay pedals.

Discography

In 1983, Satriani made his first record, a five-song EP titled **Joe Satriani**. He produced the record himself, and generated every sound with his electric guitar. Only 500 copies of this EP were pressed, and it has become quite a collector's item.

Joe's solo albums on Relativity Records all contain fine examples of his playing. These records include: **Not Of This Earth**, **Surfing With The Alien**, the four-song live EP **Dreaming #11**, **Flying In A Blue Dream**, and **The Extremist**. The double-CD **Time Machine** features live performances, several out-takes, and rarities, including four of the five songs from his self-produced EP.

Recording Sessions

Although Satriani was quite active as a studio musician in the '80s, he mainly worked on music for advertisements. In 1985 he became a member of Greg Kihn's band, and played lead guitar on the album **Love And Rock And Roll**. He recorded a few sessions with drummers Tony Williams and Danny Gottlieb, appearing on the latter's **Aquamarine** album. Satriani has guested on the following albums: Blue Öyster Cult's **Astronomy**, Stu Hamm **Radio Free Albemuth**, Paul Shaffer **Coast To Coast**, and Spinal Tap's **Break Like The Wind**. Satriani and his former student, Steve Vai, trade solos on "Feed My Frankenstein" on Alice Cooper's **Hey Stoopid**.

Typical Licks

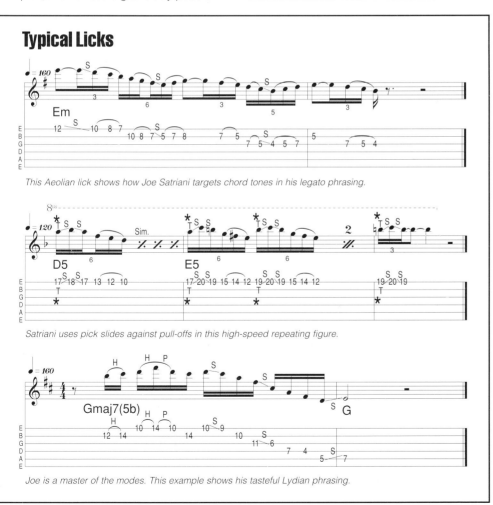

This Aeolian lick shows how Joe Satriani targets chord tones in his legato phrasing.

Satriani uses pick slides against pull-offs in this high-speed repeating figure.

Joe is a master of the modes. This example shows his tasteful Lydian phrasing.

Slash

Although Slash came to prominence in the late '80s, his playing is deeply rooted in the blues-based hard-rock and heavy-metal guitar styles from the mid-'70s. As a member of the controversial band Guns N' Roses, Slash gained notoriety for his tough, punk-inspired image as much as for his aggressive leads and raunchy rhythms. Despite his image, he quickly became a highly respected guitarist and has been asked to record with mega-stars such as Michael Jackson and Bob Dylan.

The Player

Influences

Like most teenagers who grew up during the late '70s, Slash was primarily influenced by the hard-rock and heavy-metal bands that were popular at the time. He has cited Led Zeppelin's Jimmy Page and the Rolling Stones' Mick Taylor as his biggest influences, with Eddie Van Halen and Jeff Beck following close behind. "Van Halen had just come out when I started," Slash reminisces. "I didn't think about how good Eddie was, or how good Van Halen was, except for the fact that it just sounded great and gave me a certain kind of energy. So when I started playing guitar, I just did what I wanted to do."

Some of Slash's favorite bands include Aerosmith, Ted Nugent, Cheap Trick, The Who, and Black Sabbath. Aerosmith's *Rocks*, Cheap Trick's *Live At Budokan*, and UFO's *Strangers In The Night* were his favorite albums. Slash is entirely self-taught. He learned to play guitar by listening to records and playing as much as 12 hours a day. Some of the first songs he taught himself how to play include Deep Purple's "Smoke On The Water," and a song by UFO. As his

skills developed, he spent most of his time trying to play along with Jeff Beck records. Slash also took lessons for a brief period from a guitarist named Robert Wollan.

Later, Slash became interested in speed-metal bands, such as Metallica and Megadeth, and punk groups such as Fear and the Sex Pistols. Slash revealed his affinity for punk rock on Guns N' Roses' collection of punk covers, *The Spaghetti Incident?*, a project which was largely directed and produced by him. "My influences from punk are the same as there would be from any kind of music," he stated in a recent interview. "I just dig that attitude, a certain kind of guitar sound, the lyrics, and a particular state of mind." Slash's choice of songs that were covered on this album included Fear's "I Don't Care About You," T. Rex's "Buick Mackane," and Nazareth's "Hair Of The Dog."

In sharp contrast to his hard-rock tastes, Slash also enjoys the music of singer-songwriters, such as Cat Stevens and Joni Mitchell. These preferences are reflected in some of Guns N' Roses more sensitive, melodic songs like "Sweet Child O' Mine," which was primarily written by Slash. He also enjoys classical music, and has cited Erik Satie as one of his favorite composers.

Background

1965 *Saul Hudson is born on July 23, in Highgate, London, England.*

1976 *His family moves to Los Angeles, California.*

1978 *Slash meets future Guns N' Roses drummer Steven Adler. He starts playing guitar soon afterwards, and tries to form several bands, but with little success.*

1980 *Slash announces the arrival of his new band, Tidus Sloan, with red and black graffiti around the L.A. Carthay Circle neighbourhood.*

1983 *Slash plays briefly with Los Angeles heavy-metal band London before joining Hollywood Rose, featuring future Guns N' Roses singer Axl Rose.*

1985 *Rose is recruited by L.A. Guns, which includes rhythm guitarist Izzy Stradlin. Bassist Duff McKagan and Steven Adler become members of L.A. Guns shortly afterwards, and the band is renamed Guns N' Roses. Slash joins Guns N' Roses after lead guitarist Tracii Guns quits.*

1986 *Guns N' Roses release their first EP, Live?!*@ Like A Suicide, on their own label.*

1987 *The band releases its first album, Appetite For Destruction, on Geffen. It takes one year for it to appear on the Billboard charts.*

1988 *Sales of Appetite For Destruction reach 10 million. Guns N' Roses go on tour with one of Slash's favorite bands, Aerosmith.*

1989 *Guns N' Roses release GN'R Lies. The band is attacked by critics for the racist and homophobic lyrical content of the song "One In A Million."*

1991 *In an unprecedented move, Guns N' Roses release two albums on the same day, Use Your Illusion I and Use Your Illusion II. The records debut at #1 and #2 on the charts in several countries.*

1993 *Guns N' Roses release The Spaghetti Incident?, a collection of punk-rock covers. Much controversy is generated over the inclusion of a song allegedly penned by mass murderer Charles Manson.*

Approach and Style

Slash bases his playing style around the blues and harmonic minor scales favored by his influences. Although Slash is self-taught, he possesses strong, advanced melodic sensibilities. He generally relies on pentatonic minor scales played in "blues box" positions for solos, and sometimes uses the Aeolian mode, the Dorian mode, the Mixolydian scale, and pentatonic major scale. He often branches out with major scales to expand on melodic phrases.

Slash often plays pedal-steel bends and uses the pentatonic major scale to create leads that sound similar to country, or some of the Rolling Stones' country-influenced songs. This is particularly noticeable on his leads on "Paradise City" (*Appetite For Destruction*), and "Coma" (*Use Your Illusion I*).

When playing rhythm, Slash usually relies on power chords (a two-note chord played at an interval of a fifth), riffs played on the lower strings of the guitar, or arpeggiated figures.

Techniques

Spurning the flashy tapping, sweep-picking, and vibrato-bar techniques popularized during the mid-'80s, Slash's playing techniques have more in common with the hard-rock players he listened to during the late '70s. Like many blues and '70s hard-rock guitarists, he uses a wide and fast vibrato technique. He mainly relies on his left hand for speed, using pull-offs and hammer-ons to sound notes. He makes liberal use of right-hand muting, resting his hand on the guitar's bridge to make the notes he plays sound more percussive. He uses this technique for both his lead and rhythm playing. A good example of this can be heard on the intro to "Welcome To The Jungle" (*Appetite For Destruction*). He holds his pick between his thumb and index finger, and sometimes plucks strings with the tips of his free fingers.

To achieve tonal variations, Slash often changes pickup selections while he plays. One of his favorite settings for lead is the guitar's rhythm or neck pickup, with the tone control rolled back. Known as "woman tone," this setting was also a favorite of Eric Clapton and many British blues guitarists. Slash also likes to use feedback to sustain notes on solos and song introductions.

The Hardware
Guitars, Strings, and Picks

Slash's first guitar was a modest nylon-string acoustic which had only one string. His grandmother gave him his first electric, an inexpensive copy of a Gibson Explorer. Later guitars included a Memphis Les Paul copy, a B. C. Rich Mockingbird, a B. C. Rich Warlock, a Fender Stratocaster, a Jackson Firebird copy, and a Charvel. Most of these instruments were sold to support Slash's former drug habit.

Gibson Les Pauls are Slash's favorite guitars. He owns more than 80 guitars, including several late-'50s Les Paul Standards (one of which is a '59 tobacco-sunburst Les Paul that once belonged to Aerosmith guitarist Joe Perry), a '59 Les Paul copy made by Peter "Max" Baranet of Max guitars (Hollywood, CA) featuring Seymour Duncan Alnico II pickups, '56 Les Paul gold tops, '69 Les Paul Customs, and several new Les Pauls that he plays on stage. He also has a '58 Gibson Flying V, a '58 Gibson Explorer, two Ernie Ball/Music Man Silhouettes (one with humbucking pickups, the other with single coil pickups), a '52 Fender Telecaster, a '65 Fender Stratocaster, '63 and '65 Gibson Melody Makers, a '60s Gibson SG, and a Fender 6-string bass, all of which are used for recording. Slash plays slide on a Travis Bean

electric which features five strings tuned (low to high) to *G, D, G, B, D*. His acoustic guitars include a Guild 12-string, a Gibson J-100, a Ramirez classical, and a Dobro. Slash borrowed producer Mike Clink's Yamaha guitar to record his acoustic parts for *Appetite For Destruction*. Most of Slash's guitars are kept entirely stock.

His main guitar for live performance is an '85 Gibson Les Paul Standard reissue. "It's been my main live guitar since we started," he told *Guitar Player* in January, 1994. "Unfortunately, Gibson doesn't produce that many good-sounding new guitars. They're few and far between. You should see it. It's pretty beat up. It looks like it's 25 years old at this point. It's been bashed around a few

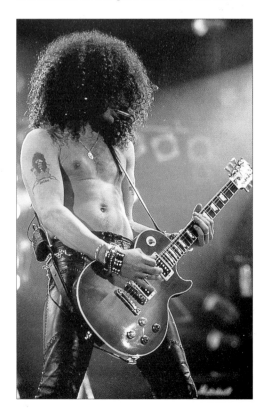

With a street-punk image, a vintage Les Paul Standard, and a handful of melodic, blues-based licks, Slash is the antithesis of the technically advanced shredders who dominated the rock guitar scene in the mid-'80s.

We don't work out our parts. If it's Izzy's song, I might turn the riff around a little bit and add something. When it comes to my tunes, I write riffs that are a lot more intricate – that's my style.
Guitar Player, *December 1991*

I just think of a particular type of guitar that will work for the song and grab whatever happens to be in the front of storage. I try to make any guitar do what I want it to do.
Guitar Player, *January 1994*

Critics pigeonhole you into talking about your influences in detail. Mine are endless. My basic roots come from a certain hard rock background. I think that's why the band is what it is, because we all have that one thing in common.
Guitar Player, *January 1994*

What They Say

Slash is completely the opposite of what I thought he'd be. He's very focused and together. He's got a great vibe and plays with a lot of intensity.
Eddie Kramer on working with Slash on Stone Free – A Tribute To Jimi Hendrix, Guitar Player, *December 1993*

Slash was somewhat of a wild card. He was suggested to me and I asked, "Does Slash play the blues?" I listened to some of his things and realized he's a good player.
Paul Rodgers on enlisting Slash to play on Muddy Water Blues, Guitar Player, *May 1993*

Slash is one of my favorite cartoon characters.
Axl Rose, Appetite For Destruction, *by Danny Sugerman, 1991*

I had a riff and it was a slow smooth melody. When we were playing with it, Slash turned up his amp and went into this bashing thing and we said, "Wow!"
Former Guns N' Roses rhythm guitarist Izzy Stradlin on the writing of "My Michelle," Guitar For The Practicing Musician, *September 1988*

times. I actually broke the neck on it one night. I lost my mind." He often uses a Stratocaster copy made by Performance guitars in Hollywood, California and a B. C. Rich Warlock on stage as well.

Slash tunes his guitars down a half-step to E♭. He uses a standard set of Ernie Ball Slinky regular light strings gauged .010, .013, .017, .026, .036, .046. He likes to play with the heaviest picks he can find. His current preference is purple Dunlop Tortex 2.0mm picks.

Amplifiers, Effects, and Devices

One of Slash's first amps was a black-face Fender Twin Reverb that, he admits with regret, he later traded for a Sunn Beta Lead. Since he started playing with Guns N' Roses,

As a member of the multi-platinum-selling act Guns N' Roses, Slash developed a raw, stripped-down, hard-rock guitar sound influenced by classic '70s bands such as Aerosmith and Led Zeppelin.

he has preferred Marshall amps. For live performance he uses 100-watt Marshall Jubilee heads along with single Marshall 4x12 cabinets loaded with Celestion speakers. In live performance he will play through two Marshall half stacks, one set to a clean tone, the other distorted. Slash uses a variety of Marshall heads in the studio. Until recently, he played through a single Marshall half stack along with a Mesa Boogie Mark III, which is used only to generate feedback in the studio control room. Currently, he likes to use two Marshall half-stacks that are connected in series. He sometimes records clean tones with a solid-state Roland JC-120 Jazz Chorus amp.

Slash does not like to use many effects other than a wah-wah pedal in the studio, preferring the tone of the guitar connected directly to an amp. On stage he uses a Boss 7-band graphic EQ for extra gain, a Heil talk box (a Dean Markley talk box was used on the first album), and custom voltage-controlled wah-wah pedals made by Matt Bacchi of EMB audio (Oakland, CA). Sometimes he will use a small amount of delay or echo, which is added at the mixing board. On stage, he connects his guitar to a Nady 1200 wireless system.

Typical Licks

E5

Double stops add colour to this typical E minor pentatonic phrase played at the twelfth fret.

C5

Slash sometimes combines the minor pentatonic scale and the Dorian mode for a bluesy mixture over a dominant chord.

A5

Playing pentatonic scales in sixteentth notes at high tempos is no problem for Slash's rock technique.

Discography

Slash's first recorded performance appears on **Live?!*@ Like A Suicide** (1986), an EP released on the band's own Uzi-Suicide label. Guns N' Roses' debut LP, **Appetite For Destruction** (1987), sold more than 10 million copies. Their second LP, **GN'R Lies** (1989), contains material from the EP and several acoustic songs. In an unprecedented move, the band released **Use Your Illusion I** and **Use Your Illusion II** (1991) on the same day. These LPs debuted at the #1 and #2 positions of record charts in several countries, including the United States, the United Kingdom, and Japan. In late 1993, the band released **The Spaghetti Incident**, a collection of punk-rock and glam covers. The record was designated platinum (one million units sold) in the United States in less than two months.

In 1994, Slash began work on his first solo album, which was scheduled for release by Geffen Records in 1995.

Recording Sessions

Although Slash is often busy recording or touring with Guns N' Roses, he has guested on several records by other artists. Guest performances include Alice Cooper's **Hey Stoopid**, Iggy Pop's **Brick By Brick**, Lenny Kravitz' **Mama Said**, Spinal Tap's **Break Like The Wind**, "Give In To Me" on Michael Jackson's **Dangerous**, "The Hunter" on Paul Rodgers' **Muddy Water Blues**, "I Don't Live Today" with Paul Rodgers, Billy Cox, and Buddy Miles on Warner Bros.' **Stone Free – A Tribute To Jimi Hendrix**, and a live performance on Carol King's **Carol King Live**.

Slash has also played lead-guitar parts on solo albums by his bandmates in Guns N' Roses, including Gilby Clarke's **Pawn Shop Guitars** and Duff McKagan's **Believe In Me**.

Andy Summers

Andy Summers came to prominence in the late '70s with the Police. Combining reggae rhythms, pop-song structures, and punk rock energy, he developed a minimalistic but sophisticated style based around sparse chords, inventive arpeggios, and a diverse palette of sonic textures. His live performances with the Police featured brilliant improvisations that never succumbed to rock clichés. One of the most influential new-wave and rock guitarists in the '80s, Summers continues to create fascinating and innovative music as a solo artist.

The Player

Influences

Starting out as a piano player, Andy Summers did not play guitar until he was 14 years old. "I was given a guitar when I was 14, and it was like an obsession immediately," he told Jas Obrecht in his '82 *Guitar Player* cover story. "I never put it down. I was always playing."

His older brother was an avid fan of jazz music, and he exposed Andy to several artists. "I grew up listening to jazz, so by the time I was 16 my *raison d'être* was to play once a week in a modern jazz club," Summers told Peter Mengaziol in *Guitar Player*. One of Summer's earliest guitar influences was Django Reinhardt, and he lists Reinhardt's "Nuages" as one of his favorite guitar performances. He also enjoyed the playing of jazz guitarists Barney Kessell, Kenny Burrell, Wes Montgomery, and Joe Pass. Later he became interested in Larry Coryell's jazz guitar explorations and the music of jazz saxophonist Charlie Parker.

As a teenager, Summers also enjoyed listening to and playing rock 'n' roll music. In the early '60s, he learned to play songs by the Shadows, featuring guitarist Hank Marvin.

Soon afterwards, he became interested in American R&B music and joined Zoot Money's Big Roll Band, which played various R&B-inspired originals and covers by Otis Redding, Ray Charles, and Jimmy Smith. Summers developed a rhythm-guitar style that was heavily influenced by Jimmy Nolen, who played with James Brown.

In the late '60s, Summers witnessed one of Jimi Hendrix's concert performances in England. "I was moved by Jimi Hendrix quite a lot," Summers remarked to Obrecht. "It was great to see him. At the time it was just mind-blowing."

Summers moved to Los Angeles and studied classical guitar at the California State University of Northridge in the late '60s and early '70s. At college he learned about harmony, music theory, composition, conducting, and 20th-century composers. Béla Bartók, Messiaen, Schoenberg, Stravinsky, and Takemitsu are among Summers' favorite classical composers. Andy played classical guitar for a while before returning to England and pursuing a career as a rock musician.

Summers also studied sitar for four years. "I used to copy Vilayat Kahn's solos when I was trying to learn Indian sitar solos on the guitar," Andy comments. "He was my

Background

1942 *Andrew James Somers is born on December 31, in Blackpool, Lancashire, England.*

1957 *Andy starts playing guitar.*

1966 *Summers makes his recorded debut on Zoot Money's Big Roll Band's* The All Happening Zoot Money's Big Roll Band At Klook's Kleek.

1967 *Records sessions for innovative jazz-rock outfit Soft Machine.*

1968 *Summers tours briefly with Eric Burdon and the Animals.*

1975 *Plays on Joan Armatrading's* Back to The Night *album.*

1976 *Plays on David Bedford's* Odyssey *album, and on* Sarabande *by Deep Purple's keyboard player, Jon Lord.*

1977 *Summers joins the Police, featuring Sting on bass and Stewart Copeland on drums.*

1979 *The Police have two hit singles from their second album, firmly establishing them as one of the decade's most successful new bands.*

1980 *The Police play a benefit gig in Bombay, the first live act to play there since Hawkwind's appearance ten years earlier.*

1981 *The BBC refuse to screen the Police's new video for "Invisible Sun," from* Ghost In The Machine, *which was filmed in Belfast, Northern Ireland. It was felt that the footage might convey messages that were not in keeping with the lyrics.*

1982 *Summers collaborates with Robert Fripp on the album* I Advance Masked.

1983 *The Police make history by becoming the first band on the A&M label to top both single and album charts in the U.S.*

1985 *The Police unofficially disband as each of the band's members pursue solo projects.*

1987 *Summers releases his first solo album, XYZ.*

1988 *He forms his own record company, Private Music.*

favorite." Summers' Middle Eastern and Indian music inspirations emerged several years later on his solo album *The Golden Wire*.

With the Police, Summers combined a variety of musical styles, including reggae, new wave, pop, and hard rock. Even now he is a fan of new artists such as Nirvana, Pearl Jam, and P. J. Harvey.

Approach And Style

Summers gained notoriety for his sparse, textural rhythm work with the Police. Because he rarely played long, extended guitar solos, he has been categorized as a rhythm player, but his instrumental works with Robert Fripp and as a solo artist reveal his proficiency beyond supporting roles.

Driven by Andy Summers inventive, textural guitar playing, the Police developed an innovative combination of reggae rhythms, pop melodies, and punk rock-inspired energy. The band was one of the most successful acts of the early '80s.

When playing rhythm guitar, Summers uses chords, arpeggios, and single-note lines in inventive ways. Many Police songs are characterized by his partial cluster-type chords and triads. He favors suspended chords, such as sus2, sus4, and add4, and he often voices major and minor chords on the top three strings only. He often omits the root notes, which are played by the bass instead, creating the effect of a full chord. Summers also favors quintal harmonies or stacked fifths, which are chords that are built around root-fifth-ninth intervals.

Inspired by reggae music, he frequently plays heavily accented comps at consistent quarter-, half-, and whole-note intervals. Sometimes he plays arpeggiated eighth-note figures, such as the patterns he plays on "Every Breath You Take" and "Message In A Bottle." Many of Summers' rhythm guitar figures are based around single-note lines and riffs, which reveal his funk and R&B influences.

Summers' solos with the Police were often short, restrained passages that adhered to punk rock's "less is more" aesthetic. Most of his solos were based around pentatonic minor scales, although a few were atonal explorations. Some of his solos made effective use of Phrygian, Lydian, Aeolian, and Mixolydian modes. On "Next To You" (*Outlandos D'Amour*) he played a slide solo on a guitar tuned to open *G* (*D, G, D, G, B, D*, low to high) and used open *E* (*E, B, E, G♯, B, E*, low to high) for the slide solo on "It's Alright For You" (*Regatta De Blanc*). Many of his solos were simply extensions of his rhythm-guitar figures or textural embellishments generated with a guitar synthesizer.

His solo work greatly expands upon the concepts he explored while playing with the Police. Summers relies more heavily upon ethnic scales, polytonality, and modal melodies, which reveal his early jazz influences. He retains a vast palette of timbres, but uses them in more of an orchestral manner that highly contrasts his sparse, minimalist work with the Police.

Techniques

Summers' most identifiable technique is his creative use of effects' processing to produce a wide variety of timbres and textures. He generally starts with a crisp, clean tone, then uses chorus and phase shifting to generate thick, moving tones. He uses Echoplexes or digital delays to generate counter-rhythms that make simple lines or chord patterns sound more complex.

Summers holds his pick between his forefinger and thumb. Although he generally uses downstrokes when he is playing rhythm, he sometimes plucks chords with his free fingers. To generate harmonics, he strikes the string with the pick and the edge of his thumb at the same time.

Summers does not use left-hand techniques – such as hammer-ons, pull-offs, and slides – as frequently as most rock guitarists. He generates vibrato with his ring finger, usually waiting until the note is decaying before applying pressure. "I like to hold the note and then, just as it's dying, give it the vibrato," Summers told Obrecht. "There's a subtle difference. It's more exciting that way." More recently he has started using a vibrato bar, although he generally uses this to simulate sitar sounds. On the rare occasions when he plays slide, Summers wears a heavy brass tube on his little finger.

One of Summers more distinctive techniques is his use of harp harmonic patterns, which he learned from studying the playing of guitarist Lenny Breau. This technique involves an arpeggiated pattern that alternates between a harmonic played on a lower string and a fretted note struck three strings higher. To execute this technique, Summers holds the pick between his thumb and middle finger. This leaves his forefinger free to generate harmonics while the pick strikes the string behind the forefinger. He plucks the following fretted note with his ring finger.

The Hardware

Guitars, Strings, and Picks

In several interviews, Summers has stated that he was given his first guitar when he was 14, but he has not provided any details as to what kind of guitar it was. Details about the instruments he played in the '60s are similarly scarce.

With the Police, Summers' main guitar was a '63 Telecaster Custom with a Gibson humbucker installed in the neck position and a built-in overdrive unit. He also frequently played a '61 Fender Stratocaster and a Hamer Prototype. After the Police disbanded and he started pursuing a career as a solo artist, Summers played a variety of electrics, including a '52 gold-top Les Paul, a Gibson ES-335, and various Steinbergers. His current favorite is a Steve Klein custom electric, which has many of the same features as a Steinberger, including a non-headstock neck and a TransTrem vibrato.

Summers also plays various acoustic guitars, and his collection includes a Gibson Chet Atkins electric classical guitar, a Dobro resonator guitar, a Gibson B-25 flat-top, a Guild 12-string, and several Martins, including a D-28. One of his recent acquisitions is a custom-made Andrew Manson acoustic.

Even in live performance, Summers switches between two different types of picks – a small Dunlop Jazz II for lead and single-note line playing and a thin, conventional-shaped pick for rhythm work. His strings are a set of .010-.046 Dean Markleys.

Summers played in several bands during the '60s and early '70s, and has had a successful career as a solo artist in the late '80s and '90s, but he is best known for his rhythm-guitar work with the Police.

Amplifiers, Effects, and Devices

Information about Summers' early amplifiers is also unknown. Onstage with the Police he used 100-watt Marshall heads and Roland JC-120 solid-state combos, which were used to amplify his guitar synthesizer. He uses a variety of small amps in the studio, including various Fenders and a Dean Markley combo.

In the early days of the Police, Summers used a pedal board designed by Pete Cornish. The board contained an MXR Phase 90, an Electro-Harmonix flanger, an MXR Distortion +, a Mu-tron III, and unspecified compressors and analog delays. He also used a pair of tube Echoplexes, each of which were adjusted to different delay settings.

In the late '80s, Summers switched to a

In His Own Words

I always was a serious musician, because it was very natural. I loved music and wanted to play, and I wanted the knowledge of music.
Guitar Player, *September 1982*

Technique is only a means to a musical end. There's no point in it otherwise.
Guitar Player, *September 1982*

For the Police the context was pop-rock songs, but the information inside the songs, particularly in live performances, was definitely from other places.
Guitar Player, *April 1991*

Compositionally and sonically, I like to be right in the front of things. Some sounds available now are very beautiful. I mean if Charlie Christian were playing now, he'd probably be playing with a modern guitar sound.
Guitar Player, *April 1991*

I've been saying this for quite a while, but doing this acoustic album with John [Etheridge] meant that I turned my back on the electric for about six months and I think that's been very healthy for me as a guitar player, because now I look at all this rack gear and realize that I don't want to go back to it.
Guitarist, *April 1994*

What They Say

A master of understatement and effects, he makes innovative use of space, sending a rainbow swath of sound through Stuart Copeland's drumming and Sting's bass parts.
Jas Obrecht, Guitar Player, *September 1982*

His playing has helped to re-define the role of a guitarist in a rock band. [He is] consciously drawing on as many different musical styles and influences as possible, and aiming to do away with the conventional concept of a rhythm section simply providing a backing for a soloist.
Ralph Denyer, The Guitar Handbook, *1982*

Bradshaw rack that contained several multi-effects units and high-end processors, including an Eventide H3000 Ultra Harmonizer and a Lexicon PCM-70. He also used a ProCo Rat distortion pedal.

Throughout his career, Summers has used a variety of guitar synthesizers. "The guitar synthesizer is a great writing instrument," he explained to Jas Obrecht. "I certainly find composition is often inspired purely by sound itself, and having all those sounds under your fingers can be a fantastic aid to inspiring writing ideas." He prefers Roland guitar synths and has used their GL-500, GR-300, and GR-700 systems.

Discography

Summers' most outstanding and accessible work was recorded with the Police, all of whose albums contain fine examples of his playing. The Police released the following records: **Outlandos d'Amour**, **Regatta de Blanc**, **Zenyatta Mondatta**, **Ghost In The Machine**, and **Synchronicity**. The **Message In A Box** box set and the compilation **Every Breath You Take – The Singles** provide a good overview of the Police's output.

Summers' solo albums display the more adventurous side of his playing style. His first solo album, **XYZ**, features several misguided vocal tracks. His instrumental works, **Mysterious Barricades**, **The Golden Wire**, **Charming Snakes**, and **World Gone Strange**, offer much better representations of his current direction.

Summers composed the scores to the following films: **2010**, **Down And Out In Beverly Hills**, and **Weekend At Bernie's**.

In the early '80s Summers collaborated with Robert Fripp on two instrumental albums, **I Advanced Masked** and **Bewitched**. In 1994, he collaborated with guitarist John Etheridge on the all-acoustic instrumental album **Invisible Threads**.

Summers was a member of several different bands in the '60s and '70s. He made his recording debut as a member of Zoot Money's Big Roll Band on the album **The All Happening Zoot Money's Big Roll Band At Klook's Kleek**. During the psychedelic era, the band changed its name to Dantalian's Chariot. Summers played briefly with Soft Machine, then became a member of the Animals and played on the record **Love Is...** In the '70s, Summers recorded several albums with Kevin Coyne, including **Matching Head And Feet**, **Heartburn**, and **In Living Black And White**.

Recording Sessions

Summers had an active career as a session musician and sideman during the '70s and performed with various artists, including Neil Sedaka, Mike Oldfield, Kevin Ayers, and David Essex. Some of his more notable sessions include Kevin Lamb's **Sailin' Down The Years** and Eberhard Schoener's **Video Magic**, which also features Sting and Stewart Copeland from the Police.

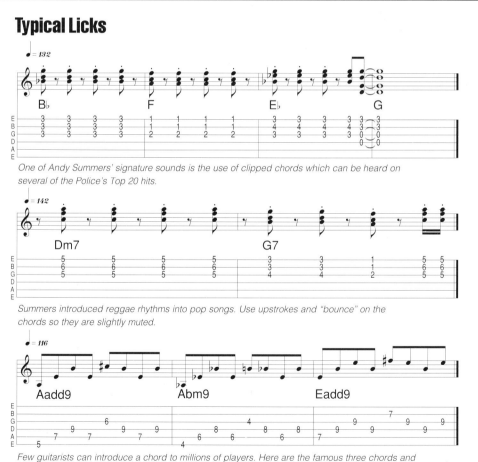

Typical Licks

♩ = 132

Bb   F   Eb   G

One of Andy Summers' signature sounds is the use of clipped chords which can be heard on several of the Police's Top 20 hits.

♩ = 142

Dm7   G7

Summers introduced reggae rhythms into pop songs. Use upstrokes and "bounce" on the chords so they are slightly muted.

♩ = 116

Aadd9   Abm9   Eadd9

Few guitarists can introduce a chord to millions of players. Here are the famous three chords and arpeggio pattern that have become synonymous with Summers.

Richard Thompson

As a member of Fairport Convention, Richard Thompson was a pivotal figure in the development of British folk-rock in the late '60s. After quitting the band in the early '70s, he pursued a successful career working as a solo artist and in a duet with his then-wife, Linda. A highly inventive and daring player, equally adept on electric and acoustic guitar, Thompson mixes several genres of music, including rock, country, Celtic, and Middle Eastern. An accomplished songwriter and musician, Thompson continues to open up new musical avenues.

The Player

Influences

Richard took an interest in music at an early age, and he often listened to the radio and records. His father frequently listened to jazz and classical records, particularly enjoying the music of Les Paul and Django Reinhardt, and his older sister was a fan of Elvis Presley. When Thompson bought himself a single of Presley's "All Shook Up," he decided that he wanted to play guitar.

Thompson's parents were from Scotland, so he was exposed to Scottish dance music. "I grew up with a lot of Scottish dance music," he told Dan Forte in *Guitar Player*. "But you don't connect it as being hip when you're a kid. What you want to hear is rock 'n' roll."

Thompson started playing guitar when he was 10. His first inspirations were Buddy Holly, and Hank Marvin of the Shadows. "The Shadows had such great records – the sound on them is phenomenal," he told Forte. James Burton was another important influence who Thompson admitted had a great impact on his playing style.

When he was 12, Thompson started taking classical-guitar lessons. Classical music remains one of his primary influences, and he is especially fond of 20th-century composers, such as Kurt Weill, Benjamin Britten, Claude Debussy, Hans-Werner Henze, Maurice Ravel, Béla Bartók, Igor Stravinsky, and Karlheinz Stockhausen. Some of Thompson's 20th-century classical influences are evident in his atonal lines.

In the mid-'60s, Thompson did not get caught up in the British blues revival like most other young guitarists because he felt that most of the artists were poor imitations of authentic American blues artists. "I didn't want to play Eric Clapton because I felt that was too easy – anyone could do that," he remarked in *Guitar Player*. He spent a brief period playing blues and studied the playing of Otis Rush and Hubert Sumlin. He appreciated the playing of only a few British blues guitarists, including Bernie Watson and Geoff Bradford (who both played with Cyril Davies) and the U.S.'s Michael Bloomfield.

He also enjoyed the playing of several American rock guitarists, including Jerry Miller with Moby Grape and Zal Yanovsky of the Lovin' Spoonful. "Yanovsky was one of the first guitarists I heard incorporating country influences into popular music," Thompson told Forte. "'Nashville Cats' – that's great guitar playing."

Background

1949 Richard Thompson is born on April 3, in London, England.

1955 He buys his first record, a single of "Four Legged Friend," by singing cowboy Roy Rogers.

1959 Richard starts playing guitar.

1967 Thompson forms Fairport Convention, with Ashley Hutchings on bass, Simon Nicol on guitar, Martin Lamble on drums, and Judy Dyble and Ian Matthews on vocals.

1969 Richard is injured in a car accident that claims the life of Fairport Convention's young drummer, Martin Lambale.

1971 Thompson leaves Fairport Convention and forms a duo with his wife Linda.

1972 He releases his first solo album, Henry The Human Fly. *He also performs on an album entitled* The Bunch *with, among others, Sandy Denny, and tours with the Albion Country Band later in the year.*

1973 Richard converts to the Sufi faith.

1974 Richard and Linda Thompson record I Want To See The Bright Lights Tonight.

1976 Following a three-year hibernation, Thompson releases Guitar, Vocal, a double album of rare and unreleased material.

1981 He writes material for Arlo Guthrie's album Power Of Love.

1982 Richard and Linda Thompson get divorced. They release Shoot Out The Lights, hailed as one of the 10 greatest albums of the '80s by Rolling Stone magazine.

1991 Richard appears, along with 24 of the world's finest guitarists, at the Guitar Legends Festival in Seville, Spain.

As a teenager, Thompson joined several bands and played various types of music, including acoustic, blues, and Cajun. At 18 he helped form Fairport Convention, which was initially inspired by American rock musicians, such as Phil Ochs, Bob Dylan, and Joni Mitchell. He particularly enjoyed the Byrds and the playing of the band's guitarists Roger McGuinn and Clarence White.

Fairport Convention then became fascinated with British traditional music. "It was the indigenous music that interested us," says Thompson. "That was what we felt we could contribute to, and would be rewarding to us." He started making efforts at emulating the sounds and melodies of Celtic instruments, such as the bagpipe and fiddle. Surprisingly, he says that he wasn't influenced by the playing of other Celtic guitarists, although he admits that he enjoys the playing of Martin Carthy, John Martyn, and Bert Jansch.

Arabic and Middle Eastern music are some of Thompson's recent inspirations. He is particularly fascinated with Andalusian

Thompson is equally adept on electric and acoustic guitars. Because he has played hundreds of solo acoustic-guitar gigs, he has developed an advanced playing style that incorporates simultaneous rhythm and lead parts.

music, which flourished in Southern Spain around the eighth century and has influenced several Northern African musical forms. Thompson has also picked up many modal ideas from listening to the music of jazz saxophonists John Coltrane, Charlie Parker, and Ornette Coleman. He is also deeply inspired by jazz guitarist George Van Eps' solos, and has studied several of Ted Greene's books for insight into chords and music theory.

Approach and Style
Thompson freely mixes several different styles, such as rock, country, Celtic, Arabic, and Cajun music, in his songs and solos. His highly melodic guitar lines are often based around the Mixolydian mode, but he also employs blues scales or Middle Eastern motifs. His on-the-beat accents and wide-interval melodic skips are influenced by Scottish music and bagpipes. Many of his solos bear the distinguishable mark of his deft chromatic phrases.

He often uses open string drones that give his music a Celtic or Middle Eastern feel, and favors the keys of *E*, *A*, *D*, and *G*, because they provide him with a wide variety of open strings for the root and fifth. When playing in other keys, he often uses open strings as drones at other intervals. When playing in *F*, for example, he might use the open-*G* string as a droning second. "I'm a constant droner, and I'm happiest when I have a free open string," he told Joe Gore.

He also writes many songs in minor keys. One of his favorite compositional devices is to change keys – either for a solo, in the middle of a solo, or over a droning open string.

Because he has spent many years performing by himself with just an acoustic guitar for accompaniment, he has developed a distinctive playing style that incorporates simultaneous rhythm- and lead-guitar parts. Sometimes he uses conventional Travis-style picking with alternating bass patterns, but

more often his bass lines and melodies interweave polyrhythmically and independently.

Alternate and open tunings are vital facets of Thompson's approach to the guitar. He generally uses standard or dropped *D* tuning ("I Misunderstood," on *Rumor And Sign*) on the electric, but he experiments with several different tunings (all low to high) on his acoustic guitars, such as: *D*, *A*, *D*, *G*, *A*, *D* ("Two Left Feet"); *C*, *G*, *D*, *G*, *B*, *E* ("1952 Vincent Black Shadow"); *D*, *G*, *D*, *G*, *A*, *D*; and *F*, *G*, *D*, *G*, *C*, *D*. "I think of acoustic and electric guitars as two totally different instruments," he told Dan Forte.

Techniques
Thompson uses a hybrid picking technique, incorporating both a flatpick and his fingers. He holds the flatpick between his right-hand thumb and forefinger, and generally uses his middle and ring fingers, though he occasionally also plucks notes with his little finger. He sometimes uses a thumbpick on acoustic guitar, but he prefers the back-picking capabilities afforded by a flatpick. Sometimes he uses only his bare fingers and thumb.

His left-hand technique involves frequent pull-offs, hammer-ons, slurs, harmonics, and bent notes. "I bend notes differently than a blues player would," he explained to Joe Gore in *Guitar Player*. He incorporates whole-step pedal-steel bends, double-stop bends, and triad bends, which reveal his country-music influences. Sometimes he presses down on the strings behind the nut to bend open strings.

To imitate the sounds of a bagpipe, he often employs half-step bends from the 7th to the root, the ♭2nd to the 2nd, and the 3rd to the 4th. Other techniques he uses to imitate a bagpipe include tapping the fretboard with his right hand an octave or higher above the notes he is fretting with his left hand, pulling off to open strings while playing in the upper register of the neck, and jerking on the vibrato bar.

The Hardware

Guitars, Strings, and Picks

When Richard started playing guitar, he used a nylon-string Spanish acoustic he borrowed from his father. Later he acquired his first electric – a Hofner V-3 with three pickups. "That was a great guitar," he told Dan Forte. "I wish I still had it." After that, he owned several off-brand guitars and eventually ended up with a Gibson ES-175. In Fairport Convention's early days, he played a '50s gold-top Les Paul with P-90 pickups, which he "foolishly sold to John Martyn."

He started playing a Fender Stratocaster in the '70s. Playing the neck/middle and bridge/middle pickup settings, he developed a signature tone based around the Strat. From the '70s through the mid-'80s, his main Strat featured a '57 body, a '55 neck, and a modified tone circuit. He then switched to a '59 Strat. Now he uses the Strat only occasionally.

His current main electric is a custom-made solidbody built by Danny Ferrington, which features a mini-humbucking neck pickup, a Telecaster-style bridge and pickup, and a basswood body. He also sometimes uses a Telecaster, a '60s Fender Electric XII, and a Vox electric 12-string in the studio.

Thompson owns several acoustic guitars. His main acoustic is a Lowden L-32, and he also plays a Lowden L-27, a '60s Martin 000-18, and a custom-made Ferrington flat-top. He uses a Sunrise soundhole pickup to amplify his acoustic guitars.

Thompson plays with a medium-gauge flatpick and uses .009- or .008-gauge strings on his electrics.

Amplifiers, Effects, and Devices

Thompson's first amp was a Selmer Select-A-Tone amp with push-button tone controls.

Although Thompson is best known for his searing lead work on a Fender Stratocaster, he uses the Strat less often because he feels that "it's become a cliché that you hear on Chevrolet adverts."

Since then, his amps have mainly been Fenders. He used a Showman head while playing with Fairport Convention, but now he favors smaller combo amps. He used a '60 and a '56 Fender Deluxe on *Rumor And Sigh* and played through a Fender Vibroverb reissue on *Mirror Blue*. Other Fender amps that he often uses for recording or performance include a mid-'60s blackface Deluxe Reverb, a 2x10 Vibrolux combo, and an early-'50s tweed Bassman with a single 15-inch speaker.

Generally preferring the tone of his guitar plugged straight into an amp, Thompson uses effects only sparingly. In the mid-'80s, his effects rig consisted of a Boss CE-1 Chorus Ensemble, an MXR preamp, a Korg digital delay unit, and a Morley volume pedal. More recently he has been using a Demeter Tremulator tremolo pedal, a t. c. electronic dual parametric equalizer, and a Boss digital delay. He played through a Hot Cake fuzz pedal from New Zealand on "Grey Walls" (*Rumor And Sigh*).

Discography

Thompson made his recording debut in 1967 with the band Fairport Convention on the record **Fairport Convention**. He recorded several albums with the band between 1967 and 1970, including **What We Did On Our Holidays** (1968), **Unhalfbricking** (1969), **Liege & Lief** (1969), and **Full House** (1970). **Heyday** features several early Fairport Convention performances that were recorded for radio broadcasts.

After quitting Fairport Convention in 1971, Thompson regrouped with several ex-bandmates and formed the Bunch, who released the albums **Rock On** and **Morris On**.

In 1972, Thompson began pursuing a career as a solo artist. His solo albums generally contain his finest guitar work. They include: **Henry The Human Fly** (1972), the retrospective collection **(Guitar/Vocal)** (1976), the all-instrumental **Strict Tempo** (1981), **Hand Of Kindness** (1983), **Small Town Romance** (1984), the acoustic live album **Across A Crowded Room** (1985), **Daring Adventures** (1986), **Amnesia** (1989), **Rumor And Sigh** (1990), **Sweet Talker** (1992), and **Mirror Blue** (1994). The three-disc compilation **Watching The Dark** is an excellent retrospective of Thompson's career up to 1993.

Thompson also recorded several acclaimed albums with Linda Peters, his wife until 1982. These albums include: **I Want To See The Bright Lights Tonight** (1974), **Hokey Pokey** (1975), **Pour Down Like Silver** (1975), **First Light** (1978), **Sunnyvista** (1979), and **Shoot Out The Lights** (1982). All of these albums contain fine examples of Thompson's guitar playing, but the first and last records are particularly noteworthy.

In the late '80s, Thompson worked on two albums with Fred Frith, Henry Kaiser, and Frank French in the group French-Frith-Kaiser-Thompson. The albums, **Live, Love, Larf And Loaf** and **Invisible Means**, show Thompson's more experimental and exploratory side to good effect.

Recording Sessions

Thompson had a fairly active career as a session musician after leaving Fairport Convention. Some of his notable early '70s sessions include Mike and Lal Waterson's **Bright Phoebus** and Gary Farr's **Strange Fruit**. Other '70s and early '80s sessions include John Cale's **Fear**, Mike Heron's **Smiling Men With Bad Reputations**, John Martyn's **Bless The Weather**, Ian Matthews **Matthews Southern Comfort**, and Gerry Rafferty's **Night Owl**. Thompson also recorded several albums with ex-Fairport Convention vocalist Sandy Denny, including **The North Star Grassman And The Ravens**, **Sandy**, **Like An Old Fashioned Waltz**, and **Rendezvous**.

Some of Thompson's more recent sessions include Crowded House's "Sister Madly" on the album **Temple Of Low Men**, Michael Doucet's **Cajun Brew**, Willie Nile's **Places I Have Never Been**, and Bonnie Raitt's **Luck Of The Draw** and **Longing In Their Hearts**. He has also appeared on albums by Beausoleil, David Byrne, the Golden Palominos, and Suzanne Vega.

Typical Licks

Richard Thompson improvises freely with a rock sound, using rhythms derived from the folk tradition.

Probably the leading expert on folk-guitar styles, here Thompson plays a "hornpipe" line in drop-D tuning.

A lot of Richard's playing uses "Travis" picking, with bluesy bends in DADGBE tuning.

Pete Townshend

Pete Townshend may be best known for his flamboyant stage antics, but he is also one of rock's most powerful rhythm guitarists. He is credited with inventing the power chord, a two- or three-note chord consisting of roots and fifths, and his experimentation with feedback and sound effects had an impact on Jimi Hendrix, Jeff Beck, and many other rock guitarists in the '60s. His influence spans several generations of rock music, and his music has inspired everyone from young punks and mod revisionists to heavy-metal guitar heroes.

The Player

Influences

Pete's parents were musicians who worked professionally in big bands (his father played saxophone and his mother was a vocalist.) His first musical instrument was the harmonica, but he switched to guitar when he was 11.

After some basic instruction from his father, Pete taught himself how to play. Although he studied chords and harmony from books, he never learned to read music. "I really wish that I had learned how to read music," he remarks. "As a composer I can't communicate properly with other writers, collaborators, and players. I can write charts, but I can't read them. I find it difficult, even to read stuff that I've written. If I had learned how to read music, I think I would feel very differently about life and about my work."

Pete started playing the banjo shortly after starting on the guitar. "My whole kind of flourishing guitar style had started on the banjo," he told Matt Resnicoff in *Guitar Player*. At this point he became interested in traditional jazz, dixieland, and bluegrass music. During the late '50s, he joined his first band, playing traditional jazz music on the banjo.

He also started listening to a wide variety of music, including jazz, pop, and rock 'n' roll. "My idol in England was Mickey Green (of Johnny Kidd & The Pirates)," he told Michael Brooks in *Guitar Player*. "He was the first big note bender, particularly on the G string." Townshend's early guitar influences include James Burton, Link Wray, Hank Marvin, Chet Atkins, and jazz guitarists Wes Montgomery, Barney Kessel, Kenny Burrell, Johnny Smith, and Charlie Christian. He studied *Mickey Baker's Complete Course In Jazz Guitar*, where he learned about chord changes.

In the early '60s, Townshend's focus shifted to R&B. While attending art school, he became exposed to the music of Muddy Waters, Bo Diddley, Chuck Berry, Ray Charles, and Jimmy Smith. "I found R&B a way to pull my jazz and pop influences together," Townshend told Resnicoff. His favorite guitarists from this era include John Lee Hooker (who guested on Townshend's *Iron Man* in 1989), Buddy Guy, B. B. King, Freddie King, Jimmy Reed, Howlin' Wolf, and Steve Cropper. He also enjoyed the music of folk artists Joan Baez and Bob Dylan.

Around the mid-'60s, Townshend was introduced to the music of 17th-century English composer Henry Purcell by the Who's

Background

1945 *Peter Denis Blandford Townshend is born in Chiswick, London, on May 19.*

1956 *Pete starts playing guitar.*

1961 *He joins his first rock band, The Detours.*

1964 *Pete makes his recording debut on the High Numbers single "I'm The Face"/"Zoot Suit." The High Numbers later change their name to the Who.*

1965 *The Who releases its first single, "I Can't Explain," and album My Generation.*

1966 *Keith Moon threatens to quit the Who when he is injured by Pete's wild stage antics.*

1967 *When Jagger and Richards are jailed on drugs charges, the Who record Rolling Stones' songs and donate the proceeds to help with legal costs.*

1969 *Townshend composes the rock opera Tommy. The Who performs at the Woodstock festival.*

1971 *The Who release Who's Next, the band's most successful album.*

1972 *Pete records his first solo album, Who Came First.*

1973 *Pete's rock opera Tommy is made into a major feature film, directed by Ken Russell.*

1975 *Tommy is premiered in New York. Eric Clapton publicly thanks Townshend for helping him quit his heroin addiction.*

1977 *The Who buy Shepperton Film Studios.*

1978 *Who drummer Keith Moon dies.*

1982 *The Who disbands.*

1983 *Eel Pie Books, Townsend's publishing company, is wound up and he announces associations with British publishers, Faber and Faber.*

1985 *The Who reforms for the Live Aid concert.*

1989 *It reforms again for its 25th-Anniversary tour.*

1990 *The Who is inducted into the Rock And Roll Hall Of Fame.*

1993 *Townshend releases PsychoDerelict and stages a solo tour. Tommy makes its debut on Broadway and wins several Tony awards.*

manager, Kit Lambert. Purcell's "Symphony Upon One Note" had a profound effect on Pete. "It was just full of Baroque suspensions," he told Resnicoff. "I was deeply, *deeply* influenced by it... I sat down and wrote all the demos for the Who's first album, and it's just *covered* in those suspensions."

As the Who's popularity increased, Pete followed pop-music trends closely, going to clubs and concerts to see Eric Clapton, Pink Floyd, and Hendrix perform. "I was happiest listening to Jimi Hendrix," he told Brooks. "That to me was like heaven." He also took an interest in American rock artists, particularly Joe Walsh with the James Gang. Walsh and he often swapped instruments, and Walsh showed him about equipment setups. Pete also became interested in electronic music, and was inspired by Terry Riley and John Cage's experimental compositions.

More recently, Townshend's tastes lean towards jazz music. Many of his songs have been inspired by the music of Charlie Parker, Keith Jarrett, and Glenn Gould. He also enjoys the music of acoustic guitarists John Fahey and Robbie Basho, and songwriters Todd Rundgren and Joe Jackson.

Approach and Style

Although he is an excellent lead player, Pete considers himself primarily a rhythm guitarist. His rhythm playing is distinguished by two characteristics: suspended and partial chords. Many of his best-known songs, such as "Pinball Wizard," feature sus4 and sus2 chords. When playing major chords, he often omits the third. His two-note root/fifth and three-note root/fifth/root chords are known as "power chords," and he is often credited as the originator of this approach in a rock context.

Many of Pete's chord progressions are based around descending major scales. He also uses modulation, examples of which can be heard on "My Generation" and "Pictures Of Lily." Perhaps his most identifiable stylistic device is his use of droning patterns or pedal tones on the upper or lower strings over a I-V-IV chord progression. The songs "Substitute," "Pure And Easy," and "Cut My Hair" are all examples of this approach, in which he often fingers a simple triad pattern and moves it up and down the neck for chord changes.

Many of Townshend's songs are written in open tunings. One of his favorite tunings is *D, A, D, A, D, E* (low to high), which he developed for the song "Parvardigar" (*Who Came First*). On 12-string guitar he drops the tuning a whole step to *C, G, C, G, C, D* (low to high). Other tunings that he uses include open *D* (*D, A, D, F♯, A, D*, low to high) for "The Seeker," dropped *D* (tuning the low-*E* string down a whole step), and *D, G, D, A, D, E* (low to high). Sometimes he tunes the entire guitar down a half-step (*E♭, A♭, D♭, G♭, B♭, E♭*, low to high) or a minor 3rd (*C♯, F♯, B, E, G♯, C♯*, low to high). He also uses a capo at the first fret ("Baba O'Riley" and "Join Together") and the third fret ("5:15").

When Townshend plays lead, he generally relies on pentatonic minor scales.

Townshend was one of the first guitarists to experiment with feedback and sound effects, such as scraping the strings with a pick or microphone stand, flicking the guitar's toggle switch, and detuning strings.

Techniques

In the mid-'60s, Pete used the electric guitar to create a variety of sound effects. One of the first rock guitarists to experiment with controlled feedback, he became proficient at getting notes to feed back at will. To imitate the sound of a machine gun, he flicked the pickup selector switch back and forth rapidly. He also produced dissonant noises by scraping his pick along the bass strings or rubbing the guitar neck against a microphone stand.

Townshend's left-hand technique is more conventional. He frequently relies on the rock guitarist's typical vocabulary of bent notes, pull-offs, and hammer-ons for his lead playing, and he generally uses blues box patterns. The key to Townshend's style lies in his right-hand technique. One of his signature strumming techniques is a succession of flamenco-style 16th-note triplets using alternating upstrokes and downstrokes. He often places the accent on upbeats. His flamboyant, "windmill" strumming technique, where he swings his arm in circles and strikes the strings violently on the upswings and downswings, is only used for its visual appeal.

The Hardware
Guitars, Strings, and Picks

The first guitar that Townshend played was a homemade instrument that belonged to a friend. When his father saw that he could play such a primitive instrument, Pete's grandmother gave him his first guitar, a cheap acoustic, as a Christmas present.

While Pete was playing in the Detours, Roger Daltrey gave him an Epiphone solidbody electric, which he considers his first good guitar. In the Who's early days, he played Rickenbacker hollowbody electrics. He went through several of these, including a model 1996 6-string and a model 1993

12-string, mainly because he was smashing them as part of the Who's stage act.

He then moved on to Fender Stratocasters and Telecasters. He used a Fender Electric XII in the studio and briefly owned a Fender Jazzmaster, until it was stolen. He also used a Gibson ES-335 before it became splinters. In the late '60s, his main guitar was a Gibson SG Special with two single-coil P-90 pickups. "I started to use the Gibson SG when I got fed up with Fenders, because they were too clean" he told Michael Brooks in the early '70s. "I went to the manager and said, 'I really need an alternative to this,' and he said, 'I think you'd like the newest SG.' I played it and it rang. It sang to me." However, like the Rickenbackers and Fenders, Townshend's SGs were mercilessly destroyed onstage.

After Gibson discontinued the SG Special and the supply of used models dried up, Townshend began using Gibson Les Paul Deluxes, which were modified with a DiMarzio Dual Sound humbucker placed in the center position. This was his main guitar until the early '80s, when he started using Schecter Telecaster-style solidbodies, featuring two humbucking pickups. He also used Giffin solidbodies for a brief period. In 1989, Pete returned to the Fender Stratocaster, playing an Eric Clapton signature model on the Who's 25th Anniversary tour.

Pete has spared a handful of vintage instruments from the violent deaths that many of his guitars have met. One of his favorite guitars for recording is a 1957 Gretsch 6120 Chet Atkins hollowbody electric that was a gift from Joe Walsh. This was Pete's main guitar on *Who's Next*. Walsh also gave him a late-'50s Gibson Flying V, which he used to record *The Who By Numbers* and his solo album, *Empty Glass*. Other vintage guitars that Townshend has owned include a '53 Les Paul and a D'Angelico New Yorker archtop jazz guitar, which he sold to buy a boat.

Townshend's flamboyant stage antics, which included dramatic leaps and violent windmill strokes on his guitar, were an extension of his explosive rhythm playing on songs such as "Won't Get Fooled Again" and "My Generation."

Pete frequently plays acoustic guitars. Since 1969, his main acoustic for recording is a Gibson J-200, which can be heard on "Pinball Wizard," "Behind Blue Eyes," and many other classic Who tracks. For the Who's 1989 tour, he played a Takamine acoustic-electric.

Pete uses generic heavy-gauge picks that he purchases in bulk from music stores, such as Manny's and Pete's Guitars. He has used several various gauges of strings at different stages in his career. In the '60s, he used a regular set of Fender strings. In the early '70s, he played with an exceptionally heavy set gauged .056, .044, .032, .028, .028, .022, from bottom to top. "It's a heavy set," he told Brooks. "If you're going to hit a note, you've got to work for it." His current preference is a set of .011-.052 Ernie Ball strings with a non-wound *G* on his electrics and a set of .013-.056 Ernie Balls on acoustic.

Amplifiers, Effects, and Devices

Townshend joined the Low Numbers because he heard that they were one of the few local bands that had a Vox amp. The amp was probably an AC30, and Pete and Roger Daltrey both played through it until Pete bought himself a Fender Pro and a Fender Bassman head, which he used during the Who's early days. For the band's first U.S. tour, Pete rented Vox Super Beatle amps.

Townshend was one of the first guitarists to stack several amplifier heads and cabinets onstage in pursuit of excessive volume levels. When bassist John Entwistle produced a Marshall head and a 4x12 speaker cabinet, Pete ditched his Fenders and built a wall of Marshall heads and cabinets. He used the Marshalls very briefly before he discovered Hiwatt. Most of Pete's Hiwatt amps were custom-made, including a special four-channel 100-watt head, but they varied little from the stock versions. From the late '60s through to the early '80s, his stacks of Hiwatt amps were a familiar fixture at Who concerts. For the Who's '89 tour, his amplification setup consisted of several Mesa Boogie Studio pre-amps connected directly to the mixing board.

Townshend uses a variety of amps in the recording studio, such as an Ampeg B15N, a Roland JC-120, and a Mesa Boogie Mark II combo. He especially likes old Fender amps, including a Dual Showman, an early '60s blonde Twin, and a 3x10 Bandmaster combo that he likes to use with his Gretsch 6120.

Pete uses very few effects. In the early '80s, his effects rig consisted of an MXR Dyna Comp, a Roland Dimension D chorus, and a Roland SDE-2000 digital delay. An Edwards volume pedal for use with pedal steel guitars is an essential link in his Gretsch 6120/Fender Bandmaster studio rig. Other devices that he has used include a Rockman Sustainor for direct recording and a Grandpiene reverb that he used in the late '60s "for distortion – it gives a kind of clear fuzz dirge."

Since the early '70s, Pete has experimented with synthesizers. He helped develop the ARP Avatar, and has owned several Roland guitar synthesizer units, including a GR-300.

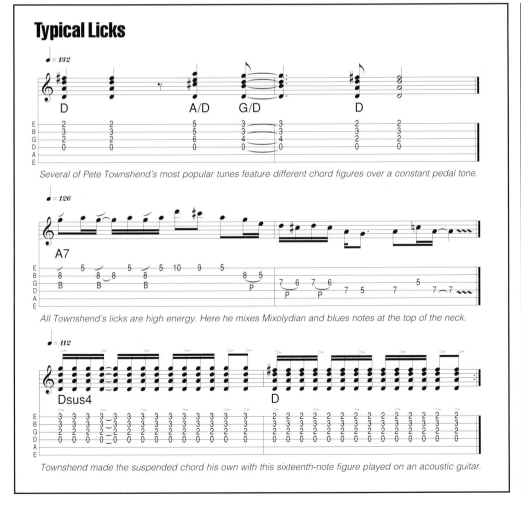

Typical Licks

Several of Pete Townshend's most popular tunes feature different chord figures over a constant pedal tone.

All Townshend's licks are high energy. Here he mixes Mixolydian and blues notes at the top of the neck.

Townshend made the suspended chord his own with this sixteenth-note figure played on an acoustic guitar.

Discography

*Townshend's recordings with the Who contain some of his best and most inventive guitar work. These albums include: **My Generation**, **A Quick One**, **The Who Sell Out**, **Tommy**, **Live At Leeds**, **Who's Next**, **Quadrophenia**, **Odds & Sods**, **The Who By Numbers**, **Who Are You**, **Face Dances**, and **It's Hard**. The box set **The Who: 30 Years Of Maximum R&B** is an excellent retrospective.*

*He has recorded several fine solo albums, including **Who Came First**, **Empty Glass**, **All The Best Cowboys Have Chinese Eyes**, **Scoop**, **Another Scoop**, **White City**, **Iron Man**, and **PsychoDerelict**. He performed several Who classics with classical guitarist John Williams for **The Secret Policeman's Ball**, and in 1977 he recorded the album **Rough Mix** with Ronnie Lane.*

Recording Sessions

*His rare guest appearances include Thunderclap Newman's **Hollywood Dream**, Mike Heron's **Smiling Men With Bad Reputations**, Eric Clapton's **Eric Clapton's Rainbow Concert**, Yvonne Elliman's **Food Of Love**, The Crickets' **Bubblegum, Bop, Ballads & Boogies**, John Otway and Wild Willy Barrett's **John Otway and Wild Willy Barrett**, the **Mahoney's Last Stand** soundtrack with Ron Wood and Ronnie Lane, and David Bowie's **Scary Monsters**.*

Steve Vai

A phenomenally talented guitarist, Vai made his debut as a teenager in the highly challenging environs of Frank Zappa's band. Achieving fame as a member of David Lee Roth's band and Whitesnake, Vai began pursuing a successful career as a solo artist in 1990. He is an extremely proficient player with an innate ability to produce a variety of unconventional tones and sound effects from the guitar. One of the most highly regarded rock guitarists of the '80s and '90s, Vai has greatly expanded the electric guitar's boundaries.

The Player

Influences

Steve was the only member of his family who was interested in being a musician. His first instrument was the accordion, which he started playing when he was 11. He disliked the accordion however, and his interests shifted to the guitar when he was 13. He took his first lessons from his schoolmate Joe Satriani, who taught him how to play songs by Jimi Hendrix and Led Zeppelin. Shortly afterwards, Vai started playing in the bands Susrat – closely patterned after Satriani's band Tarsus (they even spelled the name backwards) – and Rayge. Vai and Satriani have remained close friends, and Vai often cites Satriani as his favorite guitarist.

Vai has a thorough background in music theory. He took music classes in high school from Bill Wescott, learning about theory and composition. After high school, he enrolled in Boston's Berklee School Of Music, where he studied modal harmony and arranging for big bands. In college, he practiced for 12 hours a day, working on exercises, scales, chords, and sight reading.

While at Berklee, Vai learned how to transcribe music, a talent that eventually landed him work with Frank Zappa. Some of his early transcriptions included works by Zappa and guitar solos by Allan Holdsworth and Carlos Santana. Vai studied several music books and lists Gary Chaffee's *Rhythms* and Ted Greene's *Chord Chemistry* as some of his favorite instructional material. "I learned so much just by reading through that book and trying to utilize it," Vai remarked to Tom Mulhern in *Guitar Player*.

Vai's musical tastes are fairly diverse, but his main influences are rock guitarists. In the early '80s, he listed Jimi Hendrix, Jimmy Page, Brian May, Eddie Van Halen, Randy Rhoads, and Frank Zappa as his favorite guitarists. "I copped a lot of Hendrix," he told *Guitar Player*'s Jas Obrecht. "That's how I got the basic foundation of my whole way of approaching chords." Vai cited Van Halen's solo on "Push Comes To Shove" (*Fair Warning*) as one of his favorite guitar solos. Vai also enjoys the playing of Adrian Belew, Diamond Darrell with Pantera, Reeves Gabrels of David Bowie's Tin Machine, Extreme's Nuno Bettencourt, Dweezil Zappa, Vernon Reid, and Texas guitar legend Eric Johnson.

Jazz is probably Vai's second biggest musical influence. His favorite jazz guitarists

Background

1960 *Steve Vai is born on June 6 in Carle Place, Long Island, New York.*

1971 *Starts playing the accordion.*

1973 *Steve starts playing guitar, taking lessons from his schoolmate Joe Satriani, and later forms Susrat, playing Led Zeppelin covers.*

1977 *Vai attends Boston's Berklee School of Music.*

1978 *After recording some tunes with fusion ensemble Morning Thunder, Vai sends a tape to Frank Zappa.*

1979 *Moves to Los Angeles and starts working with Frank Zappa.*

1982 *Steve embarks on his first world tour with Frank Zappa.*

1983 *Records his solo album* Flex-Able *on his eight-track home studio setup.*

1984 *Vai joins heavy metal band Alcatrazz, replacing Yngwie Malmsteen.*

1985 *He becomes a member of ex-Van Halen vocalist David Lee Roth's band.*

1986 *Steve works with Ry Cooder on the movie* Crossroads, *playing Jack Butler, the "devil" guitar player.*

1989 *Joins David Coverdales' Whitesnake and records album* Slip Of The Tongue *after guitarist Adrian Vandenberg suffers a hand injury. Steve uses a seven-string guitar for the entire album.*

1990 *Vai releases the solo album* Passion And Warfare. *He becomes the first guitarist to win four categories in* Guitar Player*'s Readers Poll.*

1991 *Vai headlines the rock night with mentor Joe Satriani at the Guitar Legends Festival in Seville, Spain.*

1993 *Steve forms the band Vai and releases the album* Sex And Religion.

Vai has gigged with several artists and bands, including Frank Zappa, Alcatrazz, David Lee Roth, and Whitesnake. Currently pursuing a solo career, Vai is a flamboyant performer, both onstage and in the studio.

include Wes Montgomery, Joe Pass, and Al Di Meola. He ranks Ted Greene's *Solo Guitar* as one of his favorite jazz albums. "He's a maniac the way he makes the rhythm and melody go at the same time," Vai told Mulhern. He also enjoys big-band music and Broadway musical scores, such as Leonard Bernstein's *West Side Story* and Stephen Sondheim's *Sweeney Todd.*

Steve also enjoys Prince's funk music ("His grooves are priceless."), Stevie Ray Vaughan's blues guitar playing, Michael Hedges' acoustic guitar explorations, and African guitar music.

Approach and Style

Vai is an extremely versatile stylist with an advanced understanding of music theory. His playing is distinguished by his reliance on many unconventional modes, sophisticated rhythm structures, and distinctive chord voicings. He may be characterized as a rock guitarist, but his playing is far removed from the pentatonic minor and blues-based clichés of most rock musicians.

Vai's favorite mode is the Lydian mode, and he frequently bases his solos and melodies around this. He also uses the Mixolydian and Dorian modes often. "I love the sound of Dorian with a major 6th that almost implies minor, and the same thing goes for the ninth" Vai told Joe Gore in *Guitar Player.* "I like Dorian better than straight minor, and I like cadencing my melodies on the ninth." Sometimes Vai plays synthetic modes, which are not derived from the basic diatonic major scale system. Occasionally he uses conventional major scales or modern whole-tone scales. Many of his licks are based on sequenced scale motifs.

While playing with Frank Zappa, Vai became familiar with polyrhythms, and many of his songs are structured around polyrhythmic figures. Some of his rhythmic devices include displacement and shifting accents, such as a 7/8 rhythm stacked on top of an 8/8 figure.

Vai is also an accomplished orchestrator and he likes to build dense, layered multiple guitar parts in the studio. One of his main compositional approaches is a hybrid chord structure where he superimposes simple but harmonically remote chords that move in a progression over a constant bass line. Sometimes these hybrid structures involve overlapping upper-structure triads.

Vai's melodies often emphasize the ninth instead of the root. He claims that the ninth, ♯11, and ♭7 are his favorite notes. His other melodic devices include chromatic ascending licks, Hendrix-inspired chord melodies, Wes Montgomery-style octaves, wide interval skips, pedal tones, and triadic harmonies.

Techniques

One of Vai's most recognizable techniques is his frequent use of the Floyd Rose tremolo system. He uses the tremolo to create a wide variety of musical effects. He plays melodies with the bar, pulls the bar sharp until the strings touch the frets or presses down the bar until the strings go limp, and creates unusual bends by turning the bar around and bouncing his hand on it to pull notes sharp. By flicking the bar with his fingers, he makes notes warble. Before he had a guitar with a Floyd Rose tailpiece, he sometimes used to bend notes by reaching behind the nut and either pulling or pushing on the strings.

Vai uses a wide variety of right-hand techniques. Resting his right hand against the bridge, he mutes notes with his palm to create staccato tones. He is especially adept at generating artificial harmonic "squeals" by striking the string simultaneously with the pick and the edge of his thumb. To generate sitar-like tones, he picks next to the notes that he is fretting with his left hand. He uses sweep picking, a technique where the pick is lightly dragged back and forth across the strings, to play fast arpeggios and plucks the strings with several fingers to create percussive, piano-like grooves. His tapping technique is especially well developed, and he sometimes plays figures up and down the neck by walking hand-over-hand on one string. He also taps chords and harmonized lines on multiple strings.

With his left hand, Vai employs the rock guitarist's full vocabulary of pull-offs, hammer-ons, slurs, slides, and bends. He often uses legato phrasing, playing entire passages with his left hand only, for fluid tone and speed. Using string skipping, he plays wide intervals and complex melodies. Some of his unorthodox left-hand techniques include pulling the *B* string off of the neck, a trick he learned from Joe Satriani, and playing a fast single-note triplet while fretting the note with a different finger each time he strikes the string. For timbral variety, he plays the same note pattern successively on different strings.

A few of Vai's techniques involve use of effects processors. For example, on "Ballerina 12/24" on *Passion And Warfare* he used a

Harmonizer that was set to generate a fifth and third, each successively delayed after the initial note. This turned a simple sixteenth-note pattern into a complex figure that is impossible to play by conventional means.

The Hardware
Guitars, Strings, and Picks

Steve's first guitar was a Tempo electric that he bought for five dollars. He has provided little other information about his early guitars, but it is safe to assume that he moved on to a better instrument shortly after he acquired the Tempo.

When he joined Frank Zappa's band, he played a '76 Fender Strat that was modified by Zappa technician Midget Sloatman. The Strat featured a built-in overdrive unit, ring modulator, EQ, and Alembic Stratoblaster preamp. This guitar was equipped with a Floyd Rose tremolo. Towards the end of his Zappa gig, his main guitar was a blue custom-made Performance Strat-style solidbody with three humbucking pickups (a DiMarzio X2N in the bridge position and two DiMarzio PAFs) and an Alembic Stratoblaster preamp.

While playing with Alcatrazz and David Lee Roth, Vai owned several custom-made electrics made for him by Jackson, Guild, Ibanez, and luthier Joe Despagni. Most of these guitars were stolen during rehearsal for Roth's first solo tour. His main guitars at this time were a green '86 Charvel Strat-style and a pink Jackson. He also frequently used a Tom Anderson solidbody and a B. C. Rich Bitch doubleneck in the recording studio.

In the late '80s, Steve landed a deal to endorse Ibanez products and helped the company design several signature models. Ibanez' JEM-series models were all built to Steve's specifications. In 1989, Ibanez introduced the Universe, a 7-string solidbody

Vai possesses a rare combination of technical ability, music theory fluency, and emotional finesse. His main guitar is an Ibanez Universe 7-string, which he helped design.

with an additional low B string. An alder-body version of the Universe is Vai's current main guitar.

Steve has played several unorthodox guitars as well, including a three-neck, heart-shaped Ibanez, a 30-fret Guild – an experimental electric with 16 frets to the octave – and a fretless guitar.

Vai's favorite acoustic guitars are all made by Guild. He owns several 6- and 12-string Guilds, as well as a Fender 12-string acoustic.

He plays with a heavy-gauge pick and uses .009-.042 (.009-.052 on the 7-string) Dean Markley Blue Steel strings.

Amplifiers, Effects, and Devices
Steve's first amp was a Fender Deluxe that he still owns and uses for recording. In Frank Zappa's band he often plugged into Zappa's Acoustic 2x12 combo and a Roland JC-120 solid-state combo. Later he started using 100-watt Carvin X100B heads.

After leaving Zappa's band, Vai used a combination of Carvin and Marshall 100-watt

In His Own Words

Who cares if somebody says I sound like someone else? Let's face it – I'm not original. Neither is anybody else, except the Shaggs.
Guitar Player, *February 1983*

A lot of people get tangled up in scales and licks. The next thing you know, they're doing finger exercises, scales, and licks, and it sounds like it.
Guitar Player, *February 1983*

A good solo is like a good book. It'll start out in sentences, or a phrase. It will be in paragraphs, and have pauses, and then it will go and have a great ending – a climax.
Guitar Player, *February 1983*

People say, "When did you get involved in music?" I don't know; it must have been lifetimes ago. When I came out of the chute, I must have had a pair of dark glasses on and a Strat in one hand and a tattoo on the other.
Guitar Player, *October 1986*

I think we create the beautiful things we do using our intuition, which comes from inside. How much we let that flame inside become part of our product determines what type of person we are.
Guitar Player, *May 1990*

What They Say

I've heard more of him than other people have heard. Steve Vai is a huge musician. Most people hear him as a guitar player. They don't see all the different pairs of pants he owns. But I've seen the pants and I've heard the tapes.
Joe Satriani, Guitar World, *April 1990*

Watching a guy like Steve Vai is so amazing that I couldn't even call him an influence 'cause... I can't do any of that shit! It's like, way out of my league! He's incredibly amazing.
Scotti Hill of Skid Row, The Guitar Magazine, *February 1992*

heads, generally using the Carvin for clean tones and the Marshalls for distortion. His Marshalls were modified by Lee Jackson and Jose Arrendondo. Marshalls are Vai's current main amps, and he owns a variety of JCM 800, Jubilee-series, and JCM 900 heads. He also uses a VHT power amp and several Mesa Boogie and Soldano heads, preferring the Soldanos for onstage use. Sometimes he plays through an ADA MP-1 preamp. His speaker cabinets are 4x12 Marshalls with 30-watt Celestion speakers.

While playing with Zappa, Vai used a pedalboard containing MXR Distortion +, MXR flanger, Cry Baby wah-wah, and Boss CE-2 Chorus pedals, as well as an A/B box for switching between the Roland and Acoustic amps. By the time he joined Roth's band, he was using a large Bradshaw rack system, containing Roland SDE-3000 digital delays, Eventide SP-26T and 949 Harmonizers, Yamaha SPX-90 multi-effects units, an Ibanez SDR-1000 stereo digital reverb, and a t.c. electronics 2290 delay. In the late '80s he replaced the SP-26T and 949 with an Eventide H3000S Ultra Harmonizer, which he uses extensively in the studio and onstage. His current pedals include a Boss overdrive, a Mu-Tron Bi-Phase pedal, a DigiTech Whammy pedal, and a Vox Cry Baby wah-wah.

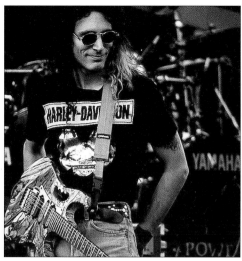

Discography

Vai made his recording debut with Frank Zappa's band, with whom he made the following albums: **Tinseltown Rebellion** *(1981),* **You Are What You Is** *(1981),* **Ship Arriving Too Late To Save A Drowning Witch** *(1982),* **The Man From Utopia** *(1983),* **Them Or Us** *(1984),* **Thing-Fish** *(1984),* **Jazz From Hell** *(1986), and the multiple volume series albums* **Shut Up And Play Yer Guitar** *and* **You Can't Do That On Stage Anymore**.

Between Zappa and his current solo projects, Vai joined several bands and played on the following albums: Alcatrazz's **Disturbing The Peace** (1985), David Lee Roth's **Eat 'Em And Smile** (1986) and **Skyscraper** (1988), and Whitesnake's **Slip Of The Tongue** (1989).

In 1984, Vai made the experimental solo albums **Flex-able** and **Flex-able Leftovers**. After playing in several heavy metal bands, he decided to pursue a full-time career as a solo artist and has released the following solo efforts: **Passion And Warfare** (1990) and **Sex And Religion** (1993). **Passion And Warfare** is regarded as his finest album to date and is a good place for the uninitiated to become acquainted with his playing style.

Recording Sessions

Vai's few guest appearances include Public Image Limited's **Album**, *L. Shankar's* **The Epidemics**, *Alice Cooper's* **Hey Stoopid!**, *and* **Guitar's Practicing Musicians**.

Typical Licks

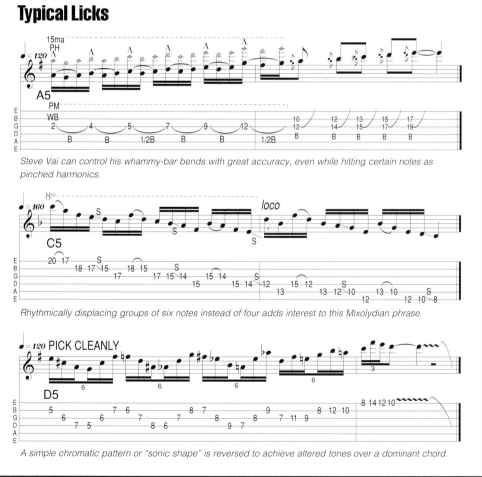

Steve Vai can control his whammy-bar bends with great accuracy, even while hitting certain notes as pinched harmonics.

Rhythmically displacing groups of six notes instead of four adds interest to this Mixolydian phrase.

A simple chromatic pattern or "sonic shape" is reversed to achieve altered tones over a dominant chord.

Eddie Van Halen

Eddie Van Halen is the most influential and innovative rock guitarist to emerge since Jimi Hendrix. Van Halen not only changed the way the electric guitar is played, he also affected the way it is made. Several guitar product innovations – most notably the Floyd Rose tremolo system – were directly influenced by Van Halen's playing style. His two-handed tapping technique is now an accepted part of most rock guitarists' repertoires. Van Halen remains one of rock music's most popular instrumentalists.

The Player

Influences

Eddie Van Halen came from a musical family. His father, Jan, was a professional clarinet player and his mother played keyboards. When he was six, Eddie learned to read music and started taking piano lessons. This gave him a solid grounding in classical music and taught him to use his hands, and fingers, independently. He also studied violin for three years.

When the family moved to California, Eddie began to develop an interest in rock music. He taught himself to play the guitar, his only instruction being a few barre chords learned from a friend. After graduating from high school, Eddie studied scoring and arranging with Dr. Fischer at Pasadena City College.

When he started to play guitar, one of Eddie's favorite players was Eric Clapton. He learned to play Eric's solos on "Crossroads," "I'm So Glad," and "Sitting On Top Of The World" with Cream, and his licks from the Bluesbreakers album. Eddie still cites Clapton as his primary influence. "I realize I don't sound like him, but I know every solo he's ever played, note-for-note, still to this day," he told Jas Obrecht in a 1978 interview

for *Guitar Player*. He also enjoyed the music of Jimi Hendrix, Jeff Beck, Jimmy Page, and Ritchie Blackmore, among others. He also said that he liked the playing of Hendrix-impersonator Randy Hansen and Cheap Trick's Rick Nielsen, and appreciated Joe Satriani and Steve Vai. He was also heavily influenced by Allan Holdsworth. "I *love* the way he plays," Eddie told Obrecht in 1982. "He's got feeling. He's got an ear that's unbelievable. I mean, he can play any chord change you want, and he can improvise over it."

Classical music influences also figure heavily in Van Halen's repertoire, primarily Bach, Debussy, and Mozart. He was inspired to write the instrumental "Spanish Fly" on *Van Halen II* after hearing a record by classical guitarist Carlos Montoya.

Approach And Style

Largely due to the revolutionary techniques he developed, Eddie created a guitar style unlike any previous guitarist. Although much of his playing is centered in pentatonic-minor and pentatonic-major blues scales, his flamboyant approach ensured that no one would mistake his playing for that of anyone else.

Eddie's rhythm style combines riffs and simple chords. He prefers two- or three-note

Background

1957 *Edward Lodewijk Van Halen is born in Nijmegen, The Netherlands, on January 26.*

1963 *Eddie starts taking piano lessons.*

1965 *The Van Halen family moves to the United States.*

1968 *Eddie starts learning to play the drums, but switches to guitar when he notices that his brother Alex is progressing more quickly on the drums. When he was starting to play guitar, Eddie learned licks off of records by slowing them down.*

1972 *Alex and Eddie form Mammoth, with Eddie singing and playing lead.*

1974 *The group Van Halen is formed.*

1976 *Gene Simmons of Kiss sponsors the group's first demo recordings, but no record companies are interested.*

1977 *Ted Templeman and Mo Ostin see Van Halen at the Starwood Club in L.A. They sign the group the following week.*

1978 *Eddie Van Halen makes his recording debut on Van Halen.*

1979 *Eddie wins Best Rock Guitarist in Guitar Player's readers' poll, edging out Page, Santana, and Howe.*

1980 *Guitar Player features Eddie on the April 1980 cover, making him the youngest cover story artist in the magazine's history.*

1982 *Records an innovative solo on Michael Jackson's Thriller album for no fee.*

1983 *Van Halen enters Guitar Player magazine's "Gallery Of The Greats" after winning the Readers' Poll for five consecutive years. Brian May of Queen invites Eddie to record on his solo album Star Fleet Project.*

1985 *Vocalist David Lee Roth quits Van Halen.*

1986 *Vocalist/guitarist Sammy Hagar joins the band. The band's album 5150 reaches #1 on the Billboard Top 200 Albums chart.*

1991 *Eddie introduces a new guitar designed by himself and the Ernie Ball/Music Man company.*

chords to full ones, and often uses fifths for major chords. He generally sticks to major and minor chords with an occasional seventh or suspended chord, feeling that these sound best in a loud rock 'n' roll context.

Most of Eddie's solos are created spontaneously, often centered around the Dorian mode, or blurring the line between major- and minor-pentatonic scales. He uses many sophisticated approaches that add variety to his solos, such as chromatic passing tones, pedal tones, and symmetrical fingerboard patterns that do not fit within any particular scales but suit the context of his music perfectly. Dominant seventh arpeggios and diminished triads give his music a semi-classical flavor. Although his style often defies common music-theory practices, Eddie feels that the only rule to follow is to make sure that whatever he plays sounds good to him.

Techniques

Eddie has developed several techniques that were quite revolutionary when he started, although they are now widely imitated. The most distinctive is his tapping technique, where he simultaneously performs pull-offs with his left-hand and strikes the fingerboard with his right-hand forefinger on a single string, producing a triplet pattern. He performs several variations of this technique, such as tapping chord shapes on several strings with both hands or holding a note with his right hand while his left taps higher up on the fingerboard. When tapping, he mutes strings with his left-hand index finger and thumb.

Van Halen holds his pick with his right-hand thumb and middle finger, leaving the forefinger free to perform tapping. Sometimes he rests the side of his right hand against the bridge to muffle the strings, producing a percussive muted effect. He uses an alternate picking pattern, feeling it gives him greater control and speed. One of his signature licks is a fast, ascending tremolo-picked line played on one string that ends with a bent note. He often employs cross-picked patterns as well, skipping back and forth between two strings. He has considerable reach with his left hand and can stretch from the fifth to the twelfth fret. He has developed a sophisticated left-hand legato technique where he pulls-off and hammers-on triads in a fluid manner.

Harmonics are also an important part of Van Halen's technique. He produces harmonics in several manners, including traditional open-string natural harmonics, muted pick harmonics, and tapped harmonics produced by striking the fret one octave, an octave and a fifth, or two octaves above a fretted note. A good example of the latter technique can be heard on the intro to "Women In Love" from the album *Van Halen II*.

Van Halen also uses the vibrato bar extensively to drop pitch and bend notes. His application of the vibrato bar led to the development of the Floyd Rose locking tremolo. "It's more of a feeling as opposed to an effect," he told *Guitar Player*. "I just grab it when I feel like it." He has developed precise control of the vibrato bar and is able to drop the bar to specific notes at will.

Although he does not consider himself a slide player, Van Halen has played slide on several of his own compositions, including "Could This Be Magic," "Dirty Movies," and "Apolitical Blues."

The Hardware

Guitars, Strings, and Picks

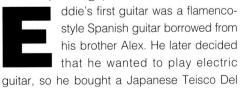Eddie's first guitar was a flamenco-style Spanish guitar borrowed from his brother Alex. He later decided that he wanted to play electric guitar, so he bought a Japanese Teisco Del Rey guitar with four pickups for $70.

Van Halen owned a number of different guitars while he was playing in bands during the '70s. He briefly played a '58 Strat, but stopped because other band members complained that it sounded too thin. He also played a Gibson ES-335, which he loved, but his band thought that the guitar did not look right for a rock band. This ES-335, which he still owns, became Eddie's guinea pig for various repair experiments, and he refinished and refretted it several times. During this time he used a Les Paul as well. Although he liked the sound of this guitar, he wanted a vibrato-bar system such as that found on a Strat.

Eddie found that the answer was to build his own guitar, combining Les Paul and Strat features. His main guitar was assembled with a Strat body and neck that he bought from Charvel, a Gibson Patent Applied For humbucking pickup, large Gibson frets, and a Strat vibrato system. This guitar had only one pickup in a slanted position near the bridge and one volume control. Eddie used this guitar on the first Van Halen album and tour.

Although Van Halen was best known for his home-made guitar, he always used a variety of guitars in the studio on his early albums. He played an Ibanez Destroyer (a Gibson Explorer copy) on much of the first album, and has used a guitar he made with a Charvel Explorer-shaped body, a Danelectro neck, and a Gibson PAF humbucker. He also played a '52 goldtop Les Paul, modified with a Tune-O-Matic bridge and humbucking pickups. Eddie doubled his solo for "Ain't Talkin' 'Bout Love" with an electric sitar. For *Van Halen II*, he made a black guitar with yellow strips, similar to his first home-made one, and played an Ovation nylon-string guitar on the instrumental "Spanish Fly."

By the time Van Halen was preparing their third album, *Women And Children First*, a designer named Floyd Rose developed a locking tailpiece and nut for Eddie. This device, called a Floyd Rose tailpiece, is now a common feature on electric guitars. Eddie made a guitar with a 2-inch-thick Boogie Bodies mahogany body and a Floyd Rose system for this record. He also played a Rickenbacker electric 12-string on "Simple Rhyme." By now, Eddie's guitar collection had grown quite a bit, and he had acquired several Gibson ES-335s, two '58 Gibson Les Paul Juniors, several Japanese Strat copies, and two vintage Les Paul Standards – a '59 flame-top and a '58 gold-top.

In the early '80s, Eddie signed an endorsement deal with Kramer guitars. The Kramers that he used were similar to his early home-made guitars, and they became his primary instruments for live performance and studio work for the rest of the decade. His main guitar was made from a Kramer Baretta body and a Kramer neck, and it featured a Seymour Duncan '59 humbucker. He also played a Kramer Ferrington electric-acoustic guitar and a Kramer Ripley stereo guitar.

For *Diver Down*, Eddie played a '61 Stratocaster on "Cathedral," a miniature Les Paul copy made by Dave Petschulat on "Little Guitars," and a Gibson double-neck 6/12 for "Secrets." A Gibson Flying V was used on *1984*'s "Hot For Teacher" and "Drop Dead Legs." On *5150*, he played a Steinberger GL2T equipped with EMG humbuckers and a Trans-Trem for "Get Up" and "Summer Nights." On *OU812*, he used a Fender Telecaster for "Run Around," a Fender 12-string on "Cabo Wabo," and an Airline guitar for "Apolitical Blues."

Just prior to recording *For Unlawful Carnal Knowledge*, Eddie signed a new endorsement deal with the Ernie Ball/Music Man company. Working with Dudley Gimpel and Sterling Ball, he developed the Edward Van Halen guitar, which featured a basswood body, maple top, two DiMarzio humbucking pickups, and a Floyd Rose-licensed Gotoh tailpiece. This is Eddie's current main guitar. Ernie Ball/Music Man also made Eddie a

doubleneck guitar featuring a 6-string hollow-body bass and a 6-string solidbody guitar.

Van Halen played several other guitars on *For Unlawful Carnal Knowledge*, including a Roger Giffin electric 12-string on "Poundcake," a Danelectro 6-string bass on "Spanked," an Ernie Ball 6-string bass for "Right Now," and a Gibson Chet Atkins steel string on "316."

Eddie's picks are light-medium .027-gauge D'Addarios. He used to use stock Fender 150XL strings, but now prefers Ernie Ball 5150s (.009, .011, .015, .024, .032, .040).

Amplifiers, Effects, and Devices

From the mid-'70s until the early '90s, Eddie's main amp was a '66 or '67 plexiglas front, 100-watt Marshall Super Lead. He has used this amp on every Van Halen album. Although he has had many of his amps modified, this particular amp is stock.

In the early days of Van Halen, Eddie used three 100-watt Marshall amps. After he

Eddie Van Halen is one of the most influential electric guitarists since Jimi Hendrix. His innovative tapping techniques, pick harmonics, and flamboyant tremolo-bar effects have been imitated by thousands of guitarists.

temporarily lost his main amp while on tour, he was using a combination of late '70s Marshall heads, Laneys, and Music Mans. For backstage warm-up he used a Fender Deluxe Reverb, and at home he likes to play through a cream-Tolex covered early-'60s Fender Bandmaster. In the late '80s he started using 100-watt Soldano SLO-100 heads.

Many of Van Halen's amps were modified by Jose Arrendondo. Eddie also liked to use a Variac variable transformer with his amps, either increasing the voltage to 130 or 140 volts or decreasing it to 90 volts.

He recently worked with Peavey to develop the 5150 EVH amplifier head, which is currently his main amp. He uses this with 4x12 cabinets loaded with 25-watt speakers.

On Van Halen's early albums and tours, Eddie used an MXR flanger, an MXR Phase 90, two Echoplexes, and a Univox EC-80 echo housed in a World War II practice bomb. Later he added an Eventide 949 Harmonizer, Rocktron RX2H Exciter, and a Roland DC30 Chorus Echo to his effects rig.

His current effects setup consists of two Roland SDE-3000 digital delays, two Eventide H-3000 Harmonizers, a Lexicon PCM-70, a Boss OC-2 Octave pedal, an MXR Phase 90, an MXR flanger, a Boss SD-1 Overdrive, and a Cry Baby wah-wah. The effects are controlled by a Bradshaw switching system and run through a Palmer speaker simulator and H&H V-800 power amp. The signals are split to three cabinets – the center cabinet gets a dry signal, and the left and right cabinets get the effected signal in stereo. Eddie also occasionally uses a hand-held E-Bow sustain device, and has created special effects with a Makita cordless drill, as can be heard at the beginning of "Poundcake."

Throughout his career, Van Halen has used several wireless systems. His first was a Schaffer-Vega wireless system, then he switched to a Nady Cordless. He is currently using a Sony WR440 wireless system.

Discography

All of Van Halen's albums on Warner Bros. contain fine examples of his playing. These albums include: **Van Halen**, **Van Halen II**, **Women And Children First**, **Fair Warning**, **Diver Down**, *1984*, **5150**, **OU812**, **For Unlawful Carnal Knowledge**, *and* **Van Halen Live: Right Here, Right Now**.

Eddie has also written and performed music for the soundtracks to **The Wild Life** *and* **Over The Top**.

Recording Sessions

Eddie has made guest appearances on only a handful of albums, including Nicolette Larson's **Nicolette**, *"Beat It," on Michael Jackson's* **Thriller**, *Brian May & Friends'* **Star Fleet Project**, *and Sammy Hagar's* **Sammy Hagar**. *He also played on the intro of Dweezil Zappa's single, "My Mother Is A Space Cadet."*

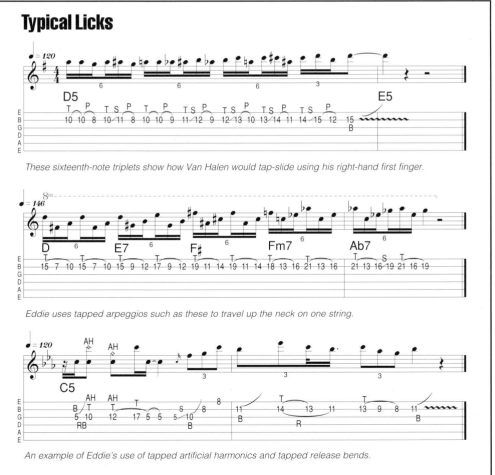

Typical Licks

These sixteenth-note triplets show how Van Halen would tap-slide using his right-hand first finger.

Eddie uses tapped arpeggios such as these to travel up the neck on one string.

An example of Eddie's use of tapped artificial harmonics and tapped release bends.

Stevie Ray Vaughan

With a thick, powerful, biting tone, a soulful playing style, and dynamic stage presence, Stevie Ray Vaughan was one of the finest modern blues guitarists. His music appealed to rock fans as well as blues enthusiasts, which helped make him the most successful blues artist to emerge since Clapton's reign in the '60s. Vaughan borrowed freely from his influences, but his music always bore the indelible stamp of his charismatic personality. Many guitarists have imitated Vaughan's licks, but few match the intensity and fire of his inspired playing.

The Player

Influences

Neither of Vaughan's parents were musicians, but they were avid music fans who used to take Stevie and his brother Jimmie to shows by Fats Domino, Jimmy Reed, and Bob Wills. Vaughan's uncles both played electric guitar, and he often watched them play at family get-togethers.

Although Vaughan said that he initially wanted to be a drummer, his first instrument was the guitar, which he started playing when he was eight years old. His brother, who later became well-known in Texas clubs and was a member of the Fabulous Thunderbirds, gave Stevie his first guitar lessons. "My brother Jimmie actually was one of the biggest influences on my playing," Stevie told Bruce Nixon in *Guitar Player*. "He really was the reason why I started to play, watching him and seeing what could be done." After his brother showed him a few basic chords, Stevie taught himself to play. He learned entirely by ear and never learned how to read music.

Stevie was attracted to blues music from the very beginning. He listened to records by blues artists B. B. King, T-Bone Walker, Muddy Waters, Howlin' Wolf with Hubert Sumlin, Magic Sam, Albert Collins, Guitar Slim, Johnny Guitar Watson, John Lee Hooker, Lightnin' Hopkins, Jimmy Reed, Elmore James, and several others. The first record he bought was a 45 of Lonnie Mack's "Wham"/"Suzie-Q." He also enjoyed rock artists, such as the Yardbirds, Eric Clapton, and Jeff Beck. Vaughan covered many songs by his favorite blues artists, including Buddy Guy's "Mary Had A Little Lamb," Howlin' Wolf's "Tell Me" and "Love Me Darlin'," Elmore James' "The Sky Is Crying," and Muddy Water's "Close To You."

Several of Vaughan's blues and rock influences are evident in his licks and phrasing. Albert King had a profound effect on Vaughan, and Stevie often incorporated King's signature licks into his solos. Many of Stevie's bent-note phrases are reminiscent of Buddy Guy's playing, and several of his fast-tempo, pull-off based riffs were based on Lonnie Mack's style. He also imitated many of Freddie King's turnarounds. But the guitarist who probably influenced Vaughan the most was Jimi Hendrix. "Jimmie brought home a Hendrix record, and I went, 'Whoa! What is this?' I'll never forget that," Stevie

Background

1954 *Stevie Ray Vaughan is born on October 3, in Dallas, Texas.*

1962 *Stevie starts playing guitar.*

1968 *He meets up with bassist Tommy Shannon and forms the band Blackbird.*

1972 *Vaughan moves to Austin, Texas, where he joins several club bands.*

1973 *Records "Texas Clover" with Paul Ray and the Cobras.*

1977 *Stevie forms Triple Threat Revue with vocalist Lou Ann Barton who later briefly fronted Double Trouble.*

1978 *Stevie forms the band Double Trouble.*

1982 *Producer Jerry Wexler enlists Vaughan for the Montreux Jazz Festival, where he meets David Bowie.*

1983 *Stevie guests on Bowie's* Let's Dance *and releases his debut solo album* Texas Flood, *which is later certified gold.*

1984 *"Couldn't Stand The Weather" is released with a video and receives good airplay on MTV. Stevie teams up with George Thorogood for a tribute to Chuck Berry at the Grammy Awards.*

1985 *Stevie is awarded a Grammy for his contribution to the* Blues Explosion *anthology. Reese Wynans joins Double Trouble on keyboards. Vaughan co-produces album* Strikes Like Lightning *with childhood idol Lonnie Mack.*

1986 *Stevie plays on James Brown's hit single "Living In America." After years of hard living and substance abuse, Stevie checks into a clinic, and finally overcomes an addiction to drugs and alcohol.*

1989 *Vaughan and Jeff Beck hit the road in a co-headlining tour.*

1990 *Vaughan dies in a helicopter accident on August 27, in East Troy, Wisconsin.*

told Dan Forte in a *Guitar Player* interview. Vaughan played covers of several Hendrix songs throughout his career, including "Voodoo Chile," "Third Stone From The Sun," and "Little Wing."

Vaughan started playing professionally at an early age. He played blues and rock covers by bands such as the Allman Brothers, and by the time he was 13 years old he was playing in clubs where he met many of his blues idols. In the early '70s, Vaughan jammed with Johnny Winter, whose bassist Tommy Shannon eventually became a member of Vaughan's band Double Trouble.

Besides the blues and rock 'n' roll, Vaughan was also influenced by R&B music and jazz. Some of his favorite jazz guitarists include Wes Montgomery, Grant Green, Django Reinhardt, and Kenny Burrell, whose "Chitlins Con Carne" was covered by Vaughan on the posthumous release, *The Sky Is Crying*.

Approach and Style

Vaughan's style was heavily rooted in the blues. He relied almost exclusively on major pentatonic, minor pentatonic, and blues scales, and many of his songs used conventional 12-bar blues I-IV-V chord progressions. He also liked to use bluesy turnarounds to bridge chord changes. However, Vaughan combined influences from rock and jazz as well, developing a style that was truly his own.

One of Vaughan's signatures was a quarter-note bass line interspersed with comped chord stabs. "Pride And Joy" is an example of this approach. He used a variety of other rhythmic approaches, including shuffles, straight-eighth grooves, and three-against-four cross-rhythms. Sometimes he played jazzy, Hendrix-inspired chord melodies and used parallel-chord motion, particularly on his slower ballads. His chordal vocabulary

After years of obscurity playing in small clubs and bars in Texas, Stevie Ray Vaughan was introduced to the masses by his appearance on David Bowie's single, "Let's Dance." Shortly afterwards he began a successful solo career.

consisted primarily of major, minor, and seventh chords, but he frequently played sixth, ninth, and thirteenth chords as well.

Vaughan made effective use of open strings. Many of his fast riffs incorporated a series of pull-offs to open strings and he often used open-string pedal tones. Occasionally he would play octave pull-offs from the 12th fret to open strings. Some of his other favorite melodic devices included Wes Montgomery-style octave melodies, quartal harmonies – such as those heard on "Lenny" – and chromatically ascending pick-ups or chords.

Vaughan's guitars were tuned to standard tuning, but he usually tuned the entire guitar down a half step. On the rare occasions when he played slide guitar, he tuned the G string up a half step.

Techniques

The most distinctive element of Vaughan's playing style was his right-hand picking technique. Holding his pick between his right-hand thumb and forefinger, he often switched between playing exclusively with the pick and playing with both the pick and his middle finger. For tonal variation he would turn the pick around and pluck the strings with the blunt, round end. Occasionally, he would tuck the pick up into his palm and snap the strings percussively with only his fingers.

Vaughan had great control of dynamics with his right hand. He often struck the strings quite forcefully with the pick, but he also played soft passages with a light touch. He used alternate- and tremolo-picking techniques for fast phrases, and sometimes he would use upstrokes for entire passages, picking with the flesh of his thumb or forefinger. One of his signatures was a raking technique where he would drag the pick quickly across several strings while his left hand muted all but one of the notes. By resting his right-hand palm against the bridge, he would mute the strings to produce a percussive tone or to damp open strings.

Vaughan's left-hand string-bending technique was particularly well-developed. He would use bends ranging from a half step to two whole steps, and he often made effective use of microtones. He could bend strings with any of his left-hand fingers, including his forefinger, which he employed for Albert King-style phrases. He used a variety of other bending techniques, including released bends, double-stop bends, and atonal bends that he produced by catching several strings with his fingertips.

Vaughan's left-hand techniques included hammer-ons, pull-offs, and slurs, and he often used legato phrasing to play entire passages. Sometimes he would drape his left-hand thumb over the fretboard to play chords. He was adept at several different left-hand vibrato techniques, such as fast, narrow flutters and slow, wide modulations. He also used the tremolo bar for vibrato as

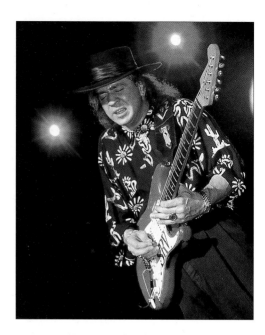

Although Vaughan is best known for his fiery blues guitar work, he also played stunning Jimi Hendrix covers, rocking Lonnie Mack-style instrumentals, and haunting ballads. His main guitar was a battered '59 Fender Stratocaster.

well as for dramatic, Hendrix-inspired dive bombs and special effects.

The Hardware

Guitars, Strings, and Picks

Vaughan's first guitar was an inexpensive Masonite acoustic that he was given for his seventh birthday. He owned a succession of guitars before acquiring his all-time favorite, a Fender Stratocaster. His main guitar was a '59 Strat with rosewood fingerboard. "I didn't even try it out in the store," he told Bruce Nixon in *Guitar Player*. "I looked at it and I knew. It's the first Strat I was ever really attached to." Vaughan added a few modifications to the Strat, including a left-handed tremolo and large Gibson frets.

Stevie played a variety of Strats during his career. He owned a '57 Strat that he got from his brother, an early '60s Strat with a maple fingerboard that he nicknamed "Lenny," an orange-finished '60 Strat, and a yellow '64 with one DiMarzio pickup in the neck position that was modified by Charley Wirz. He also had several custom-built Strat-style guitars, including a white Strat with Danelectro lipstick-tube pickups and a Hamiltone that featured Vaughan's name inlaid on the fingerboard, neck-through-body construction, an ebony fingerboard, and EMG pickups.

Although he was rarely seen playing anything but a Strat, Vaughan owned several other electrics, including a 1958 Gibson ES-335, a Kay Barney Kessel model, a '48 Airline, a couple of Fender Telecasters, and a Gibson Johnny Smith, which he used for "Stan's Swang." Vaughan's main acoustic guitar was a '28 National Duolian resonator guitar that once belonged to Blind Boy Fuller.

Vaughan played with a heavy D'Addario Delrin .043-gauge pick. He used heavy strings, preferring a .013, .015, .019, .028, .038, .058 set.

Amplifiers, Effects, and Devices

Vaughan's amplifier choices were a key element of his thick, powerful tone. Onstage, he ran several amps in parallel in combinations that changed throughout his career. In the early '80s, he used two '63 Fender Vibroverb 1x15 combos. The Vibroverb was one of Vaughan's favorite amps, and late in his career he used a Vibroverb to power a Leslie speaker cabinet onstage. In the late '80s, he used a pair of mid-'60s Fender Super Reverb 4x10 combos onstage. Sometimes he augmented his amp setup with a Dumble Steel String Singer 150-watt head.

Vaughan also played through various Marshalls, both onstage and in the studio. In the early '80s he used a Marshall Club And Country 2x12 combo. While recording *In Step*, Vaughan played through several

In His Own Words

I'd call it R&B, but sometimes we get out there with it. A lot of people think of it as blues-rock, although I'd like to have it thought of as just music.
Guitar Player, *August 1983*

In Texas there seem to be a lot of musicians interested in pulling for each other and working together, and it really, really helps a lot. It makes everybody a tighter unit, and it keeps you right in your heart.
Guitar Player, *October 1984.*

I'm just trying to find the most tone I can get. There are these nights when it doesn't seem that I've got anything to do with it. That's the one you always play for.
Guitar Player, *February 1990*

I'm not Jimi Hendrix – I can't play every rhythm part in the world and then sing at the same time and act like nothing's wrong. And do somersaults.
Guitar Player, *February 1990*

What They Say

Stevie Ray Vaughan is exactly what I wanted to be when I was 16 years old.
Eric Clapton, Guitar Player, *July 1985*

Stevie gets plugged into his soul's emotions. He wails and he's mellow, all at the same time, without ever playing it the same way once, much less twice.
Jimmie Vaughan, Guitar Player, *July 1986*

I think Stevie's playing state-of-the-art blues at the moment. There's no one who has that tone, and the venom that goes with it.
Jeff Beck, Guitar Player, *February 1990*

I remember we played "Baker Street" by Gerry Rafferty. I was so surprised to see Stevie Ray play over those changes, how he incorporated his blues style into a non-blues song. Watching him do that, it stuck in my head that night how blues truly is the foundation.
Will Lee, session bass player, Guitar World, *December 1990*

Marshall heads, including a 100-watt JCM 800 and 200-watt Marshall Major Super P. A. and Super Leads. The Majors were connected to Marshall 4x15 and 8x10 cabinets. Other amps used on the *In Step* sessions include a '62 Fender Twin, a '59 4x10 Fender Bassman, a Fender Harvard, and a Magnatone.

There were only a few pedals in Vaughan's effects rig. His favorite effect was an Ibanez Tube Screamer, which he used primarily to boost his signal for solos. His other effects pedals were a Fuzz Face, an Octavia, and a Vox wah-wah. In the studio, he sometimes used two wah-wah pedals, a Univibe, and a Fender Vibratone unit for Leslie effects.

Discography

Vaughan made his first recordings in the early '70s with his band Cast Of Thousands. One of their songs appeared on the various artists compilation, **A New Hi**.

In the '80s, Vaughan recorded several fine albums with his band Double Trouble. These include: **Texas Flood** *(1983),* **Couldn't Stand The Weather** *(1984),* **Soul To Soul** *(1985), the live album* **Live Alive** *(1986), and* **In Step** *(1989). The following albums were released after his death:* **The Sky Is Crying** *(1991) and* **In The Beginning** *(1992), taken from a live radio broadcast in 1980.*

The following various artist compilations include fine Vaughan live performances: **Blues Explosion** *(1984), which was recorded at the '82 Montreux Jazz Festival, and* **Sacred Sources 1 – Live Forever** *(1993), which features a stunning live rendition of "Riviera Paradise."*

Vaughan made one record with his brother Jimmie, **Family Style** *(1990), which was released within days of Stevie's untimely death.*

Recording Sessions

Vaughan guested on many records during his career. One of his first sessions was for Paul Ray and the Cobras' single "Other Days"/"Texas Clover" (1973). He also appeared on W. C. Clark's single "My Song"/"Rough Edges" (1979).

Vaughan's appearance on David Bowie's **Let's Dance** *(1983) brought him to the attention of the general public. After that he guested on several other blues and rock albums, including Marcia Ball's* **Soulful Dress** *(1983), Johnny Copeland's* **Texas Twister** *(1984), James Brown's* **Gravity** *(1985), Roy Head's* **Living For A Song** *(1985), Lonnie Mack's* **Strike Like Lightning** *(1985), Bennie Wallace's* **Twilight Time** *(1985), Don Johnson's* **Heartbeat** *(1986), Teena Marie's* **Emerald City** *(1986), Jennifer Warnes'* **Famous Blue Raincoat** *(1986), A. C. Reed's* **I'm In The Wrong Business** *(1987), the* **Back To The Beach** *soundtrack (1987), where he teamed up with Dick Dale for a cover of "Pipeline," Stevie Wonder's* **Characters** *(1987), Bill Carter's* **Loaded Dice** *(1988), Brian Slawson's* **Distant Drums** *(1988), Bob Dylan's* **Under A Red Sky** *(1990), and Doyle Bramhall's* **Bird Nest On The Ground** *(1994).*

Typical Licks

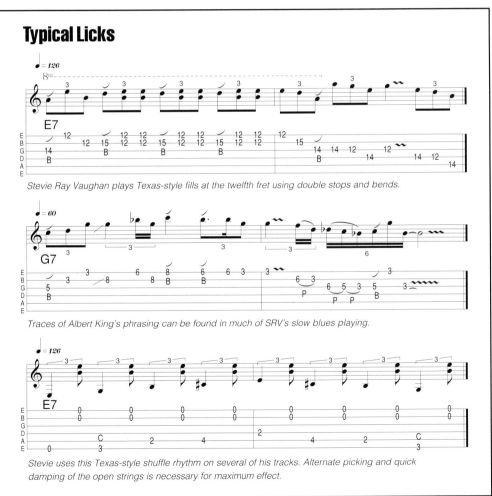

Stevie Ray Vaughan plays Texas-style fills at the twelfth fret using double stops and bends.

Traces of Albert King's phrasing can be found in much of SRV's slow blues playing.

Stevie uses this Texas-style shuffle rhythm on several of his tracks. Alternate picking and quick damping of the open strings is necessary for maximum effect.

T-Bone Walker

With his blend of swing rhythms, big-band accompaniment, and horn-influenced single-note lines, T-Bone Walker was a seminal figure in the development of urban blues. One of the first musicians to embrace the electric guitar, he helped establish it as a featured solo instrument. Many of his licks have become standard fixtures of the rock and blues guitarist's vocabulary. His distinctive soloing style was highly influential on dozens of blues and rock guitarists, including B. B. King, Buddy Guy, Chuck Berry, Eric Clapton, Jimi Hendrix, and Stevie Ray Vaughan.

The Player

Influences

T-Bone was raised in a musical household. "The first thing I can remember was my mother singing the blues as she would sit alone in the evenings in our place in Dallas," he told Nat Shapiro and Nat Hentoff in *Hear Me Talkin' To Ya*. "I used to listen to her singing there at night, and I knew then that the blues was in me too."

Another primary influence during T-Bone's youth was spiritual music. He used to hang around outside the Holiness church near his home in Dallas and listen to the service. "When the hand clapping started, the spirituals would begin," he told Helen Oakley Dance in the book *Stormy Monday*. "I'd be kneeling in the dirt, my heart pounding. Their time was so *great*."

Walker's mother, stepfather, and uncles played guitar and various other stringed instruments. "They used to play for their own kicks," T-Bone told Jim and Amy O'Neil in *Living Blues*. "Like on Sundays everybody would get together in the house and have a little drink, and they would tune up their instruments and play to themselves. People used to come and stand around and listen to them while we'd play. No money was involved. It was just one of those things. Everybody was happy."

Blues guitarists Blind Lemon Jefferson and Huddie "Leadbelly" Ledbetter used to come by Walker's house, and he watched his mother play along with them. Playing a home-made guitar, he imitated his mother's string-bending technique. When Walker was 12, his mother started letting him play her guitar.

With money he had saved, he bought a banjo and started learning to play. He also learned to play the guitar, violin, ukulele, mandolin, and piano, and says that his banjo-playing experience inspired him to play single-note lines on the guitar. Walker would hang around with Blind Lemon Jefferson, leading Jefferson around while he played for money on the streets and in clubs and beer joints. "I was really crazy about him," Walker told *Living Blues*. "He'd come over every Sunday and sit with us and play his guitar, and they sang and had a few drinks." Impressed with Walker's interest in the guitar, Jefferson gave him a few lessons.

Walker learned to play by listening to records and other musicians. Leroy Carr was

Background

1910 *Aaron Thibeaux Walker is born on May 28, in Linden, Texas.*

1922 *T-Bone starts playing the guitar.*

1928 *He records a record for Columbia Records as "Oak Cliff T-Bone."*

1929 *He wins the Cab Calloway contest and plays in Calloway's band for a week.*

1933 *Walker meets and befriends Charlie Christian and they both take electric guitar lessons from Chuck Richardson.*

1935 *He becomes one of the first professional musicians to play the electric guitar.*

1937 *T-Bone moves to Los Angeles.*

1940 *Marili Morden books Walker at the Trocadero, in Hollywood.*

1942 *Walker joins Freddy Slack's band and starts recording for Capitol Records.*

1945 *He stars at the Rhumboogie Club in Chicago with Milt Larkin's or Marl Young's Orchestras.*

1946 *He signs a recording contract with Comet Records.*

1947 *T-Bone records his biggest hit, "Call It Stormy Monday."*

1950 *Imperial Records signs a recording deal with Walker.*

1955 *He starts recording for Atlantic.*

1960 *Walker plays with the Count Basie band.*

1962 *He goes on his first tour of Europe.*

1972 *T-Bone wins a Grammy.*

1974 *He suffers a massive stroke, from which he never truly recovers.*

1975 *Walker dies on March 16 in Los Angeles, California.*

1987 *He is inducted into the Rock And Roll Hall Of Fame.*

one of his favorite artists, and Walker imitated both Carr's vocals and his guitarist Scrapper Blackwell's playing. T-Bone was also heavily influenced by a Lonnie Johnson performance he saw in Dallas.

Walker started playing professionally by the time he was 16, working on street corners or at carnivals, social functions, dances, parties, and medicine shows. He played country blues during this time, but soon he took considerable interest in big bands and swing music. He got gigs backing singers such as Ida Cox, Ma Rainey, and Bessie Smith, playing blues, spirituals, and popular ballads.

When he lived in Oklahoma City, T-Bone took a few lessons from Chuck Richardson, who also instructed Charlie Christian. Walker

and Christian became friends and started doing shows together. "We'd go dance and pass the hat and make money," Walker told *Living Blues*. "We had a little routine of dancing that we did. Charlie would play guitar while I would play a bass, and then we'd change and he'd play bass and I'd play guitar. And then we'd go into our little dance." Not coincidentally, both men later became seminal figures in the popularization of the electric guitar.

Approach and Style

Walker was one of the first musicians to use an electric guitar to play solos in a big band. Imitating lines and phrases used by saxophonists and other horn players, he developed a single-note soloing style that influenced many blues and rock guitarists.

Walker's solos were based on pentatonic minor, pentatonic major, and blues scales. His lines emphasized 6ths, 7ths, and 9ths,

and many of his most distinctive licks involved interplay between the ♭3rd, 3rd, and 4th. He was one of the first guitarists to recognize the electric guitar's sustain characteristics, and he used bent and sustained single notes to good effect in his playing. Sometimes he would also bend diminished chord triads during his solos.

Walker's rhythm style greatly contrasted from that of other blues artists from his era. He moved away from the I-IV-V 12-bar blues format, preferring more sophisticated and varied chord progressions. He frequently played ninth chords, and his chromatic walk-ups and descending half-step ninth-chord figures are a signature of his rhythm style.

Many of his songs used similar chord progressions, but Walker gave each of them a distinctive character by varying the rhythm. Most of his songs were based on swing rhythms, and his use of syncopation, double timing, and arpeggios gave his music a jazz-like flavor. Walker is often credited as the inventor of the Texas shuffle, a rhythmic style associated with several Texas blues artists, including Albert Collins, Freddie King, and Stevie Ray Vaughan.

Techniques

Waker had an unorthodox playing technique. He wore the guitar almost perpendicular to his body, holding it away from him, and curled his left hand around the neck. He did not use his left-hand little finger, relying instead on the other three fingers to voice chords and fret notes.

Walker usually bent notes with his left-hand ring finger, supporting the bend with the forefinger and middle finger. His note-bending vocabulary was diverse, with phrases ranging from subtle microtones to accurately intonated whole-step bends. For variety, he would sometimes use slides instead of bends.

Walker, a superb showman, often performed stunts, such as playing the guitar behind his head and doing the splits. His stage antics were a big influence on Chuck Berry, whose duck walk was an imitation of one of Walker's stage moves.

Clutching his flatpick between his right-hand forefinger and thumb, Walker used several different strumming patterns to play rhythms, including alternating strokes and downstrokes. When playing solos or single-note fill lines, he usually utilized alternate picking.

Walker played a seminal role in the development of urban blues and in establishing the electric guitar as a featured solo instrument. He wore his guitar in an unorthodox manner, holding it in a perpendicular position away from his body.

The Hardware

Guitars, Strings, and Picks

T-Bone made his first guitar from a Prince Albert tobacco can made of tin, and some nails and wire. When he was 12, he had saved up enough money to buy himself a banjo. During his junior year in high school, he bought himself his first guitar.

Walker claims that he got his first electric guitar in 1935. "Oh, yes, I was before Charlie Christian on electric guitar," he said in a *Melody Maker* interview with Max Jones. "He was about the next one to have it. I was out there for four or five years on my own before they all started playing amplified. I recorded my 'T-Bone Blues' with Les Hite's

band in 1939, but I'd been playing amplified guitar a long time before that. The band didn't like the sound of it in the rhythm section, so I played ordinary guitar there."

The electric guitar was Walker's main instrument from the late '30s onward. When he joined Les Hite's band, he was playing a late-'30s Gibson ES-250 archtop electric with a single "Charlie Christian"-style pickup in the neck position. He owned a couple of ES-250s, including one with "open-book" neck inlays and another with double-parallelogram inlays. In the early '50s, he purchased a blonde Gibson ES-5 archtop electric, featuring three P-90 single-coil pickups. This was his main guitar until the early '70s, when it was stolen during a European tour. In the late '60s, Walker sometimes played a Gibson Barney Kessel Regular archtop electric with two humbucking pickups. After his ES-5 was stolen, he played a sunburst Gibson ES-335 semi-hollowbody.

Details about Walker's picks and strings are unknown, other than that he used an unwound *G* string that made it easier for him to bend notes.

Amplifiers, Effects, and Devices

Precise details about the amplifiers that Walker used are also unknown. He probably used a Gibson EH-150 during the late '30s and early '40s. Later, he expressed a preference for Fender amplifiers, and during the '50s he was occasionally pictured playing a tweed-covered 4x10 Bassman combo.

T-Bone Walker used no effects.

Typical Licks

T-Bone often used long, triplet-based blues-scale lines.

Two devices T-Bone used regularly are double-stop bends on the top two strings and 3rd-string bends repeated successively.

T-Bone often used to play his intros with 9th and 13th chords going down in tone intervals.

Discography

Walker recorded more than 250 sides during his career. Credited as Oak Cliff T-Bone, he made his first recordings, "Trinity River Blues" and "Wichita Falls Blues," in 1929 for Columbia Records. It wasn't until 1944, when he recorded "Low Down Dirty Shame Blues (Married Woman Blues)," that he made his next record as a featured artist. He worked for the Rhumboogie and Old Swingmaster labels before scoring his first hit, "Call It Stormy Monday," with the Black & White label in 1947. From 1950 to 1954, he recorded for the Imperial label, then switched to Atlantic Records in 1955 until 1959. After that, he recorded for several labels, including Brunswick, Prestige, Polydor, Wet Soul, Pablo, Blues Way, Black & Blue, Chess, and Reprise.

*Mosaic's **The Complete Recordings Of T-Bone Walker 1940-1954** is a comprehensive 6-CD set of recordings from Walker's most influential years. Capitol's **The Complete Imperial Recordings, 1950-1954**, paired with **His Original 1945-50 Performances**, is a highly recommended starting point for the uninitiated. Atlantic's **T-Bone Blues** features the best material from Walker's late '50s recordings. Bluesboy's **T-Bone Walker** features 17 tracks, ranging from 1929 to 1953.*

*Other T-Bone Walker albums of interest include: **Good Feelin'** (Polydor), **Dirty Mistreater** (MCA), **Stormy Monday Blues** (Charly), **T-Bone Jumps Again** (Charly), **Plain Ole Blues** (Charly), **The Natural Blues** (Charly), **Feeling The Blues** (Black And Blue), **The Inventor Of The Electric Guitar Blues** (Bluesboy), **Singing The Blues** (Liberty), and **I Get So Weary** (Imperial).*

Recording Sessions

*Walker appears on a handful of recordings as a sideman or guest. In 1939, he recorded "T-Bone Blues" with Les Hite And His Orchestra. His playing with Freddie Slack And His Orchestra during the early '40s can be heard on Capitol's **The Complete Freddie Slack, Vol. 1** and **Vol. 2**. He recorded several songs with Roy Hawkins in 1952, which are included on the albums **Why Do Everything Happen To Me?** and **Highway 59**. In the '60s, he guested on Jimmy Witherspoon's **Evenin' Blues**, Jay McShann's **Confessin' The Blues**, and Eddie Vinson's **Wee Baby Blues**.*

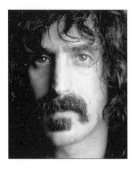

Frank Zappa

Although he was always critical of his playing abilities, Frank Zappa was one of the electric guitar's most original stylists. Many of his recordings feature extended guitar excursions that display his unique legato phrasing, horn-like distorted tone, and complex sense of rhythm. He was also a brilliant composer who pursued his musical vision without conceding to popular trends. His success, coupled with his commitment to artistic excellence, has provided inpiration and motivation to countless musical iconoclasts worldwide.

The Player

Influences

Frank Zappa's parents had a limited musical background. His father played guitar in college, but never aspired to a professional musical career. His first musical instrument was the drums. He started playing drums when he was 12, and later he took drum classes. By the time he was 15, he had acquired a drum set, and played in local bands. While he was still in high school, he enrolled in music-theory classes at a nearby junior college, where he studied Walter Piston's *Harmony* and started experimenting with 12-tone music.

Around the time that he turned 18, Zappa started collecting R&B records. The guitar solos that he heard on blues records inspired him to start playing the guitar. "The solos were never long enough, and I figured the only way I was going to get to hear enough of what I wanted to hear was to get an instrument and play it myself," Zappa told Steve Rosen. Zappa says that he did not know any chords, but he learned to play single-note lines immediately. Later, he bought one of Mickey Baker's instructional books and learned how to play chords.

Zappa's primary guitar influences were blues guitarists. His favorites included Johnny Guitar Watson, Clarence "Gatemouth" Brown, Guitar Smith, Matt "Guitar" Murphy, Hubert Sumlin, and B. B. King. He particularly liked the solos on Watson's "Three Hours Past Midnight," Guitar Slim's "The Story Of My Life," Frankie Lee Simms' "Lucy Mae Blues," and Elmore James' "Happy Home." "I like all blues-type guitar players," he told Tom Mulhern in *Guitar Player*. "I happen to think that what they play really means something, as opposed to most of what happens on most rock 'n' roll records."

By the time he was 21, Zappa was gigging with R&B bands around San Diego. Later, he worked casual lounge jobs with a band called Joe Perrino And The Mellow Tones. Zappa was particularly disillusioned with playing in lounges. "At the end of it I put my guitar in the case and stuck it behind the sofa and didn't touch it I guess for a year," he told Don Menn in *Zappa*. "It was nauseating."

He also listened to classical music, and he started buying classical records while at high school. Later he started writing chamber and orchestral music. He was mainly interested in 20th-century composers, such as Pierre Boulez, Stockhausen, Stravinsky, Edgar Varese, and Anton Webern, whose non-traditional uses of

Background

1940 *Frank Vincent Zappa is born on December 21, in Baltimore, Maryland.*

1956 *Zappa plays his first gig on drums with The Ramblers, a high-school R&B band.*

1958 *Frank starts playing guitar and forms The Blackouts. He writes his first movie score for a modest cowboy movie,* Run Home Slow.

1962 *Using the profits from* Run Home Slow, *Zappa purchases a five-track recording studio from Paul Buff.*

1964 *Frank joins the Soul Giants, who eventually become the Mothers.*

1966 *Zappa and the Mothers release their first album,* Freak Out!, *and start touring.*

1969 *The Mothers of Invention disband and Zappa sets up his first record label, Bizarre/Straight Records.*

1970 *Frank gives birth to the movie* 200 Motels, *which includes appearances by Ringo Starr and Keith Moon.*

1971 *Zappa is pushed from the stage while performing at London's Rainbow Theatre. He spends the next year in a wheelchair, but still manages to produce three albums.*

1975 *He loses in a long court battle with London's Royal Albert Hall over cancelled performances several years earlier.*

1983 *The London Symphony Orchestra records some of Zappa's orchestral works. He is unhappy with their performance.*

1984 *After 25 years on the road, Zappa ceases touring.*

1985 *Zappa testifies before the U. S. Senate against the censorship of rock and pop albums.*

1987 *He wins a Grammy Award for Best Rock Instrumental,* Jazz From Hell.

1988 *Zappa publishes his autobiography. He goes on his last rock world tour.*

1992 *Using a unique six-channel surround-sound P. A., Zappa gives his finest orchestral concerts with the Ensemble Modern in Europe.*

1993 *Zappa dies of prostrate cancer in Los Angeles, California, on December 4.*

harmony, rhythm, and orchestration influenced many of his compostions. He studied several classical-music-theory books, including Nicolas Slonimsky's *Thesaurus Of Scales And Melodic Patterns*, which introduced him to new chords. In the early '80s, he invited Slonimsky to perform on stage with him.

Several different ethnic music styles were also influential on Zappa's music and playing. He particularly enjoyed the modal character-istics and use of drones in Indian music. Some of his ethnic influences include Sardinian and Bulgarian music, especially that of the Bulgarian Women's Choir.

He also appreciated a few jazz and rock musicians. One of his favorite jazz albums was Wes Montgomery's *The Montgomery Brothers*. He enjoyed the work of Captain Beefheart, and worked with him on several occasions. In vari-ous interviews from the '70s and '80s, he stated that he liked the playing of guitarists Allan Holdsworth, John McLaughlin, Jimi Hendrix, Jeff Beck, Eric Clapton with Cream, Brian May, Eddie Van Halen, and Warren De Martini.

Approach and Style

Zappa's guitar style was primarily dominated by single-note lines. Many of his records feature lengthy improvised guitar solos, character-ized by their rhythmic complexity. "My solos are speech-influenced rhythmically, and harmonically they're either pentatonic or poly-scale oriented," he told Steve Rosen.

For soloing, he preferred the Lydian and Mixolydian modes and fourth and eleventh intervals. He liked to combine tonalities, such as playing in the key of *A* over an *E7* vamp. Most of his solos were played over pedal tones or one- or two-chord vamps. "I don't like chord changes," he said. "I like to have one tonal center that stays right there, or possibly with a second chord that varies off the main tonal center." Instead of playing chord changes, he often played notes that imply chords.

To keep his solos musically interesting, he employed unusual rhythms and syncopations, such as subdivided time signatures, ritardan-dos and accelerandos, and polyrhythms. "The rhythms of Frank's guitar playing never come to a full resting point," Kent Nagano commented in *Zappa*. "They phrase the way a phrase will, but they actually never come to sit on a big, fat, ripe cadence." Other distinguishing features of Zappa's playing style are frequent use of sextuplets, septuplets, and 64th notes.

Techniques

The most distinctive aspect of Zappa's play-ing technique was his left-hand legato phrasing. "If I pick one note with my right hand, I'm playing five with my left," he said to Steve Rosen. "I don't pick everything that I play." Sometimes he played exclusively with his left hand, generating notes with hammer-ons and pull-offs for several measures before he picked a note with his right hand.

From the mid-'70s, Zappa frequently used right-hand tapping techniques. He usually struck the fingerboard with the tip of his pick when tapping to create "bagpipe noises." Examples of this can be heard on "Inca Roads" and "Po-Jama People," from *One Size Fits All*.

Zappa held his pick with his right-hand thumb, forefinger, and middle finger. He used alternate picking, which helped him play many of his exceptionally fast and accurate passages. In the early '80s, when he got a guitar equipped with a Floyd Rose locking tremolo, he frequently experimented with the vibrato bar, pulling notes sharp and depressing the bar until the strings went limp.

Zappa also enjoyed experimenting with feedback. Many of his guitars were equipped with special EQ circuits that enhanced midrange frequencies that cause the guitar to feed back more easily.

Zappa's concerts often featured extended improvised guitar solos that displayed his fluid legato phrasing and advanced sense of rhythm. Many of his finest solos can be heard on Shut Up 'N Play Your Guitar *and* Guitar.

The Hardware

Guitars, Strings, and Picks

Frank's first guitar was an old, second-hand archtop f-hole acoustic that he bought for $1.50 when he was 18. Three years later, he got his first electric guitar, a Fender Telecaster that he rented from a music store. Later on, he bought a Fender Jazzmaster, and then purchased an ES-5 Switchmaster hollow-body archtop electric with money he made from composing music for the movie *Run Home Slow*. He used this on his first three albums.

After that, Zappa owned a succession of Gibson solidbodies. He played a Gibson Les Paul gold-top for a while, then switched to a Gibson SG, which was his main guitar throughout most of the '70s. A fan in Phoenix, Arizona, custom-built an SG-style guitar for him that featured 23 frets and a built-in preamp. Some of Zappa's SGs had Barcus Berry contact pickups installed on the bridge. He also owned a cherry sunburst Les Paul Custom with DiMarzio pickups that he frequently played onstage.

From the latter part of the '70s through to the '80s, Zappa preferred Fender Stratocasters and Strat-style guitars. He owned a Fender Strat that once belonged to Jimi Hendrix, who set it on fire at a Miami Pop Festival in the '60s. This Strat had a Barcus Berry contact pickup installed in the neck, a built-in preamp, and an out-of-phase switch. Zappa also played several custom Strat-style electrics with Floyd Rose tremolo systems. "The Strat has a drier sound – it has more of an acute, exact sound – and I use the Gibson for more of a sweat-hog type of sound," Zappa told Tom Mulhern in *Guitar Player*.

He also played a few unconventional electrics, including an Acoustic fretless guitar, D'Mini miniature Les Paul and Stratocaster copies, and a Fender Electric XII.

Zappa used acoustic guitars only

Zappa may have been best-known for his sarcastic social commentary and his battles in the U. S. Senate against censorship, but he was also a brilliant composer who had his works performed by the London Symphony Orchestra.

occasionally. He rarely played acoustic on his records and he only used electric guitars onstage. He once owned a Gibson J-200 and various Martin and Ovation acoustics.

Zappa used heavy-gauge Fender picks and .009, .012, .017, .024, .034, .046, .052 Ernie Ball strings.

Amplifiers, Effects, and Devices

Zappa used a Fender Deluxe amp on his first album with the Mothers, *Freak Out!* In the late '60s, he started using Acoustic 270 amps, which he had throughout his entire career. During the '70s, he played through a combination of Acoustic and Marshall 100-watt amps onstage, and in the '80s he added a Carvin 100-watt head to this setup. He usually connected the amps to a Vox 4x12 speaker cabinet and a Marshall cabinet loaded with four 12-inch JBL speakers.

In the recording studio he often played through a tiny Pignose practice amp.

In His Own Words

I'm not really a fast guitar player, because I'm not picking everything I play. I only play fast when I think it's appropriate to the line I'm doing.
Guitar Player, *January 1977*

Once I get out onstage and turn my guitar on, it's a special thing to me – I love doing it. But I approach it more as a composer who happens to be able to operate an instrument called a guitar, rather than "Frank Zappa, Rock And Roll Guitar Hero."
Guitar Player, *January 1977*

Once you learn the 28 or 29 most commonly used rock guitar doodads (a few country licks, a little Albert King, a pentatonic scale here 'n' there, get your heavy vibrato together), you are ready to live; to be what will be known in the future as "The Guitar Player Of The '70s."
Guitar Player, *January 1977*

Guitar playing as currently understood has more to do with sports than it has to do with music. It's an Olympic-challenge type of situation. The challenges are in the realm of speed, redundancy, choreography, and grooming.
A Definitive Tribute To Frank Zappa, *1994*

What They Say

The stuff I've learned from Frank you can't acquire for money. Just working with the man's genius inspires you to become as much of a perfectionist as he is.
Steve Vai, Guitar Player, *February 1983*

He's a fascinating guitarist. I learned a lot by watching him play guitar – his phrasing, his timing, the way he can create dramatic tension.
Orchestral conductor Kent Nagano, Zappa.

One wouldn't have to be interested in guitar very long to discover Frank Zappa. And the more you explore that, the better, because he's put out unabridged recordings of just great music.
Warren De Martini, Zappa.

Occasionally he experimented with other setups, such as a 200-watt Marshall head connected to an 18-inch speaker.

Zappa used a variety of effects, but he mainly relied on a wah-wah pedal and a phase shifter. One of his favorite effects was Mu-Tron bi-phase. He used several other Mu-Tron effects, including an Octave Divider and a wah-wah pedal. He generally employed the wah-wah as a tone control, instead of sweeping the pedal back and forth. Some of his other more conventional effects included a '60s Octavia pedal and an Echoplex.

Many of Zappa's effects were unusual custom-made units or studio devices. He used an Oberheim VCF, which was triggered by a sample-and-hold unit to generate brief rhythmic figures. He also had a Systech Harmonic Energizer equalization unit, several MXR digital delays, MicMix Dynaflangers, and Aphex compressors.

Zappa frequently experimented with guitar synthesizers. One of his first was an Electro Wagnerian Emancipator unit built by Bob Easton at 360 Systems. It worked as a frequency follower, playing chords that tracked single notes. He also used a guitar interface with his Synclavier, but eventually he preferred to use the typewriter keyboard to enter data into the system.

Discography

Zappa had a prolific career as a recording artist. His earliest recordings were soundtracks that he recorded in the early '60s for the movies **The World's Greatest Sinner** and **Run Home Slow**. In 1966, Zappa released his first album with The Mothers, **Freak Out!** Zappa released more than 60 albums, most of which feature excellent examples of his guitar playing. All of the following albums are available on Zappa's Barking Pumpkin label: **Absolutely Free, We're Only In It For The Money, Lumpy Gravy, Cruisin' With Ruben & The Jets, Mothermania, Uncle Meat, Hot Rats, Burnt Weeny Sandwich, Weasels Ripped My Flesh, Chunga's Revenge, Live At The Fillmore East – June 1971, 200 Motels, Just Another Band From L.A., Waka/Jawaka, The Grand Wazoo, Over-Nite Sensation, Apostrophe, Roxy & Elsewhere, One Size Fits All, Bongo Fury, Zoot Allures, Zappa In New York, Studio Tan, Sleep Dirt, Sheik Yerbouti, Orchestral Favorites, Joe's Garage Acts I, II, & III, Tinseltown Rebellion, Shut Up 'N Play Yer Guitar, You Are What You Is, Ship Arriving Too Late To Save A Drowning Witch, The Man From Utopia, Baby Snakes, Them Or Us, Thing Fish, FZ Meets The Mothers Of Prevention, Does Humor Belong In Music?, Jazz From Hell, Guitar, You Can't Do That On Stage Anymore, Vol. 1-6, Broadway The Hardway, The Best Band You Never Heard In Your Life, Make A Jazz Noise Here, Playground Psychotics, Beat The Boots!,** and **The Yellow Shark**.

The albums **Shut Up 'N Play Your Guitar** and **Guitar** are collections of extended guitar solos, and are highly recommended for those interested in Zappa's guitar playing.

Recording Sessions

During the early '70s, Zappa made guest performances on albums by Flint, Grand Funk, and John Lennon and Yoko Ono. After that, he concentrated solely on his own recording and performing career.

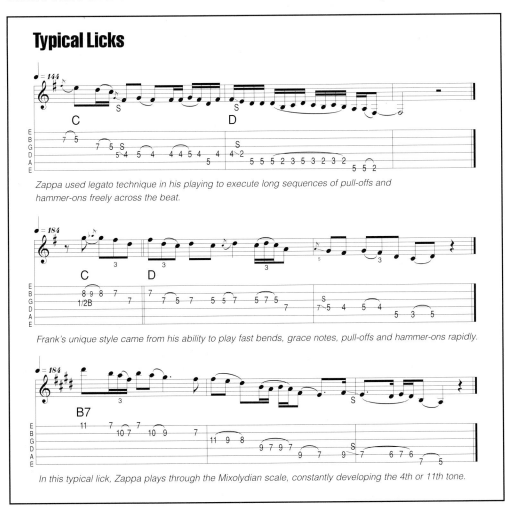

Typical Licks

Zappa used legato technique in his playing to execute long sequences of pull-offs and hammer-ons freely across the beat.

Frank's unique style came from his ability to play fast bends, grace notes, pull-offs and hammer-ons rapidly.

In this typical lick, Zappa plays through the Mixolydian scale, constantly developing the 4th or 11th tone.

Index

Acknowledgments

The publishers gratefully acknowledge the following publications for the quotations used in this book: *Guitar Player*, *Guitar World*, *Musician*, *Guitarist*, *New Musical Express*, *The Guitar Magazine*.

All illustrations in *Guitar Legends* are strictly copyright. The publishers wish to thank the following sources and photographers for supplying the photographs in this book:

© **Terry Cryer**: 102.

© **Rob Finnis**: 52, 53, 55.

© **Juke Blues**: C. Meyer 78; Don Bronstein 101.

© **Jak Kilby**: 61, 129, 130.

Courtesy **Albert Lee**: 54.

© **London Features International Ltd**: 15, 21, 28, 29, 33, 42, 46, 59, 62, 76, 84, 97, 104, 112, 124, 126, 136, 149, 152; Ebet Roberts 10, 145, 146; Michael Ochs Archive 12, 22, 31, 83; Neal Preston 90; Geoff Swaine 37; Phil Loftus 44; George DeSota 45; Ann Summa 47; Adrian Boot 50, 51; Jill Furmanovsky 56; Michael Putland 69; Postal 88, 144; Gabi Rona 98; Derek Ridgers 108; Kevin Mazur 137; Laura Levine 140; Rick Sins 142; Chris Walter 35.

© **Dave Peabody**: 79, 131.

© **Pictorial Press Ltd**: 43, 99; Joe Sia/Starfile 13; Colin Escott 81.

© **Sylvia Pitcher**: 8, 60, 63, 100, 103.

© **Barry Plummer**: 16, 30, 49, 57, 58, 70, 71, 80, 85, 86, 89, 92, 114, 120, 123, 125, 132.

© **Redferns**: P. Niemeier 2, 65, 67; Ebet Roberts 11, 48, 119, 147, 154; Gems 14; David Redfern 17, 20, 34, 39, 77, 82, 115, 150; © Val Wilmer 19; Fin Costello 24, 25, 139; Dieter Radtke 27; Mick Hutson 32, 121; Michel Linssen 36; Colin Streater 38; Elliot Landy 66; Max Jones Archive 73, 148, 151; Colin Levy 96; Ian Dickson 105, 153; Graham Wiltshire 106, 134; Richard Aaron 113; Jim Steele 122; Dave Peabody 128.

© **Relay Photos**: 93; Chris Walter 18; Ross Halfin 26; Andre Csillag 9, 87, 117, 127; Ray Palmer 116, 118; David Wainwright 138.

© **Retna Pictures Ltd**: 41, 68; Michael Putland 133.

© **Rex Features Ltd**: 40; Stills 94; Lenquette/SIPA 95; Mark Sharratt 64.

© **Alex Solca**: 143.

© **Val Wilmer**: 72, 74, 75.

© **Graham Wiltshire**: 23, 91, 109, 110, 111.

Key to licks abbreviations

B	Bend up one tone
2B	Bend up two tones
RB	Release bend
C	Blues curl
S	Slide
P	Pull-off
H	Hammer-on
T	Right-hand tap
TL	Left-hand tap
PM	Palm mute
AH	Artificial harmonic
PH	Pinched harmonic
*	Slide with the edge of the pick
WB	Whammy bar

The "typical licks" have not been directly transcribed from the artists' recordings. They have, nevertheless, been modelled on aspects of each guitarist's individual style.